D1060324

MELODIES AND MEMORIES

NELLIE MELBA

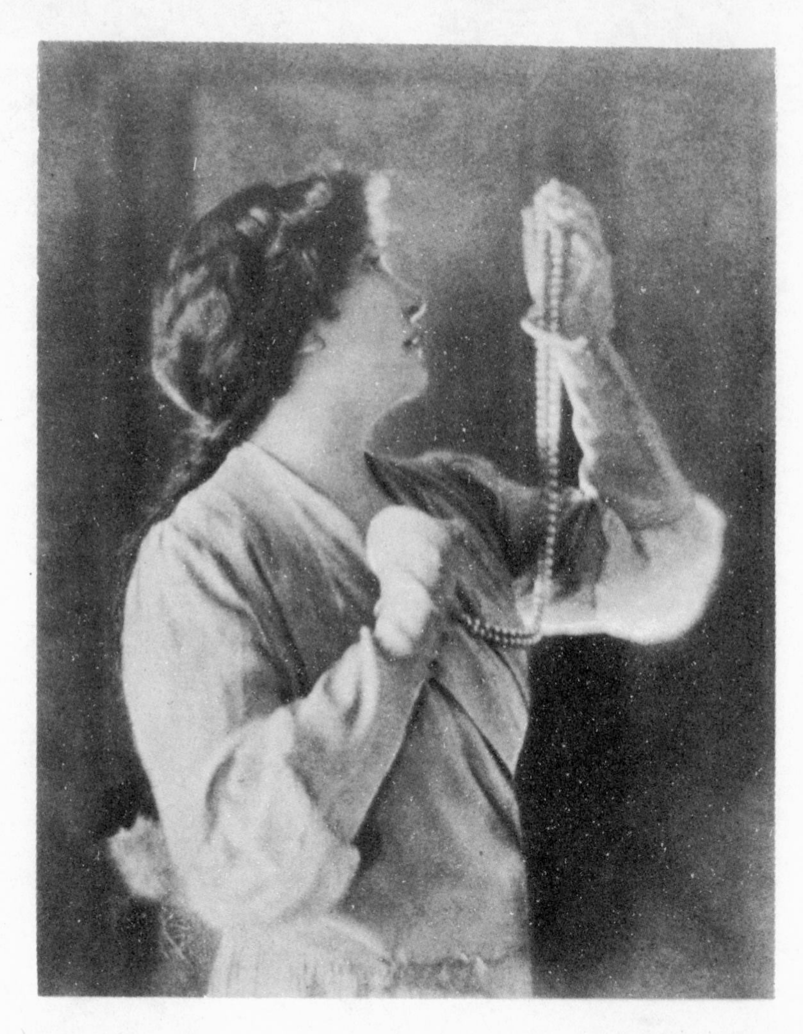

Photo: Baron de. Meyer

MELBA AS MARGUERITE IN FAUST

MELODIES AND MEMORIES

by

NELLIE MELBA

Illustrated

BOOKS FOR LIBRARIES PRESS
FREEPORT, NEW YORK

First Published 1926
Reprinted 1970

STANDARD BOOK NUMBER:
8369-5192-1

LIBRARY OF CONGRESS CATALOG CARD NUMBER:
73-107821

PRINTED IN THE UNITED STATES OF AMERICA

TO
PAMELA

CONTENTS

ILLUSTRATIONS

MELODIES AND MEMORIES

CHAPTER I

EARLY DAYS IN AUSTRALIA

If you take the long white road from Melbourne out towards the great Australian Bush, leaving behind you the little wooden-built townships of Lilydale and Coldstream, you will eventually arrive at what seems to be the fringe of civilization—a turning of the roads on rising land from which you can see over hill and valley, out to the great blue mountains on the horizon.

At this turning of the roads I have built my Australian home, Coombe Cottage, almost within sight and sound of the same trees and vineyards in which I played as a child, under the same brilliant sunshine, facing the same sudden storms that sweep in, like giants from the hills. There was no Coombe, years ago. There were no firm white roads over which motors speed by from a vast city, no telephones straggling through burnt-up branches of the gum trees. But there were always the same quiet, eternal things—the hum of crickets at evening, the flash of the green and scarlet wings of parrots, the spring of yellow wattle every winter, the liquid cry of magpies in broken branches, outside my window at dawn. And it was from these sights, these sounds and scents, that the first bars were written in the impromptu of my life.

If you wish to understand me at all (and to write an autobiography is only to open a window into one's heart) you must understand first and foremost that I am an Australian. Most people seem to imagine that any artist who has been honoured by many countries, who is equally at home in New York or Paris, London or Rome, must of necessity be a cosmopolitan. I do not believe that that is true. There was always something of the sun of Italy in Caruso's dark, laughing eyes, always a longing for the mists of Paris streets, even in the strange, wild heart of Sarah Bernhardt. And for me, whatever adventures may be in store, whatever songs there are still to sing, I shall always come back to rest in the shadow of the blue mountains, in the heart of this vast, deserted continent which gave me birth.

Childhood memories are often apt to have a sameness about them. But I feel that perhaps there may be some appeal in the very wildness of my early days, their untamed, almost mediæval simplicity.

Forty-five miles from Melbourne there stands an old house, thickly shaded by immense gum trees, on the side of a steep hill which leads down to one of the few rivers in Australia. The name of that house was Steel's Flats, and that is really the first memory that I have.

Drive with me in imagination from Melbourne towards that beloved place, many years ago. First of all there is a great bustle and excitement as the old stage coach arrives, very rickety and dusty, with its four patient horses flicking the flies with their tails. We clamber up—children, nurses and carpet bags being stuffed in hurriedly and haphazard. I always insist on sitting next to the driver, because, to my mind, all exciting things happen there. For instance, it is from there that I see my first glimpse of the blue mountains. Sometimes, too, we may meet a black snake—very venomous and deadly—and then the driver must descend, creep up to it, and break its back with his long whip. At other times we might actually run over it. But we never let a snake, once seen, escape. From our earliest childhood we were taught to strike and kill.

How clearly I see it all—the flocks of sheep and herds of cattle being driven to market—the glaring heat—the burnt-up fields—the strange remoteness, as though we were alone in the world, when Melbourne was left behind. Nowadays I can motor in to Melbourne in little over an hour, but on those days we must start at eight o'clock in the morning, arrive at Lilydale (only twenty-five miles out) at 12.15, have lunch, and then do the rest of the thirteen miles in time for a late tea in the family wagonette, an abominable vehicle in which one sat sideways in a draught. Even to this day there are similar wagonettes in the streets of Melbourne.

Oh—the mountains round Steel's Flats—the clean, sweet air—the tall, waving "tree ferns"—the *everything.* No sooner had we arrived than I would plunge down the hill, through the undergrowth, heedless of snakes, and sit by the old water-wheel, with the water dripping round me to keep me cool.

I suppose that from my very earliest days I must have been a lover of beauty. In the old dining-room at Steel's Flats there was a mirror that faced the window, and whenever possible I would sit in the seat opposite it, at meals, with my back to the window, because I thought the mountains looked even more beautiful in the reflection of dusky silver than in real life. And many is the hour I have spent, as a tiny child, huddled up under the piano, as quiet as a mouse, while my mother was practising.

Throughout my life there has always been one man who meant more than all others, one man for whose praise I thirsted, whose character I have tried to copy—my father. And if in these early pages I can repay some of the eternal debt which I owe to him, I shall have done all that I wished.

David Mitchell, the son of a small farmer in Forfarshire, arrived in Melbourne with one golden sovereign in his pocket—no more. He died leaving a will of nearly half a million golden sovereigns, and the history of his endeavour is a romance before which I feel that my own history is commonplace.

His adventures started on the journey out. His widowed mother had entrusted him, before he sailed, with a purse containing two hundred sovereigns. He carried that purse with him by day and slept with it under his pillow at night, until one early dawn he was suddenly wakened, to find that a mutiny had broken out. He rushed on deck, and with a few other sturdy Scotsmen stood by the captain. The mutiny was quelled, but when, after some hours of hand-to-hand fighting, he dragged himself back to his cabin, David Mitchell's money was gone, all except one coin in his waistcoat pocket. And that coin was the foundation of the fortune which made it possible for me to come to Europe and to sing.

But the fight was hard. Picture to yourself a young man, not tall, but very broad and thick set, with a mop of dark hair, tramping through the raw city of Melbourne, up to the gold-fields, denying himself, sleeping in cattle-sheds, even hard put to it to find shoes, until he had scraped together the little pile of gold which enabled him to start on his own. From the first he showed foresight. He said to me long afterwards: "I saw that Melbourne was going to grow beyond our dreams. A growing city needs bricks. 'Why should I not make those bricks?' said I. So I *did* make them." That was his simple recipe for success, carried through with such untiring vigour that by the time he died he was one of the landmarks of Australia, and most of the finest buildings in Melbourne are built with his bricks.

My father was never a great talker. He was very reserved, very Scotch and, you might think, very shy. He did not talk so much as twinkle. He could say more with his eyes than most men with their lips. And he admired reserve in others as much as he practised it in himself. I remember, long afterwards, when I came back to Australia in 1902, he took me aside and said, "Well—have you saved any money?"

Myself (hesitating): "Yes, a little."

Father: "How much?"

Myself (fibbing): "Perhaps £20,000."

Father: "Well, lass, you're much richer than I am."

There was a pause, and he solemnly winked at me, and I winked at him; then, taking me by the arm, he said: "You're quite right, lassie. Never tell anybody what you've got. Not even me."

My father shared my love of life in the open air—riding, fishing, tramping through the bush. Many were the rides I went with him, and though he never gave me much encouragement, he was a good master. If my hat blew off, he never paused to allow me to pick it up, but rode steadily on until I galloped up, very out of breath, to apologize for my foolishness. If I was ever one minute late, he went without me and turned a deaf ear to all excuses.

But if he was a stern master, I was a willing pupil. When I was twelve years old, I had already developed a positive passion for playing the organ, and every week on Tuesdays and Fridays I used to take lessons at St. Peter's. My father never told me that I played well, nevertheless he spurred me on in his own way. "Learn twelve pieces by heart, lass," he said to me, "and I'll give you a gold watch." I learnt the twelve pieces in as many days, and sure enough the watch was mine, for my father never broke a promise. But I fear I broke the watch. Running home one day in the brief twilight of the Australian autumn, I dropped the watch in a gutter, and when I went back to look for it, dark had already come. It was found, weeks later, by a detective and returned to me, ruined. I shall never forget the look of black disapproval on Daddy's face when he saw the ruins of the watch in my hand. "You will never get another from me," he said. And I never did, but I keep that old watch to this day in one of the drawers reserved for happy memories.

Many silhouettes are etched vividly on my memory—especially the strict Presbyterian Sundays of gloom and solemnity, in which no one might smile or hum a tune—so great a nightmare to me that one day I deliberately fell in the mud in order to avoid going to church. One Sunday, in particular, I shall never forget, for a very old parson, of great piety and excessive dulness, came to our house to conduct a service in the drawing-room. Towards the end of the service, which had been rapidly driving me to distraction, I was asked to play a hymn. I marched defiantly to the old cracked harmonium, and out of sheer light-headedness played—with all the stops out—the popular tune of the day—"Can't you dance the polka?" I was seized bodily from the stool, bustled from the room, and kept in disgrace for a week.

Of my schooldays I do not wish to write at length. They were much as other girls' schooldays, though perhaps some of them may have been more Spartan than nowadays. At one of the first schools I attended, in Bridge Road, Richmond, it was compulsory every morning to take a cold shower—at six o'clock in the morning.

A sybarite strain in my nature revolted against this custom, and I hit upon the idea of entering the bathroom with an umbrella, under which I shivered while I pulled the shower and allowed its splashing to echo through the house, deluding my mistresses with the thought that I was doing my duty. One fateful day the attention of the head mistress was drawn to the fact that there was always a terrible chaos in the bath-room after Nellie Mitchell had used it. She tramped upstairs to investigate, and there in the corner discovered the emblem of my guilt—a wet umbrella, still dripping. After that discovery I took my baths under supervision.

When did I begin to sing? Ah! That is a difficult question, for I can never remember any time when I was not singing. It was as natural to me to hum as to breathe; in fact, my mother, who was a very patient woman, sometimes would call out in desperation, "For heaven's sake, child, stop that humming." But I am glad, to-day, that I did not follow her advice, for that humming was a vocal exercise which stood me in good stead in later years.

At six years old I made my first public appearance, and incidentally received probably one of the most honest criticisms I have ever had. It was a concert at Richmond Public Hall, and I sang with great delight, "Comin' thro' the Rye," followed by a song which my grandmother had taught me, entitled "Shells of the Ocean," delivered, for greater effect, from the height of a stool. I do not know if I had much artistic success, but certainly one little girl, a great friend of mine, was impressed, for when on the following day I asked her eagerly what she thought of my song, she looked at me with a frown and said six words:

"Nellie Mitchell, I saw your drawers!"

At least, there was no flattery there!

When I was still young, my mother died. Although she had been ill for years, death had hitherto been a mere name for me, and it seemed to add a whole host of new problems, hitherto unguessed, to my existence. Just before she died she summoned the family into the room, and there was some message for each of us. For me it was, "Always be a mother to little Vere." Vere was my sister, four years old.

I carried out my mother's dying wish, and Vere's cot was moved into my room. And then, three months afterwards, Vere was suddenly seized with an illness. I and the nurse put her to bed, and did all we could for her. As it was too late to send for the doctor, I thought I would go to bed too, trusting that she would be better in the morning.

I went to bed early, put fresh wood on the fire, and lay back in bed dozing under the flickering shadows on the ceiling. Suddenly, I saw that there was a third person in the room, and peering into the half-light, I saw that the third person was my mother, dressed in the simple black dress in which I had last seen her on earth. Speechless, I watched her walk very slowly across the room to my sister's bed, raise her hand, point to the figure in the bed, make a strange, sweeping motion with her arm, and disappear.

With a quick beating heart I ran to my sister's bed. She was sleeping peacefully, and seemed better.

In the morning, I mentioned the incident to my father before he went out, wondering if it would make him feel that the illness was more serious than we thought, and if we ought to send for the doctor at once.

"Tut, tut! girl . . ." he said, in his broad Scottish burr. "Get those foolish notions out of your head."

As for sending for the doctor, he decided to wait till he returned in the evening.

In the evening it was too late. My sister died at four o'clock.

These are the facts, bare and unadorned. I do not seek to explain them.

I needed a thorough change of atmosphere. The sudden appearance of death on my youthful horizon had shocked and bewildered me. And so, in order to bring back some of my old vitality and high spirits, my father decided that he would take me for a change to Queensland. It was a significant journey for me, because it was in Queensland that I met the young Irishman, Charles Nesbitt Armstrong, who became my husband.

Queensland is a wild enough place even in these days, but then it was positively barbaric. However, as I was still in mourning for my mother, it was decided by the family that instead of returning to Melbourne, I should be married straightaway in Queensland. And there, in Brisbane, one hot dusty day in midsummer, I became Mrs. Armstrong.

A strange period ensued—a period which to most modern girls would sound something of a nightmare. My husband lived in the heart of the Bush, as the manager of a sugar plantation in Port Mackay, and it was there, after our honeymoon, that we retired. We had a little house with a galvanized iron roof, desolate and lonely, with no other company than that of the birds and especially of the reptiles. Soon after we arrived it began to rain; and rain in Queensland is rain indeed. It rained for six weeks. My piano was mildewed; my clothes were damp; the furniture fell to pieces; spiders, ticks, and other obnoxious insects penetrated into the house—to say nothing of snakes, which had a habit of appearing underneath one's bed at the most inopportune moments. It rained and rained, a perpetual tattoo on the roof, and as the days passed by, and the weeks, I felt that I should go mad unless I escaped. My only recreation was to sit on the veranda and to watch the luxurious tropical vegetation, burdened with water, yet so hot that one could actually see the leaves unfold.

Sometimes I would try to bathe. But as I walked, hot and disconsolate, towards the river, I would see green snakes hanging from the branches, and even in the water itself there would be leeches that fastened with painful precision on to one's hands and legs and arms. Nor did I forget the tales which I had heard of a giant crocodile only a hundred yards upstream. Bathing became for me an over-rated amusement. And had it not been for my dear friends, Mr. and Mrs. Charlie Rawson, I do not know what I should have done.

It was here, in the following year, that my only child, George Armstrong, was born. Two months after his birth I returned to my father's house. I never went back.

It was now that I, who all my life had been studying music in some form or another, decided that I would make a serious effort to sing in public. It was not a sudden desperate venture—it was a perfectly natural, almost inevitable development in my life.

As a girl I had studied singing at school with Madame Christian, and afterwards with Signor Cecchi, who was an old Italian opera singer who had come out to Australia some years before. It was therefore to Cecchi that I went, being told by him that as he had given me lessons as a girl he was willing to teach me for love.

Alas! What a rude awakening I was to have. Signor Cecchi gave me the lessons, and I appeared in public, of which I will speak later; but for the moment I cannot help recalling the shock of disappointment which Signor Cecchi was to give me, for it was one of the first blows of that nature that I had ever had.

I must look ahead to the time some six weeks before I went to England. I was thrilled at the expectation at last of visiting the country of my forefathers, when suddenly I heard rumours that Signor Cecchi was threatening to seize my trunks if I did not pay his bill before I left. I was overcome with astonishment. Cecchi, who had said that he was teaching me for love, to behave in this manner—it seemed utterly impossible. I went to see him, and I shall never forget his small, dark, swarthy figure and the bright avaricious eyes that examined me coldly as he remarked:

"You owe me eighty guineas. That money must be paid before you leave."

I was in despair. I had given a farewell concert, at which the nett takings had been £67 4s. 8d. Most of that had already gone to pay bills. I did not dare to ask my Daddy, because he had already paid my passage. Had it not been for a dear old uncle and a friend, I might never have gone to England; but at last I raised the eighty guineas and stuffing them into my purse, I went to Cecchi and threw the money, purse and all, on his table.

"Here," I said, "is the money you say I owe you. We had been friends for so many years that I thought you knew me better than you evidently do; for surely you must have known that if I made a success I would repay you tenfold."

He shrugged his shoulders, and put the money into his pocket.

"That is not all," I said. "If I ever do have a success, I shall never mention your name as having been a teacher of mine. I shall never refer to you in any way whatever. So good-bye, Signor Cecchi, and may this gain bring you happiness."

I never did mention his name, in spite of the fact that when I had made my success I was constantly being asked who had first taught me the elements of singing. And I honestly believe that Signor Cecchi died of apoplexy talking of me and my ingratitude. But I realize that he was not a good teacher, for all that he taught me I had to unlearn when I was privileged to study under Madame Mathilde Marchesi. However, I am looking forward too quickly.

I must now recall the first concert of my life, the beginning of so much wonder and so much that was glorious.

It took place in the Melbourne Town Hall on Saturday, May 17th, 1884, and was for the benefit of Herr Elsasser, who in his prosperous days had been the conductor of the Liedertafel Concerts for many years. When I woke up in the morning before this great occasion, I thought that I had a sore throat. I laugh to think how many times since then I have suffered from the same illusion. The day went on, and as the evening approached I grew more and more nervous. By five o'clock I was already dressed in my simple gown of golden satin, and was sitting with my Daddy wondering why I had ever undertaken this devastating task. The hours went on. I thought of my relations and my friends, those who had known me as a tomboy in the Australian Bush, and I wondered what they would think of my impudence in having the effrontery to appear before the great people of Melbourne in such a rôle. And then, at about a quarter to eight, I put on my cloak, and tremblingly stepped into the buggy that was to carry us to the Town Hall. After that my memory merely recalls two hours of wonderful triumph.

And here is the first criticism of my entire career:

". . . Mrs. Armstrong, whom her friends have long known as Nellie Mitchell, and who it may here be said is both a vocalist of the first rank, a pianiste of surpassing finish, and a painter of more than amateur excellence, but who until last Saturday night had most modestly confined her performances in all of these several capacities to private circles, and who consented to go out of her delightful domestic circle only in the holy cause of charity. If therefore her success as a vocalist had been but moderate, she would have merited the warmest recognition for placing her services at the disposal of the Elsasser Fund committee, but when it is said that she sings like one picked out of ten thousand the obligations due to her are obviously all the greater. *The Elsasser concert, therefore, if it were to be remembered in no other way, will never be forgotten on account of the delightful surprise afforded by Mrs. Armstrong's singing, and everybody who heard her will desire to hear her again and everybody who did not hear her is at this moment consumed with regrets at not having been present.*"—*Australasian.*

It was this concert that made me realize that there must be something in my voice. You must remember that I had never heard a great singer in my life, that I had never been to an opera, that I had no possible means of comparing my own voice with the voices of singers who had already made their reputation. But still, I felt, the people of Melbourne could not be after all so very different from the people of Europe, and if I could have this success before them, surely I could at least command a hearing in other places. And from now onwards, to go to England was my ruling ambition.

And then luck came my way. My father was appointed a Commissioner to the Indian and Colonial Exhibition. He came down to breakfast one morning and told me of the fact, and putting his arms on my shoulders he said, "I am going to take you too, lassie; we sail in six weeks." I believe that that was the greatest thrill of my life.

But here again an upset occurred which very nearly prevented me from going, and which, had it not been for another stroke of luck, would have kept me in Australia for the rest of my life. One night I went to the theatre with an old friend and his sister. When we came out, our carriage for some reason or other was delayed, and so my friend suggested that we three should fill in twenty minutes by going to a little adjoining restaurant for supper. We went; we ate some oysters, and then we departed.

It happened that a certain Frenchman whose wife (I thought) was a friend of mine, was in the restaurant at the same time. He went straight home, and he lied to her by saying that he had seen me with a strange man, alone, late at night, in an oyster saloon. She repeated this gossip to my father.

I knew nothing of this, but the next morning my father said to me:

"I am very sorry, Nellie, but I have made up my mind not to take you to England."

I was astounded. I said:

"Why? What have I done?"

He merely shook his head, looked at me sadly, and said: "Ask your conscience."

I was plunged into utter despondency, and went about the house like a ghost, not wishing to sing or hum, not taking any interest in life, and asking everybody if they knew what I had done.

A little later the Frenchman and his wife came to dine. I still thought they were my friends, and I tried to be as charming to them as possible. I threw off my low spirits, I played, I sang, I laughed and chattered with them as though they were the only people in whom I was interested in the world. It may have been this behaviour, it may have been a sudden remorse, but when I woke up the next morning I saw a strange figure standing beside my bed. It was the wife of the Frenchman. She fell on her knees.

"I've come to apologize," she said.

I sat up, rubbed my eyes, and said:

"I don't understand."

And then she explained. "My husband lied to me. He told me that you were alone in a little restaurant late at night. And that is the reason why your father will not take you to England."

Looking her straight in the face, I answered:

"You will go immediately to my father and explain the whole affair to him, and you will tell him that I am as innocent as you are, and that your whole story was a malicious invention."

She left the room, and a few minutes afterwards my father came in to see me.

"I'm sorry, lassie," he said. And that was all. And then he bent down and kissed me. I was to go to England after all.

I had not the faintest shadow of an idea of the life that was in store for me. Why should I? And yet, there came to me, when I was only a little girl of ten, an amazing prophecy. I am not "psychic," but I think the prophecy is worth recording if only for its complete mystery.

It happened at a school picnic. I and two other little girls had wandered off by ourselves, and plunging deep into the bush we suddenly came upon a cottage, with a youngish woman standing in the doorway.

"What are you doing here, little girls?" she called out.

"Nothing," we answered shyly.

"Then come inside and have a glass of milk," she said.

We hesitated for a moment, and then the prospect of milk sounded so refreshing that we walked in.

When we had drunk our milk, and were saying our "Thank yous," the woman said suddenly, "Would you like me to tell your fortunes?"

We were thrilled at the idea, and said "Yes."

"Very well, then; show me your hands."

One by one the grimy hands were produced. Nothing very exciting was foretold for the two other girls, but when my turn came, she bent over my hand closely, and her brow wrinkled.

"Little girl," she said at length, "you are going to travel a very great deal. You will visit almost every country in the world. Not only that, I see you everywhere in great halls, crowded with people. And you are always the centre of attraction—the one at whom all eyes are directed."

I giggled, as any little girl (especially, years ago in the remote Australian Bush) would have done. "I don't know what you mean," I said.

"You may, some day," replied the woman.

CHAPTER II

STUDY IN PARIS

TULIPS in the Park—tulips golden and crimson and yellow—that is my first memory of London as I saw it on the 1st of May, 1886. We had come through Tilbury, and the sight of the grey skies, the dirty wharves, the millions of grimy chimney-pots, had struck a chill to my heart.

"How can I sing in such gloom?" I thought; for from the moment when I first caught sight of the English coast the thought of song had been uppermost in my mind. But Tilbury passed, the rest of London with its gay hansom cabs, its vast shops, its crowds of people, and more than anything, its tulips in Hyde Park, struck me with a sense of incredible adventure, and as I stepped over the threshold of the house which my father had taken in Sloane Street, I sang a little trill of welcome, the first note that I ever sang in London.

I had not been in London forty-eight hours when I set off with my letters of introduction to teachers and musicians. I was nervous and anxious, for my father had told me that unless their reports were exceptionally favourable, he would not allow me to consider the idea of becoming a singer.

One of the first letters I had was to Arthur Sullivan, who was then at the height of his fame as a composer of light music. "If only he would give me some encouragement," I thought.

The hour of the appointment arrived, and feeling timid and diffident, I presented myself at Sullivan's flat in Victoria Street. When I entered he was sitting down at the piano, playing a little tinkling tune in the treble with the soft pedal on. I held my breath. Here at last was a composer, a man who created.

He received me politely enough, but it was obvious that he was bored by the idea of having to listen to an unknown Australian girl. (Australia was so far away then!)

"What would you like to sing me?" he said, with the hint of a sigh.

"Is there anything in particular . . . ?"

He shook his head. "No. One thing is just as good as another."

And so I sang him, "*Ah! Fors è lui.*"

When I had finished I looked at him, waiting with parted lips for his opinion. For a moment he said nothing, and then, with another little weary sigh:

"Yes, Mrs. Armstrong. That is all right." My face fell.

"Quite all right," he continued. "And if you go on studying for another year, there might be some chance that we could give you a small part in the *Mikado*—this sort of thing," and he started to play one of the little tunes which all London was later to be whistling.

My eyes filled with tears. I did not wish to listen to his tunes. I had thought that at least he might have said something a little better than that. He had said nothing about the *timbre* of my voice: nothing about its compass; nothing indeed that could give me the slightest encouragement to go on.

The next person I went to see was Brinsmead, who was at that time the most fashionable maker of pianos.

As soon as I had entered the room, Brinsmead seemed at first to be more interested in his piano than in my possibilities as a singer. He was sitting at a large, highly-polished grand, around which he kept walking, as if it were something almost human. I sat down and played, and he listened with a rapt expression as if he were listening to some heavenly music and then he told me to sing. I sang. He then turned to me and said:

"The *timbre* of your voice is almost as pure as the *timbre* of my pianos."

I looked at him in astonishment. It had never occurred to me that my voice was at all like a piano. But as I saw his kind smile I realized that he was in reality paying me the highest compliment of which he could think. But that was all. He did not suggest any means by which he could help me. And I went away from Brinsmead more depressed than before.

The next day I went to see the famous singing teacher Alberto Randegger. He was, I suppose, the *beau idéal* of a singing teacher, beautifully dressed, very *chic,* very glad to see one, very complimentary. I thought as I listened to his charming phrases, that here at last I was in luck. But no. He regretted with an exquisite shrug of his shoulders that he had no time to teach me, although perhaps in a few months he might squeeze me in a few hours a week.

And then at last I went to Wilhelm Ganz. I thought to myself: "If I do not make an impression on him, I shall give up the idea of singing for ever." Ganz's most popular song at the moment was "Sing, Sweet Bird," which I had already sung in Australia at several concerts.

The next morning I found myself in Ganz's studio, listening to the opening bars of this famous song. I sang it, and before I had sung half of it he stopped and jumped to his feet and said:

"I am enchanted. You have a very beautiful voice. I will arrange for you a little concert in the City."

I went home in the seventh heaven of delight. Here at least was a man whose opinion I reverenced, who was willing to go to the trouble of arranging a concert for me, an unknown Australian girl whom he had never seen before. I had visions of conquering London, of singing before vast audiences, of waking up to find myself famous. But alas! the concert itself was to break that illusion. It was arranged in a little hall in the City. The day was foggy, and the audience so minute that I felt, "This is not an audience at all." There was a certain amount of genteel applause, congratulations from Ganz, and the concert was over. Nobody of any importance had been there. No step had been taken in my progress to fame. And this was perhaps the most disheartening experience of all.

But that concert of Ganz's proved to be the darkest hour before the dawn, for luckily for me, about this time I remembered a letter to Madame Mathilde Marchesi, given me by Mme. Wedermann Pinschof in Australia, who had been a pupil of Marchesi in Vienna and who was a great singer herself. I looked at that letter, turning it over and over, wondering what would be the outcome of it. Holding it in my hand I went to my Daddy and said:

"Will you give me one more chance? They don't seem to think anything of me here. I do not believe they understand. I wish to go to Marchesi. If Marchesi does not like me, I promise you faithfully that I shall return to Australia and try to be happy."

My Daddy looked at me, patted me on the head and said: "Very well. But this must be the last time."

J'adore ma Nellie
Mathilde Marchesi
1899

MELBA WITH MADAME MATHILDE MARCHESI

I suppose that most girls who arrived in Paris for the first time, especially if their vision had been practically bounded by the Australian Bush, would have been delighted by the magic of the city in which they found themselves. But when I arrived in Paris, I saw nothing of the boulevards, the gay laughing crowds, the glittering shops—my mind was bent on one thing and one thing only—singing to Madame Marchesi; and early on the morning after I had arrived I went round to Madame's house in the Rue Jouffroy, bearing my letter in my hand. I rang the bell, and the door was opened by a resplendent footman, who on learning my name and mission, after many gestures and explanations, disappeared for ten minutes, to return telling me that Madame Marchesi would receive me the next day at ten o'clock. I bit my lip, feeling very much inclined to cry. Here was another day lost. How I grudged it!

The next morning twenty minutes before the time of my appointment (so like me) I was sitting in a heavily gilt room with my hands in my lap, waiting to be shown into the Presence. At last the door opened and Madame Marchesi entered.

Terror struck me to the heart as soon as I saw her. She seemed to me a mixture of alarm and attraction, standing very upright in the middle of the room, dressed all in black, a small grey-haired figure, but one which it was impossible to overlook. And then she smiled, and her whole face, with its long upper lip and its intelligent eyes, seemed to be transformed. I felt at last that I had found a friend.

She began to question me, speaking sternly and directly, more in the manner of a business man than in the manner of a musician, as I conceived one. There were other pupils sitting in the room to be heard, and after my cross-examination I was told to sit down too, and to wait. I sat down, trembling with excitement, and I waited and I listened, and as soon as I had heard one or two of the other pupils my heart began to beat with excitement, for I felt that I had nothing to be afraid of.

My turn came. I was told to stand on a tiny platform and was asked what I wished to sing. Madame seemed tired and a little bored, as though anxious to get the whole business over. I said:

"I shall sing the Aria from *Traviata*."

"*Eh bien*," said Madame, and began to play my accompaniment.

I sang, glancing nervously from time to time at Madame's profile to see how she was liking me. She listened very attentively, and before I had finished she suddenly stopped, turned swiftly on the piano stool and said:

"Why do you screech your top notes? Can't you sing them *piano?*"

I was more terrified than ever. She struck a note, and for a moment I was tongue-tied. Then I thought to myself:

"This is your last chance."

So I sang as softly as I could the top B.

"Higher," said Madame Marchesi, striking the C, and I sang the C as softly as possible. And when I glanced at her I saw that a little sparkle had come into her eyes. I sang another note—I think it was the top E, still *pianissimo*—and suddenly without a word, Madame darted up from her piano and rushed from the room. I was left standing, trembling, on the platform. I wondered if all was over. I looked at the other girls, who had begun to chatter among themselves as if they were contemptuous of my efforts. Then the door opened and

Madame Marchesi came back. Once more she made me sing, and then she took me by the arm and led me out of the room. And it was then that there came the turning point in my life.

I can see her now, sitting on the sofa by my side, looking me straight in the face, and I can hear her as she said:

"Mrs. Armstrong, are you serious?"

"Yes," I whispered.

"*Alors,*" she continued, "if you are serious, and if you can study with me for one year, I will make something *extraordinary* of you."

The old lady pronounced the words "extra ordinary" with so much emphasis that I realized that she meant what she said, and I felt that at last I had begun.

Months afterwards Madame Marchesi told me what had happened when she darted from the piano stool. She had run upstairs to find her husband, and she had bustled into his room, snatched from his hand the newspaper he was reading, and had cried in his ear:

"*Salvatore, j'ai enfin une étoile!*"

But she showed me nothing of her exuberance at the time, and I thought that I was merely an ordinary pupil, though even that was more than I had dared to hope a few days before.

The next day I went round for my first lesson. I had never realized before the amazing art into which it was possible for a woman like Madame Marchesi to transform the profession of singing-mistress. She was one of the greatest artists I have ever known. She was not only a superb technician; she had also a burning spirit of enthusiasm which made one feel even when one was singing a scale that one was singing something beautiful. From the very beginning she showed me how inferior all my other teachers had been. For example, those who are interested in singing will be interested to know that I had been taking my chest notes too high, and that Madame Marchesi, after a month, was able to cure me of that error. How grateful I am!

She took me alone for one month. At the end of that month she opened the book in which she dotted down the list of her classes, and said to me:

"Mrs. Armstrong, I find that I have no room for you either in my First Class or my Second."

My face fell, and I took her by the hand.

"Please, please, Madame Marchesi," I said, "do not send me away."

She looked up at me and smiled.

"I am not going to send you away," she said. "You are going into the Opera Class."

And so it came about that I never had to study the exercises or the wearisome routine which it is necessary for most singers to study, as this clever woman saw that I did not require them.

I could write pages about Madame Marchesi, for she was the first woman who really began my education. Not only was she my artistic mother—she was my guide and sponsor in other things as well. I knew nothing of life. I had no ideas of the dangers and temptations which beset any young woman in Paris: such things simply did not occur to me. I was to all intents and purposes alone in the world, nor had I the advantage of an independent income; for my Daddy (who had remained in London and would shortly be returning to Australia) had given me a certain sum of money which he told me must last until I began to earn my own living. He still did not consider seriously that I should be able to make a career as a singer, and he only gave me this money as a means of indulging a wish that he saw was very near to my heart.

You may imagine, therefore, the debt which I owed to Madame Marchesi, not only for encouraging me and teaching me, but for explaining to me the ways of the world. She did more than that. She endeavoured to give me a polish which I fear I sadly lacked. And her methods of doing so were sometimes so abrupt that although they were prompted by kindness, they upset me terribly.

As I said above, I was extremely poor. I had no income—only the little sum of money which my father had left me. Out of this I had to pay the rent of the small apartment, to buy clothes and boots for my baby, and to provide the necessaries of life. It was not an easy task, and many is the time that I have walked through the cold and the rain to my lessons in order to avoid the expense of a bus. Naturally, under these circumstances, it was impossible to spend any considerable sum on personal adornment. In fact, I had only one winter dress. When I think of it to-day, it seems that it must have been a very ugly dress. It was of thick blue and white striped serge.

It had seemed to me in Melbourne exceedingly smart, but in Paris things somehow look different. However, I determined to put up with it, knowing that I would need every penny in the world to pay for my lessons.

But the dress was too much for Madame Marchesi. She bore it in silence for some weeks, but each time I went for my lesson I saw her eyeing it with a greater disapproval. And then the day came when she could bear it no longer. She turned to me and said in her most severe tone:

"Mrs. Armstrong, you are never to wear that dress again."

I blushed.

" I am very sorry. I have not got another warm one, and when it is cold I must wear this."

" Why? "

" I cannot afford another one."

Madame made a little clicking noise with her tongue.

" Nonsense," she said. " You have a rich father. Go and order another dress and put it down to him."

And there the subject closed for the moment. I hoped that Madame would forget my blue and white striped dress. But when I appeared in it the next day, the first thing she said to me was:

" I did tell you not to wear that dress any more."

" But I can't afford another one," I said. " It is very cruel of you to talk about it at all."

She insisted, gesticulating violently, and telling me that she could not possibly continue to teach me if I did not get a new dress; that I looked ridiculous; that the dress was an eye-sore. I burst into tears and left the room, vowing from the bottom of my heart that I would never speak to her again.

As I reached the front door there was a whirl of footsteps behind me, and looking round I saw the face of Marchesi with a little apologetic smile as though she were asking for forgiveness.

" Nellie, Nellie," she said, " I am so sorry. You must not go. Run to Worth's now, and buy yourself the most beautiful dress you can find. I pay! I pay! "

I shook my head.

" No, dear Madame," I replied. " Either you must put up with me in this dress, or I cannot come any more."

She shrugged her shoulders and kissed me. I wore that dress for weeks more, day in and day out, in rain and sunshine, and never a word did she say, although I know it must have cost her agonies.

At first I found many of her ideas somewhat strange to me. One day I had a bad cold, and I remarked to her that I could not think how I had caught it. She looked at me with a frown and said:

" Have you washed your head? "

I nodded.

" Certainly," I said. " I washed it two days ago."

She shook her finger vehemently at me.

" A singer never washes her head," she said. " She cleans it with tonic. She cleans it with a fine tooth comb. But she never washes it."

I was astonished by this revelation, which I must admit I did not take to heart. But I was not so astounded as when afterwards I went to stay with her and learnt that I could not have a " *grand bain,*" because the bath was the receptacle for the boots of the Marquis, her husband. So I had to content myself with splashing in a tub.

It went to my heart, too, when she persuaded me to give up riding, because she said that no singer ought ever to ride, that it was bad for the vocal cords. I know better now, but in those days her word was law, and I abided by it.

I think it must have been her sense of humour which made that sort of situation bearable. That sense of humour never seemed to desert her, even till the last. One day in later years when I had been singing at the Opera I came in to see her, and found her ill and depressed.

" I am going to die! I am going to die! " she cried. " I know it, and there will be nobody to send flowers to my funeral." And she turned and gripped me by the hand, saying, " Nellie, Nellie, you promise you will send a big wreath to my funeral? "

I laughed and replied:

"Yes, if you will promise to send two to mine."

And as soon as I said that she burst out laughing and the whole cloud of depression was lifted.

My last scene with her was infinitely pathetic. She was then over ninety—although it was not till three years later that she died—and old age had wrought havoc with her faculties. She whom I had known as trim, strict, and alert, with a brain as keen as steel, was now only a sad shrunken figure, almost lost to the world.

She was sitting in a chair when I entered the room. She raised her head, looked at me with unseeing eyes, and then her head sank again.

"Who are you?" she whispered at length.

"But Madame, I'm Melba—Nellie Melba," I said.

She took no notice and I asked her—still instinctively a pupil—if I might sit down.

"I'm rather tired," I added. "I've only just come from a rehearsal at Covent Garden."

"You. Singing at Covent Garden? But you've never been taught by Marchesi!"

The idea of my singing at Covent Garden seemed to amuse her immensely, and she laughed out loud, if one could call it laughter. Then she stopped, and raising her head repeated:

"Who *are* you?"

"Only Melba, Madame Marchesi."

"Melba? What nonsense. Melba?" She scanned me more closely. "Yes. You have a slight look of her. But you, *Melba!* Ridiculous!"

She spoke to me no more, and I left her house feeling that I had lost one of my dearest friends, to whom I owed the deepest debt of gratitude, for she was indeed more than a mother to me. And I loved her.

AMBROISE THOMAS

LASSALLE

My student days were hard days indeed. It would be an exaggeration to say that I was living in a garret, but I was certainly living in a very unfashionable quarter in rooms that were poorly furnished, with nothing but the bare necessities of life to keep me going. Had it not been for the sweetness to me of two dear old Irish ladies, the Misses Hyland, who would come fluttering round me when I came back from my work, with little gifts of fruit or flowers, I do not know how I should have pulled through. Their kindness was inexhaustible. I remember that once when I had no money with which to pay my rent, the elder Miss Hyland, who was like a Jane Austen old lady with her white hair and her starched caps, came up to me and said:

"Do let me lend you five pounds. I know that one day you are going to be famous, and that then you will repay me. Till then it does not matter."

It was only the burning desire to succeed and the absorbing interest in my work that kept me going at all.

At Madame Marchesi's house all the great men of the artistic world were wont to congregate, and it was here during my student days that I first met such great men as Gounod, Ambroise Thomas, Délibes, Massenet. To meet Gounod at all was to me, who had been so thrilled by hearing Arthur Sullivan tinkling his little tunes on the piano, an adventure; to be taught by him, to arouse his interest, and, I think I may say, his admiration, was a dream. I shall never forget the first time that he asked me to go and visit him in his house in the Place Malesherbes.

As I entered the room he was sitting writing letters at his desk, and before he got up he took a big stoppered bottle that was standing by his side and sprinkled sand all over the wet ink. I had never seen anything like that before and it puzzled me; but I forgot to be puzzled as soon as he had risen to his feet, because Gounod was one of the most picturesque figures. He always wore a velvet skull cap and a velvet smoking jacket. Round his neck there was a flowing bow. He was the very best type of Bohemian; but there was nothing Bohemian about his methods of work. He was, like all true artists, the sternest self-disciplinarian. He never left anything to chance. It was Gounod who taught me Faust, Romeo, and Mirelle, and while he was teaching me he would sing the other parts himself. At one time he would be the Nurse, at another the Devil, at another Romeo; and whichever rôle he sang, he seemed to adapt himself both in voice and temperament to the character he was interpreting. He was exactly like a nurse; and he was positively Satanic as the Devil. And I believe that had there been any listeners in that long room with its great organ and its innumerable photographs, they would have thought that there were a dozen people singing, instead of only Gounod and myself.

Gounod *saw* his characters as human beings. I remember him telling me the difference between Marguerite and Juliette—Marguerite, the simple peasant, but *Juliette était une affrontée.* He added that it was she who proposed to Romeo, not Romeo to her.

He had an eternal bubble of humour. In the chorus of the First Act of Juliette come the words:

> "*Qui reste à sa place*
> *Et ne danse pas*
> *De quelque disgrace*
> *Fait l'aveu tout bas.*"

Gounod, with his hand up to his mouth, whispered "*Ca voulait dire qu'il avait des cors aux pieds.*"

Two other memories of my student days stand out sharp and clear. One of them was when I met Carlotta

Patti, who was Patti's sister. The idea of meeting anybody even remotely connected with Patti thrilled me to the core, and when I entered the room, and when she limped towards me (for she was very lame) I bent down and kissed her hand, feeling as I did so that I was paying in some dim way reverence to the woman whom I thought to be the greatest in the world.

The other was when I went for the First Night to the Paris Opera. I stood in the entrance to the *foyer,* desolated and amazed by the bigness of it all. It seemed to me incredible that so wonderful a place could exist, and when I was sitting in my stall and the curtain had risen, when I heard the first strains of that marvellous orchestra, the first echoes of the perfect chorus, I leaned back in my seat and thought that if I only could sing on that stage for once, I would die happy. The friend at my side, Mlle. Mimaut, turned to me at the end of the First Act and said:

"It will not be long before you are singing here, too."

I laughed out loud.

"What an extraordinary thing to say," I remarked.

But Mlle. Mimaut was right, for not so very long afterwards I was to make my début before one of the greatest audiences that the Opera House had ever known.

CHAPTER III

MY FIRST OPERA

I AM not sure whether I " believe in " luck. At least I can say that I am inclined to distrust any young artist who attributes her lack of success to bad luck. If one is a good artist, one succeeds; and if one is a bad artist one fails—that is the rule that I have found, in ninety-nine cases out of a hundred, to be most practicable.

But there are occasions, and I am just going to write of one, when at a critical moment Fate does seem to give an extra turn to the wheel of life.

One morning, unknown to me, when I was having a lesson, the great Maurice Strakosch, who had been Patti's impresario, was calling on the " Marquis," and after coffee and liqueurs, and his usual lamentation of the dearth of new voices, he prepared to go.

On the stairs he suddenly stopped. " Listen," he said, " listen to that voice! "

(The voice was my own, singing the *Caro Nome* from *Rigoletto.*)

The Marquis, who was not particularly anxious that Strakosch should meet me, merely replied, " Yes, I see that they have not closed the door. I will shut it."

Strakosch stopped him. " But no. I must have that voice. Nobody but I in the whole world. I will possess that voice. Tell me," and he took the Marquis by the arm. " Tell me, who it is."

The Marquis shrugged his shoulders. " It is only a

young Australian," he said, " who my wife thinks may have a career."

" I don't care," cried Strakosch. " She may be young or old, beautiful or hideous, but I must meet her." Without any more ado he entered the room, and was presented. I sang to him one song, two songs, while he listened, his twinkling eyes lifted to the ceiling. And then, when I could sing no more, he took me aside and in ten minutes had arranged a ten years' contract, by which I was to receive the enormous sum of a thousand francs a month for the first year, two thousand for the second, and so on.

I was enchanted. Such wealth at once lifted me in my own eyes to the highest pinnacle of achievement. I felt made for life.

A month later, an extraordinary development occurred. The directors of the Théâtre de la Monnaie in Brussels arrived one morning to hear the pupils sing. Pupil after pupil was produced, who duly sang, but Lapissida and Dupont (as the two directors were called) remained unmoved. At length they said, " But we have heard about a young Australian, who they say has a beautiful voice." Mme. Marchesi spread her hands in a swing of impatience.

" But she is engaged—by Strakosch. She cannot sing for you. It is useless."

However, I did sing, and while I was rendering the Mad Scene from *Hamlet,* I saw a look of astonishment on their faces. Dupont nodded to Lapissida, and Lapissida winked at Dupont. When I had finished there was silence. They departed mysteriously to the next room, from whence I heard low voices in earnest conference. Eventually I was called in myself.

Mme. Marchesi was all smiles. She advanced towards me, and said with a tremendous gesture: " These gentlemen wish to engage you for the Théâtre de la Monnaie in Brussels."

"But, Madame, my contract with Monsieur Strakosch?"

She waved it aside with her long white fingers. "That is nothing at all," she said. "Strakosch is a great friend of mine. He will perfectly understand. I will arrange everything."

Knowing nothing whatever about business, I considered this a charming idea, especially when I learnt that I was to receive no less than three thousand francs a month, exclusive of my costumes, which were also to be provided. I signed that contract with a hand that trembled with delight as I thought of my good fortune.

I continued my work till one day a few weeks later, while I was sitting in my little apartment, a knock sounded at the door, and Strakosch entered. He was purple in the face, and very much out of breath after climbing five flights of stairs, and for a moment he was unable to speak. I rose and offered him a chair. He waved it aside with his immense stick.

"No," he said. "I want no chairs. I want the truth. There is an amazing rumour, which circulates in Paris, that you have signed a contract with the Théâtre de la Monnaie. Of course, it cannot be true."

I looked at him with a puzzled expression which he must have found very irritating. "But it is certainly true," I replied.

He shook his stick with tremendous vigour in my face.

"But your contract with me? What of that? Is that nothing?"

I explained as gently as possible the circumstances of the case. How Mme. Marchesi had said that she would arrange everything, that Strakosch was such a friend of hers, and that he would not mind. "*Do* you mind?" I added gravely.

"*Mind?*" he screamed. And then I had to listen for a quarter of an hour to a tirade against the wickedness of Mme. Marchesi, the stupidity of myself and the ingratitude of the world in general to famous impresarios. Finally the last spasm of rage was over, and he blew himself out of the room, leaving me to continue my book as he stamped down the five flights of stairs.

The scene shifts to Brussels, in a little house off the Avenue Louise. I had arrived at Brussels nervous and frightened, knowing that the entire trend of my fortunes would be regulated by the success or failure of my début at the Théâtre de la Monnaie. And I was eager to start rehearsal at once.

And then, suddenly, the full gravity of the situation was revealed to me. On the day after my arrival I drove up to the theatre for my first rehearsal. I stepped out of my carriage and walked to the stage door.

To my astonishment, a formidable arm extended itself across the entrance, and stepping back, I saw a blue document being waved in my face.

"*C'est pour vous, Madame.*" And the *gendarme,* or *concierge,* or whoever it was, smiled. "*Pour vous.*"

I took it, and as I read it, my heart sank. It was a legal order, stating that in view of my contract with Strakosch, I could not be permitted to appear at the Théâtre de la Monnaie.

I was in the depths of despair. Immediately I went round to see Lapissida. He threatened, he entreated, he sent telegrams right and left. He could do nothing. To use force would have caused an open scandal. Only seven days remained before the first night, and it seemed that, unless some miracle occurred, I should not be able to sing at all.

The miracle did occur—a stroke of luck like a bolt from the blue, so sensational that ever afterwards I have remembered it when difficulties have been thick about me and the way seemed dark.

It was early on the morning of the Monday before the *première.* In all the days that had intervened I had not been able to go to the theatre. I was lying in my room with drawn blinds, having spent a restless night, from sheer weariness and anxiety, unable to sleep, looking at the ceiling. Suddenly there was a knock at my door, and the head of my maid peered through the entrance.

"It is Monsieur Lapissida, Madame. He demands to see you."

And before I could answer I heard the voice of Lapissida shouting upstairs:

"Put on your dressing-gown!"

Hastily, and wondering whether some new disaster had occurred, I threw a wrap round my shoulders and hurried out on to the landing. Leaning over the banisters, I saw Lapissida below, a look of wild excitement on his face.

"Yes—yes—what is it?"

Like a torrent the words came bubbling out: *"Strakosch est mort! Il est mort hier au soir, dans un cirque. Et je vous attends au théâtre à onze heures!"*

The date is October 13th, 1887. It is raining outside my window in the Rue du Bac, and as I look out on to the dingy street it seems to me that Brussels is indeed a dull place after the sparkling streets of Paris. And yet Brussels will always remain for me one of the dearest cities in the world, for it was here that I was first to taste of success.

You must remember that with one exception I had

MELBA AT THE TIME OF HER DÉBUT IN BRUSSELS

never been on the stage of a theatre before, and even that exception was not a glorious one. It had occurred in Paris, when I had had a special audition with the Directors of the Opera, and had sung a few songs on a darkened stage with a single gas jet flaring on my face. Apart from that, my dramatic experience was *nil.*

You may imagine therefore that when I went down to the Théâtre de la Monnaie, accompanied by my dear M. Lapissida, and saw outside the theatre, in huge letters of crimson:

MADAME MELBA

you may imagine that the sight of my name in such a conspicuous position struck a chill almost of terror to my heart.

I turned to Lapissida and brushed the raindrops from my face.

"Why is my name so much bigger than the others?" I asked him.

"Because you are the star."

I laughed. "Not yet," I said. "Cannot we wait until I have proved myself?"

But Lapissida merely shook his head.

And then it arrived. It is a day of memories so vivid and yet so crowded that I hardly know how to describe it. I remember Marchesi coming to me fluttering and excited in the morning, with Salvatore very dignified and with a big flower in his buttonhole. I remember pacing up and down the room, thinking all the time of sunshine on the gum trees so far away in Australia, and I remember that as the light faded, my spirits sank. I went to the theatre. I sat in front of the glass. I knew nothing about making up—indeed, I felt I knew nothing about anything. In a sort of a dream I allowed my dresser to get me ready; and suddenly as I looked into the glass

I saw that she was putting a fair wig over my head. I began to cry. I said:

"I hate that wig. It is not *me*. I won't have it."

The dresser shrugged her shoulders. And then in the glass I saw the cheery face of M. Dupont, one of the directors. He said:

"Let her use her own hair. It is much prettier."

And so for the first time on the stage of a European theatre, a new Gilda made her début in *Rigoletto* wearing no other adornment than her own two plaits of hair with which she had been born.

I am not going to describe my reception. I think that is better done by the critics who heard me. I only know that from the first note which I had to sing, in the Second Act, there was a hush that hardly seemed human, a hush in which I heard my voice floating out into the distance as though it were the voice of someone other than myself. Nor shall I forget the thunders of applause which broke after the end of the Second Act. I said to myself:

"This cannot be for me. They are clapping and cheering for somebody else."

But when after the Third Act I was summoned to the Royal Box to make a trembling curtsy to the Queen, I believe that then I did begin to realize something of the triumph I had enjoyed.

My first Queen! How gentle and sweet she was, this long-suffering wife of King Leopold, with her grey hair and her diamonds, and the soft voice in which she told me, "You are wonderful!" She made me love her from the first moment that I saw her.

And then the supper party after the Opera! It was all like a dream, and I believe that the only person who completely kept her head was Madame Marchesi. I can hear her voice even now, cutting straight through a babble of excitement clear and businesslike, saying to me:

"*Ma chère* Nellie, how is it that you forgot the two notes in the Quartette?"

My face fell, for I was still the student—I had not yet learned to be the Prima Donna.

"Oh, Madame," I said, "I hoped you hadn't noticed it. I'm sorry."

And then Dupont, who had been my *chef d'orchestre,* leant across the table, shook his finger at Madame, and said:

"Don't bother her. She has had the most marvellous success of any singer in the world. Why don't you think only of that?"

The next morning, when I woke up, I found that I was famous all over Europe.

Among the people who came to see me in Brussels was Paderewski. To see Paderewski for the first time was to experience an unforgettable sensation. He was brought to my house one late afternoon by Mr. Elkins, who was a sort of patron of many young artists. And my brightest memory of Paderewski on that first occasion when I met him is of his eyes. He stood in the doorway with the sun shining straight in his face and his eyes glistening as though they were lit by some inner fire. They hypnotized me so much that it was not until I had been talking to him for some minutes that I began to realize the other salient features of this remarkable man—his magnificent head, his flowing hair, and above all, the radiant personality which flowed from him like a light.

We were both very nervous, for we were both more or less beginners, shy at the thought of being regarded as artists. But soon the nervousness wore off.

It was also during this period that I first heard Jean de Reszke. One day when I was studying one of my rôles in my little room in the Rue du Bac, a friend came into the room and said to me:

"Wouldn't it be wonderful if we could go and hear the revival of *Romeo and Juliet* in Paris next week! Gounod is conducting, and Patti is Juliet, and Jean de Reszke is Romeo, and Edouard de Reszke is Père Laurent."

I sprang to my feet.

"I am going to Paris," I said, "whatever happens. I do not care if I have to postpone performances. I don't care if I never sing again. To hear Patti and Jean de Reszke would make up for anything, any sacrifice."

My excitement was all the more intense because the Directors of the Paris Opera had asked me to sing Juliet, and I had been forced to refuse because, naturally enough, the Théâtre de la Monnaie would not allow me to be released.

Ah, that First Night in Paris! I wonder if it is prejudice that makes me think that something of the glamour, something of the glory, and not a little of the magic, has departed from such occasions when they occur to-day. Were there gods in those days greater than the gods of the present? Or was it only the imagination of a girl that seemed to feel the whole theatre trembling like a human breast, that seemed to hear in the first silent throbbing of the orchestra as Gounod lifted his baton, the beating of heavenly wings? It may have been, of course, and yet that performance will always stand out in my memory.

First of all, Patti! When the moment for her entry came, and when I saw the light suddenly shine on the woman who had always been my goddess, I felt as though

I should choke. I did not know, I did not care, if Patti was in her prime; I believe that already her best days were past. But all the same, hers was perhaps the most golden voice to which I have ever listened. The *timbre* of it was exquisite, the diction crystalline. I took my lesson from her, for she had much to teach.

Patti, I believe, was nervous. After all, she had not sung in Opera for some time. There was a something a little old-fashioned, too, in her appearance, a quality which I myself felt to be not without its charm. I would not have had her different. And when in the waltz song she made just a tiny slip, I could have kissed Gounod for the cleverness with which he managed to conceal it, with a mere twist of the wrist and a sudden gesture with his baton.

As for Jean de Reszke, he was a god—not only in his voice, which he used with an artistry which can only be called perfection—but in his appearance, his acting, his every movement. So utterly wonderful was he that when some time later I found myself singing in *Lohengrin* with him without a rehearsal, I burst into tears in the last Act, and thanked my stars that my singing rôle for the evening was practically finished. Jean de Reszke—so perfect, so gallant! Never has there been an artist like him.

One of the most wonderful people I met during this time at Brussels was Félix Gevaert, who, though he is not known as a composer, has left to those who know an imperishable mark upon the music of his time. He was a superb interpreter, a genius at arrangement, and in addition, a very fine executant.

When he first came to see me, I thought that I had never seen so ugly a man in my life, but I very soon forgot his uncomely appearance, for when I began to study *Hamlet* with him I realized that I was in the presence of a genius. He told me with regard to *Hamlet* that when it was first given at a *Répétition Générale* in Paris, with Christine Nilsson in the leading rôle, it was a dead failure. Thomas came round to Gevaert immediately afterwards, wringing his hands and saying:

"What am I to do? A year of my life wasted!"

"Postpone it for a month," said Gevaert; "and" (then he paused) "put in a Swedish folk song. Do not mind how you get it in—but get it in. Think it over."

Thomas did think it over, for as all those who heard this beautiful opera know, one of the main *motifs* of the Fourth Act is an exquisite old folk song of Sweden, of which Christine Nilsson, who was of course herself a Swede, made a thing of exquisite beauty. The opera was a colossal success, and when Ophelia had sung this particular *motif,* floating down the river, the acclamations of the audience were overwhelming.

One of the first things that Gevaert said to me was:

"You know, of course, that I was a shepherd boy. My father said to me that he did not know whether to make me a priest or a sabot-maker. He decided in favour of the boot-maker, because, as he said, there were already plenty of priests in the world, but people will always need to wear sabots. However, I decided instead to be a musician. And when I came down to Brussels to compete in my first examination, clad as I was in my peasant's dress, all the other students roared with laughter. However," he added, "I am afraid that I beat them."

My time at the Théâtre de la Monnaie, from a professional point of view at least, was one long round of happiness, because I have never had a management who treated me with more courtesy. And I am sure that my utter inexperience of things theatrical must frequently have been very trying to Lapissida, and Dupont. I remember, for example, that one day when I went to the office to receive my princely salary of three thousand francs a month, I stuffed the notes into my purse and was about to go, when Lapissida said:

"Aren't you going to say 'thank you'?"

"I don't understand," I replied.

He laughed. "But I have just given you what you have not earned. You missed two performances."

Still I did not understand; and then I remembered that in my contract there was a stipulation that if I were to miss any of the ten performances that I was due to give each month, the amount would be deducted from my salary. However, M. Lapissida paid me, in spite of that.

Again, when the end of the season came, I spent a very happy day packing up all the dresses which I had worn in my various rôles, to take with me to Covent Garden. I was just watching my dresser stuff into my trunk a particularly charming costume which I had worn in *Lucia,* when I looked up and saw, watching me with ill-concealed amazement, the face of Lapissida.

"What are you doing?" he said.

"Only having my dresses packed."

"But they are not your dresses."

I rose from my knees, feeling very hurt and indignant.

"But——" I stammered, "surely—these dresses belong to me?"

Lapissida shook his head. "Oh, no," he said, "I am very sorry, but they are the property of the theatre."

Feeling very sad at heart, I began to take the dresses out, and Lapissida went to the door, put his finger to his lips, and said, "Wait a moment!"

A few minutes later he came back and said with an angelic smile:

"You may keep those dresses. They are all yours."

That was one of the most generous actions I have ever known.

Nor can I refrain from mentioning another graceful little action which they paid me at this time. Having, as I have said, very little money, it had naturally been impossible for me to buy any jewels. I think that the Directors of the Théâtre de la Monnaie must have guessed my feelings of anxiety at the thought of going to London (where I should have to appear in the richly-dressed part of Traviata) with no other adornment than the thin gold necklace which I wore round my neck. And so, on my last day in Brussels, Lapissida came into the room bearing with him a large leather box. He placed it on my table and then said mysteriously:

"Here is a little present for you. Perhaps it will be useful in *Traviata.*"

He had gone from the room before I could open the box, but when I threw back the cover, there glistened from the velvet lining a beautiful set of paste—a necklace, ear-rings and a brooch. I held it up to the light, watching the colours glittering in the sunlight. It seemed to me a happy omen for the future.

It was.

CHAPTER IV

MY DÉBUTS IN LONDON AND PARIS

If the English people are conservative in their musical tastes to-day, they were more than conservative in their tastes thirty years ago. I have now reached the spring of 1888, the time of my début before the English public, and I think I may say that it was as unhappy a month as I have ever spent.

Apart from my reception with the public, my surroundings and the atmosphere in which I found myself all seemed calculated to depress me. I lived in Bayswater, in one of the most gloomy streets in London. I knew nobody, my father had gone, and as yet I had made no friends, and after the triumph of Brussels I felt so depressed that I wondered how I was going to bear London at all. Had it not been for the thrill with which I anticipated my first appearance at Covent Garden I do not think I should have borne it, and had I foreseen the unhappy issue of that first appearance, I should probably have packed my trunk and gone straight away.

Covent Garden—my beloved Covent Garden!—never shall I forget the first time I saw you sparkling in the sunshine thirty-seven years ago. I had walked to the theatre through the market, and as I stepped over the cabbage tops and the fruit skins and the straw, and paused in front of the stage door, I said:

"Surely this is not Covent Garden! Surely the National Opera House is not in a place like this?"

It took several minutes to persuade me that it really was Covent Garden, and even then when I went in and asked for Mr. Augustus Harris, I felt that by some strange mischance I was standing in a great fruit store.

I saw Mr. Harris—perhaps the first real friend that I made in London. He was very kind, very courteous, and very determined. He said to me:

"You will make your début on the 24th."

I naturally concluded that I should be able to choose the rôle in which I desired to appear, and I said to Mr. Harris:

"I suppose it will be convenient for me to sing *Rigoletto?* I would much rather do that than any other part, because it was in *Rigoletto* that I made my European début in Brussels."

Mr. Harris shook his head.

"No," he said, "I am afraid that Madame Albani has the right to that rôle."

And it was then that I realized that Albani was the reigning star, that she must always have first choice in the opera, and that I must take what she left. It was of course a disappointment to me, but I had too much respect for all I had heard of Madame Albani's art to complain, however much I wished that things were otherwise.

And then the first night came. Let me tell you at once that there was nothing thrilling about that First Night. It certainly was not a "Melba Night." There had been no sort of announcement of my appearance in the papers; there had been none of the usual preliminaries which are necessary to arouse the public to any state of expectancy. I do not believe that the greatest critics had even bothered to look in at all.

The House was half full. There was a general air of

apathy over the stalls and boxes. Even the orchestra, with whom I had had one hasty and slovenly rehearsal, seemed half asleep, and it was thus that I sang my first rôle in Covent Garden. It is true that those who were there were wildly enthusiastic, but they were so few that they hardly seemed to count.

I woke up in the morning feeling that I had passed through a nightmare, and as soon as I had remembered the events of the night before I sat up in bed and reached with trembling hands for the newspapers which were beside me. As I read them one by one, I was filled with a feeling, first of indignation, then of astonishment, and then of amusement. Of my voice they said practically nothing. They seemed to be concerned solely with my powers as an actress, and of these they spoke in terms too generous for my capabilities. Here are a few of them:

Standard: "Her capacity *as an actress* is quite sufficient to render all possible justice to the character."

Pall Mall Gazette: "Accomplished *acting*."

Daily Chronicle: "She appears to have mastered the *dramatic* features of the characters she represents."

Observer: "Genuine *dramatic* instinct."

Morning Advertiser: "Intelligent *dramatic*ally."

Stage: "As an actress she has much in her favour."

They seemed altogether to have forgotten that my job was to sing, not to act! And I know that in those days I could *not* act.

My second night at Covent Garden, in which I was allowed to sing *Rigoletto,* was equally depressing, and so was the third. It was true that the audience, such as they were, were as enthusiastic as they had been the first night, but again the house was only half full, the critics were apathetic, and the performance of a standard very much lower than that to which I had been accustomed in Brussels. Two days later I was again in Mr. Harris' office. He offered me the rôle of the Page in the *Ballo in Maschera*—and my reply was to pack my trunks and to go straight back to Brussels.

So ended my first experience of Opera in London.

I had left London vowing that I would never return, and when I make a vow of that sort to myself, I usually keep it.

And then Fate intervened in a manner so unexpected that even now I find it difficult to recall without amazement. When I had sung at Covent Garden I imagined that nobody had been present at either of the three performances who had taken the faintest interest in me. I was soon to be pleasantly disillusioned.

I was sitting one day at breakfast in my little house in Brussels, when the English mail arrived, and taking it up I saw a letter in a strange handwriting. Letters were rather luxuries in those days, and I opened it at once. It was from Lady de Grey, the greatest patron of art that England has ever known. It was to tell me that a new Juliet was wanted for London, and that she had been asked to approach me to learn if I was willing to sing the rôle at Covent Garden.

I was of course flattered, but that was about the only sensation I experienced. I had not the faintest intention of returning to London, and I wrote to Lady de Grey saying that while I deeply appreciated her kindness, I had been so badly treated in London on my first visit that I had determined never to venture on a second. I posted the letter, and thought that there the matter would end. But by the next post I received another letter from Lady de Grey: I should like to quote from it. She said:

"I did not tell you in my first letter that one of those who are most anxious for your return is the Princess of Wales (later Queen Alexandra). She was present at your performance of *Rigoletto,* and she was deeply impressed by your singing. I know that things were badly arranged for you before, but if you come back I promise you that it will be very different. You will be under my care and I shall see that you do not lack either friends or hospitality."

So after all there had been somebody there who had appreciated me! It had not, after all, been a waste of time; and immediately I sat down and wrote to Lady de Grey saying that I should be only too happy to return for the next season.

But many adventures were in store for me before my return. The very mention of those sad early days in London makes my pen long to run on to the time when things were very different. However, an autobiography, even of a *prima donna,* must be to some extent chronological.

On May 8th, 1889, I made my début as Ophelia in *Hamlet* at the Paris Opera House. There! That is the quickest way of describing a very dramatic episode.

I had chosen *Hamlet* as the Opera in which to make my début because of the unusual success which I had had in that rôle in Brussels—so unusual indeed that I was offered the enormous sum (to me at any rate) of six thousand francs a month. To sing in Paris seemed to me a very much more arduous ordeal than to sing in Brussels. The theatre was larger, the critics, as I was well aware, were more difficult to please; the audience, as I was informed, almost impossible to sway to any sort of approval unless they were presented with something superlatively good. Most nerve-racking of all was the fact that I knew there to be an unnatural prejudice against artists who were not of French extraction. How different from London! There, the possession of a foreign name was almost an essential for anybody who desired to succeed.

That reminds me of something which, perhaps, I should have mentioned before—how I came to take the name of Melba. It is a name which has been printed fairly often, and I suppose it will figure on menus long after I am gone. And the reason I adopted it was just because Madame Marchesi told me that if I were to appear under the name of Mrs. Armstrong, I should have an eternal handicap all my life. " But why? " I asked her, " surely whether I am called Armstrong, or Mary, or Jane, I shall sing just the same? " She shook her head and told me I must think of a name. And so, I sat down and thought. For some time, nothing occurred to me. And then suddenly I thought, " Why not use something to do with my own home? Melbourne—Melbourna—Melba! that's it! " that is how the name of Melba came into being.

To add to my natural alarm before my Paris début, there were other circumstances which were calculated to unnerve me. The production was postponed several times on account of the illness of Madame Richard, who was playing the Queen, and late on the afternoon of the day which was at last fixed for my début, M. Lassalle, with whom I had rehearsed, had a sudden attack of laryngitis so that I was forced to appear with a Hamlet whom I had never even seen.

But ah! how marvellous was that evening! Would it seem very conceited of me if I quoted from a review which appeared next day in the *Figaro,* above the name of that famous critic, Monsieur August Vitu? "Madame Melba possesses a marvellous soprano voice, equal, pure, brilliant, and mellow, remarkably resonant in the middle register, and using with a perfect *pastosità* up to the acute regions of that fairy-like major third which is called *ut, re, mi,* above the lines. Her personal appearance was an advantage to her: tall, slender, gifted with an expressive physiognomy. . . . It was Ophelia herself who charmed all eyes and touched all hearts while interpreting with supreme virtuosity the Mad Scene. That which ravished us was not alone the virtuosity, the exceptional quality of that sweetly timbred voice, the facility of executing at random diatonic and chromatic scales and the trills of the nightingale. It was also that profound and touching simplicity which caused a thrill to pass through the audience with those simple notes of the middle voice—'Je suis Ophelie.' And when at length the echoes of the tone wafted to us the last high note of the poor young creature, an immense acclamation saluted in Madame Melba the most delicious Ophelia that has been heard since the days of Christine Nilsson. She was recalled three times after the fall of the curtain, and, as statisticians, we have calculated that three recalls like those in the Opera at Paris are quite equivalent to seventy-five recalls in Italy at the very least."

Those days at the Paris Opera were, I should imagine, the most brilliant that have been known. Not only were Jean and Edouard de Reszke singing there but Lassalle, Plançon and Rose Caron—a galaxy of stars that one seldom meets nowadays. Nor was the Opera less brilliant socially. It was practically a necessity to have a box at the Opera—much in the way as in London it was a necessity to have a house in the country as well as in town.

And in those days Parisian Society had about it much of the glitter, the polish, exquisite *chic* of the old days when Napoleon held court at Versailles.

After *Hamlet,* I appeared in *Rigoletto* and followed that by *Lucia.* An amazing coincidence occurred in the first performance of this latter opera. Signor Cossira was my principal tenor but as soon as he had opened his mouth to sing his first notes I realized that he had no voice. It was indeed pitiable. He was hoarse, flat, breathless, in fact he seemed to be suffering from the very worst stages of an acute cold. The House was packed from top to bottom, and in order to prevent any immediate collapse, I whispered quickly to Cossira that I would sing his recitatives, and so for as long as I could do so, I sang his part. But when it came to duets I found that, try as I could, I could not give the impression of having more than one voice at a time, and so the curtain had to come down in the middle of the act.

The curtain came down, the directors rushed on to the stage, everything was confusion. Signor Cossira was profuse in his apologies, everybody else seemed profuse in their execrations. I tried to keep my head in spite of the alarming fact that I had suddenly been informed that there was no under-study available. I should have been perfectly justified, I think, in protesting against the extraordinary lack of foresight which made an emergency like this possible. But there was nothing to be gained by protesting and so I held my peace.

Suddenly an idea entered my head. I went up to one of the directors and said:

"I gave M. Engel two tickets for to-night's performance. He sang this rôle with me in Brussels. He is in front now, so I should not waste any time in going to look for him."

MELBA AS OPHELIE IN HAMLET

MELBA AS JULIETTE

Like a streak of lightning the director precipitated himself through the wings, rushed to the front of the House, seized M. Engel and told him that he must sing at once. M. Engel was exceedingly calm, and exceedingly businesslike. He bowed, said he was much honoured, and added that he would be delighted to sing, at a certain price, if they would also give him a contract to sing in the next three performances. So great was their desperation that I fear they would have given him a contract to sing for the rest of his natural life. In any case he did sing, having dressed in an incredibly short time, and the performance was saved, after a delay of only twenty minutes.

And now all Paris with its marvellous people, its marvellous gifts, lay before me. One of the first people whom I met was the great Sarah Bernhardt. Her performance in *La Dame aux Camelias* was then electrifying all Paris. I was taken to see her by Madame Marchesi, and perhaps it was lucky that when we entered the room Sarah Bernhardt was still dressing, for I had time to look at the room, which was calculated to amaze people far more sophisticated than myself. It was an immense room that gave the impression at first sight more of a circus than of the *salon* of a great theatrical star. There were heavy stuffs hanging over the ceiling, drooping down and catching the dust. There were the skins of animals on the floor, the heads of animals on the walls, the horns of animals on the mantelpiece—there were stuffed tigers, stuffed bears, even a stuffed snake. And side by side with this extraordinary menagerie were busts of Sarah herself, busts of mythological persons, easels, pieces of tapestry, dying plants—an endless collection of bric-à-brac. I even remember that under one of the tables there was a huge bowl of water in which several somewhat adipose goldfish swam round and round in their dusty watery world.

And then Sarah came in—ran in, it would be more correct to say—and as soon as she had greeted us she jumped up on to a sort of box which stood in a corner of the room and sat on it, waggling her legs like a schoolgirl, and talking with extreme rapidity and a wealth of gesture.

How did I like Paris? Had I seen her? What did I think of her? Did I like Madame Marchesi? (This in front of Madame Marchesi's astonished face), and then suddenly she leaped from her box and taking my hand she said to me:

"You sing like an angel. I want to teach you to act like an angel too. Listen." And then without more ado she started to go through with me the part of Marguerite in *Faust*. It was a revelation. Little points of character which I had overlooked were made to live before my eyes. Subtle touches of gesture were introduced—all the more marvellous when one remembers that Sarah had never played the part herself, and had only seen it once or twice on the stage. Nor was it merely an inspiration which she gave me. It was a very practical and essentially useful lesson. For instance, she said:

"When on the death of Valentin, he curses you, and tells you that owing to your sin with Faust your white hands will never be called upon to spin any more—what must you do? You must hide your hands behind your back, terrified, ashamed, as though you wished that you might cut them from your body. See!"—and she whipped her hands behind her back, staring me straight in the face with an expression in her eyes of such utter torture, that every time in the years to come when I listened to Valentin singing those words "*Sois maudite*" it called up the vision of Sarah Bernhardt.

A few days later she came round to my dressing-room after hearing me singing Juliet, seated herself on the dressing table, to the imminent peril of her exquisite satin dress, seized my box of grease paints and, waving my dresser away, said:

"Bah! You make up your face like a school-girl. You have no idea how to do these things. You are too innocent. Take a lesson from me, the wicked one!"

And she took my face in her hands and proceeded to apply deft touches with rouge and blue pencil, with powder and lipstick, forbidding me as she did so to look in the glass until it was all over. When it was over, she leapt down again, threw out her hands and said:

"*Voilà!* Now you may look, my pretty!"

I looked in the glass, and I was astounded at the transformation which Sarah had effected. I turned to her and said:

"Ah! if you could only be here every night to do that!"

But it was not Sarah, but M. Pluque, the *maître de ballet* at the Paris Opera House, who eventually gave me the address of a beautiful danseuse, who was in the ballet, and who taught me all I know about make-up. For a whole month I went to her every day, experimenting with grease paints under different conditions, and by the end of the month there was not much to know about make-up which I did not know. She told me, for example, that one must always make up differently according to the theatre in which one was playing, but that however large the theatre, and however near the audience, there should never be visible the faintest trace of cosmetics. I am well aware that many modern actresses will claim that this is an impossibility, and that if one has to appear natural to the gallery one must inevitably appear unnatural to the boxes. People who say that sort of thing are merely ignorant of one of the first principles of technique in dramatic art. My dancer was quite right. If make-up is applied properly it should be invisible, whether you are in the first row of the stalls or in the back row of the gallery; it is merely a question of knowing how to do it.

It was always a source of wonder to me that Sarah, who will always be remembered by her voice of gold, had not a single note of music in her. Music to her was simply a noise, nothing else. I learnt to my amazement that she was so incapable of singing any sort of tune that during her rôle of Jeanne d'Arc, in which she was supposed to sing, she overcame the difficulty by opening her mouth in time to the music, keeping strict silence meanwhile. It would be wrong to say that Sarah *despised* music. She *ignored* it. It meant nothing to her. It was the same with the English language. She would not learn English, because she simply would not be bothered to do so. I once heard a rather amusing conversation between her and Mr. Henry Abbey, the famous impresario. They were both speaking to each other in languages which the other did not understand. Abbey was saying:

"You *must* go there. It is extraordinarily important for your career that you should do so." Sarah replied, "I will not go because . . ." She paused. "Because of what?" asked Abbey. "Because," repeated Sarah. And then, with a shrug of her shoulders, she suddenly burst into rapid French, and I gathered that "I will not go because" was a set phrase which somebody had taught her, and that she knew no others.

France and things French were everything to Sarah. She talked of Australia as though it were barbaric and mediæval (although she loved to go out shooting "possums" with my brother when she was out there, and would cheerfully keep an audience waiting a whole hour if she was having good sport). And she dismissed America as merely "uncomfortable" (although, again, I think she was grateful for the many kindnesses she had received out there).

To write of Sarah Bernhardt is to be impregnated with her personality. I cannot write the name without thinking of the time when, years later, I went to see her in Paris, when she was dying. There was little left of the lithe, tigerish figure that had swept into my room in the years gone by. She was lying in bed propped up with pillows, a shadow of her former self, and yet somehow the radiant, fiery spirit was still there.

"Ah, Melba!" she said, clasping my hands in hers, "*tu as toujours ta voix d'or—Ma voix d'or n'a plus besoin de moi, car je meurs.*" (Ah, Melba! you have always your golden voice. My golden voice needs me no longer, for I am dying.)

Yes, she was dying. But even in the face of death, she was acting. As I gazed at the tragic figure, with the fair wig, the scarlet lips, the rouged cheeks, I could not help marvelling at the indomitable spirit which, even at the last, urged this amazing woman to make up for the last time, that she might leave the stage of life looking her best.

She knew, too, that she was dying. When I said good-bye she clung to me, pathetically, feverishly, as though she were loth to be left alone.

I walked into the next room, and paused for a moment, too upset to go out until I had pulled myself together. I stood looking straight in front of me, thinking of all that Sarah had been—all the triumphs and glory that had now almost gone. Suddenly I realized that I was looking straight into a mirror, and though I noticed something curious about my reflection, I was too distraught to pause. However, when I got outside my great friend, Emily Yznaga, who had been waiting for me, said: "Why, Nellie, what have you been doing to yourself?"

I asked her what she meant. For answer, she took me to the nearest mirror. With a shock, almost of horror, I saw that my cheeks were covered with rouge—Sarah's rouge. With a shudder I took out my handkerchief, but it would not come off. And whenever I think of Sarah, I put my hand instinctively to my face, as though the rouge were still there.

"*Ma voix d'or n'a plus besoin de moi!*" I have heard many golden speaking voices in my day, voices that made words travel on wings, voices that seemed to give a deep and poignant meaning to even the most commonplace phrases, but no voice ever had the same effect upon me as Sarah's. Unless, as an afterthought, I may add that of Ellen Terry. She too had a divine speaking voice, and a pronunciation which should be a model for all young artists. Oh, those melodious vowels and those crisp, telling consonants! Shall we ever hear the like of it again?

When I first met Ellen Terry, she was at the height of her glory, electrifying London with Henry Irving (whom she always called His Nibs) in her perfect creation of Beatrice.

Nobody would associate so exquisite an artist as Ellen Terry with anything even remotely connected with drink, and so I think that the one occasion on which she was intoxicated deserves to be put on record.

One day she said to me, "Nellie, have you ever been tipsy?" (To hear her pronounce the word "tipsy" was in itself an education, so clear and resonant did she make it sound.)

"Never," I replied firmly.

"I have," she said proudly. And then with an impetuous gesture, "Shall I tell you about it?"

Before I could say "Yes" (as I certainly should have done) she went on: "It happened when I was in Dublin with Henry Irving. He had come to my dressing-room at the theatre and said, 'Nell, will you come to supper with some friends of mine to-night if you are not too tired?'

"So out we went. It was a terrible night, Nellie, with snow on the ground and one of those piercing *Dublin* winds, you know."

She shivered at the memory of it. "When we got in," she added, "His Nibs said to me, 'you're shivering.' 'No, I'm not,' I said. 'Oh, yes, you are,' he insisted (you see, Nellie, he was very strong-minded), and he began to make a bowl of punch. So many things he put into it—brandy, and hot rum, and sugar, and slices of lemon. 'Drink this,' he said, so of course I drank it. It was really rather nice and I said, 'D'you know I like that! I think I'll have another glass.' 'I don't think you ought to,' he said, but I got my way, because I can be strong-minded too. Then I began to feel *delicious,* warm and comfortable, and not in the least afraid of the snow or the Dublin winds, or even of His Nibs. We went downstairs, opened the front door, and then—the pavement hit my face."

When I had recovered from this story, she added, reflectively: "That's what they call being 'tipsy.' Parts of it are lovely."

This was just the time when Paris was being more and more flooded with Americans, when droves of rich sightseers were pouring over from the other side of the water. Some of them who came to see were so intrigued with what they found that they remained to stay.

Mrs. Pless Moore, whom everybody knew in Paris in those days, was among the latter. She was in some ways the most American woman I have ever met, and her Americanism was heightened by her determination on every possible occasion to speak French. Even when she left her home in Paris to go on a flying visit to London or New York, she would always be bursting into the Gallic tongue with an excess of gesture and a complete lack of pronunciation. I shall never forget meeting her one day at Victoria Station hurrying along to catch a train. She paused for a moment and said:

"*Bonjour, Melba.*"

In English I replied:

"Good morning. Why are you in such a hurry?"

"*Oh, ma chère,*" she said, waving her arms, to the imminent peril of the porters around her, "*ma chienne vient d'avoir des pups. Elle est mourante. Je suis obligée de partir pour Paris tout de suite.*" And with this sonorous phrase she made her departure.

One could not help admiring Kate Moore, as everybody called her, because by sheer doggedness she had succeeded in building up such a position for herself in Paris as very few Americans have ever rivalled. She achieved even the astounding feat—more astonishing then than now—of inviting Bourbons and Murats to the same dinner party! Had anybody else done such a thing it would probably have ended in bloodshed. But under her roof nobody seemed to care.

One day she called on me at tea-time. I wondered what she wanted, for she seemed restless, as though she wished to ask me something. I was therefore very much surprised when after an hour's aimless conversation, she took her departure. However, soon after she had left, the mystery was explained. A "*petit bleu*" arrived and opening it I found that it was from Kate Moore. It read, "I am giving a very *chic* little dinner on Thursday. It would be so nice if you would come and sing a little song afterwards. P.S.—I forgot to ask your fee." I wrote and told her what my fee was, and received a letter back by return in which she said that the sum I mentioned was "certainly the largest she had ever heard of any 'cantatrice' receiving." I replied that if she could not afford it, I could tell her of lots of charming singers who would be only too delighted to sing for a thousand francs, but that my fee could not be diminished. Apparently she still wanted me. At any rate, I went. I sang. I got my fee.

However, she once tried to bribe me, and that was a thing I would not stand from anyone, not even from a woman so goodhearted and amusing as Kate Moore. She called on me one morning and asked if I would dine the following week. I looked at my engagement list and told her that I would be delighted. Mrs. Pless Moore bridled with satisfaction.

"I have Prince and Princess —— coming," she said.

"Really?"

Here she drew from her bag a small necklace of seed pearls and held it out in front of me, rather as one would hold a biscuit in front of a dog.

"Do you think, dear Madame Melba, that it would be possible for you to give us a little song?"

I was exceedingly annoyed.

"Now, Kate Moore, put those seed pearls in your bag," I said. "I shall not come to your dinner. You can have your princes and princesses to yourself."

CHAPTER V

LONDON AND WINDSOR

To look back into one's life is like looking down a long curving road, dotted ever and anon with signposts marked "To Failure" or "To Success." Perhaps, if we but knew the truth, those signposts that we remember so well may not have been so significant as we think them now. Perhaps after all, the road would have led on to much the same destination, whichever route we had chosen. But at least it is certain that at this period of my life, on my return to London for the season of 1889, my signpost was clearly marked "To Triumph."

When I think how near I had been to refusing ever to set foot in London again, I marvel at the luck which had sent me that letter of Lady de Grey's, telling me that "everything would be different this time." How different, though, I had not even dared to guess.

I date my success in London quite distinctly from the great night of June 15th, 1889, when I appeared as Juliet to Jean de Reszke's Romeo. It was the first time that *Romeo and Juliet* had been given in French in England. What a night it was! And what a cast! Apart from the unforgettable singing of Jean, that dear little soul and great little artist Mlle. Bauermeister was the nurse, Edouard de Reszke was the friar, Mancinelli was conducting, and at last, at long last, there was a packed house. I had been so used to singing to poor houses during my three appearances in England that I wondered if I should have to wait till I was middle-aged before people came to hear me. And so, when I heard the roars of applause, and when I read, the next day, the criticisms, I felt inclined to say, "It's been a fight—a hard fight—but London really is awake now." The *Standard* wrote: "Madame Melba seems absolutely incapable of a false intonation, and is almost unsurpassed in the purity and sweetness of her tones. Her shake is close and even, the few embellishments she introduces are almost invariably in good taste, and in all she does, sincerity and dramatic force are conspicuous."

Yes—everything was different, not only from the point of view of music, but from the point of view of friends. And no woman has ever had a truer friend than she who had induced me to return, who stood by my side from first to last—Lady de Grey.

I have said that Gladys de Grey was a great patron of art. She was more, she was a *grande dame,* a type of aristocracy of which London can boast only too few to-day. There was an instinctive nobility about everything she did or said. I shall never forget the first time that I met her, before I had returned to London. It was in the Hotel Scribe in Paris, in the morning, and the spring sunshine was drifting into her apartment, lighting up the gorgeous green foulard dress which she was wearing. She was sitting at her writing table, and as she turned round the sun illuminated her lovely profile, making me catch my breath with the beauty of it.

It was Gladys who gave me my first London party; that is to say, the first party to which I went after I became a somebody. I was thrilled by the very thought of going to a party, but far more thrilled after I had been sitting in her beautiful *salon* in Bruton Street for about ten minutes. Never shall I forget the succession of women who drifted into that room—the Duchess of Leinster, robed in white satin with marvellous sapphires round her neck, holding her head like a queen. Lady Dudley, with her lovely turquoises, so numerous that they seemed to cover her from her head to her knees; and Lady Warwick, then at the height of her beauty, the old Duchess of Devonshire, making somewhat pointed comments on those around her, the brilliant Duchess of Sutherland, Lady Cynthia Graham, Lady Helen Vincent, and many others.

Gladys de Grey was among the last of the women who have been capable of holding a salon, with all that that word implies. She did not confine her hospitality to one class alone, she invited every type, and by some magic of personality seemed to blend them all into a harmonious whole.

For example, one day she was giving a party at the same time as her daughter Juliet (now Lady Juliet Trevor), who was giving another party downstairs. The Princess of Wales was holding court upstairs, but as soon as she heard that there was a Punch and Judy show below, she almost ran from the room in order to enjoy the fun. Many of us followed her, and as we went down the stairs Princess Victoria touched me on the arm and laughingly said: "Mamma is such a baby!"

As for the Prince of Wales (afterwards King Edward VII) he could never be accused of conventionality, and at Lady de Grey's he always gave one the impression of a happy schoolboy, although there were occasions when he was tired with affairs of State and did not hesitate to show his disapproval of anybody who annoyed him. For example, there was an unforgettable occasion when a lady from the other side of the water was presented to him. Instead of dropping the conventional little curtsy, she swept down almost to her knees, rather in the manner of a leading lady in a musical comedy at the end of her duet with the principal man. The Prince looked at her calmly, and then said in particularly penetrating tones:

"Have you lost anything?"

Poor woman! I shall never forget her face as she rose to her feet.

But there was nothing about the Prince of Wales which made one feel that he was not after all an ordinary human being. One night Arthur Sullivan gave a supper party at which the Prince was present. I had guessed that I should be asked to sing, and as Oudin was also going, he and I had practised a duet from *Romeo,* which when requested, we started. The Prince of Wales was sitting on a sofa, talking in a subdued but audible loud voice. He went on talking. I saw a glitter in Oudin's eye which made me feel that there were dangerous moments ahead. And indeed I began to feel a little awkward myself. I felt that I wanted to listen to what he was saying. How we got through the duet I do not know, but at the end of it the Prince paid me a charming compliment and I gathered afterwards that it was only because he had been obliged to discuss affairs of State, that he had talked at all.

How absolutely natural they were, those rulers of England! To me, who had been brought up to regard the Kings and Queens as something very much akin to deities, it came with an almost overwhelming shock to hear, for example, the Princess of Wales telling me that she hated to sit next to the Shah of Persia because he used to throw peach stones on her skirt! And when one night at Lady de Grey's she came to me and, picking up my poor little pearls, which were not worth more than a few hundred pounds, said softly, " What lovely pearls! " I felt like saying to her, " You darling."

It was at Gladys de Grey's house in Paris that I first met Oscar Wilde. I had never seen anything in the least like Wilde before (we did not seem to breed that type in Australia)—and my memory of him is firstly the inimitable wit and brilliance of his conversation, and secondly a strange, almost *macabre* element in his character which made me feel always a little uneasy when he was in the room.

When I entered the room where I was first to meet him, I had a momentary impression either that I had interrupted a reading of poetry or that some dreadful scene had just occurred, for nobody was talking except a large heavy-jowled man, of a sallow and unhealthy appearance, clad in a frock coat, with a large bunch of violets in his buttonhole. I soon learnt that this was Wilde, and that while he was talking, the rest of us were expected to be silent. However, nobody minded, for as long as that brilliant fiery-coloured chain of words fell from his coarse lips, one felt it would be almost an impertinence to interrupt. If only he had had a Boswell, what a treasure we might have inherited.

Most of his wit I have forgotten, but one of the first things he ever said to me was: " Ah, Madame Melba! I am the Lord of Language, and you are the Queen of Song, and so I suppose I shall have to write you a sonnet." He never wrote the sonnet, although he wrote me some charming letters—lost long ago—and often came to see me. If I happened to be out, I could always tell when he had been, by the quantity of cigarettes which were afterwards discovered in the fire-place. In fact, so insatiable was his appetite for cigarettes that he used to have his pockets stuffed with cigarette-cases. I counted no less than six once—gold, silver and leather—and soon saw the reason for them, for he would light a cigarette, take two puffs and then throw it away, and light another five minutes later.

I think Wilde used to reserve his best stories for the public, but a thing he said once to me lingers in my memory, because, as one knew later, it was terribly true. He had been talking to me about his little sons. "I was telling them stories last night," he said, "of little boys who were naughty and who made their mothers cry, and what dreadful things would happen to them unless they became better, and do you know what one of them answered? He asked me what punishment could be reserved for naughty papas, who did not come home till the early morning, and made mother cry far more?"

My last meeting with Wilde was terrible in its contrast to those happy times. I was walking one morning along the streets of Paris, three years after his *débâcle,* when there lurched round the corner a tall shabby man, his collar turned up to his neck, a hunted look in his eyes. I was about to pass on, when he stopped.

"Madame Melba—you don't know who I am? I'm Oscar Wilde," he said, "and I'm going to do a terrible thing. I'm going to ask you for money."

I could hardly bear to look at him, not from hatred but from shame and pity. I took all I had from my purse—about ten louis—and he quickly took it—almost snatched it—muttered a word of thanks and was gone. I never saw him again.

I have mentioned Wilde at this early stage because in some ways he was typical of a society which was rapidly drifting towards the extravagances of the *fin de siècle.* Perhaps, had I been brought up in London, I should not have noticed the glitter and the fantasy of that society at all. But you must remember that, even now, I was still a comparatively unsophisticated being, and perhaps my first fresh impressions of that amazing time may be truer than when everything seemed ordinary and familiar.

It was not only an age of lovely women. It was a spacious age, when hospitality was far more lavish, probably, than it will ever be again. Who to-day, for example, would give a dinner party in which there was a pearl in each soup plate? And yet, that was the way in which Hector Baltazzi celebrated his winning of the Derby. Who would spend £2,000 on flowers for a party? Who would engage artists at fabulous prices, as a matter of course? Who, in fact, would think nothing of spending £5,000 or even £10,000 on a single party, again a matter of course? Some of those nights were indeed Arabian Nights. I wonder if those to come will ever see what we saw then!

Food was used with an extravagance that made me shudder, brought up as I had been in a strict household where Scottish frugality was the order of the day. I remember lunching one day in a room at the Savoy Hotel. It was in the height of the season and the first peaches were just arriving, fragrant and delicious in their cotton wool. I had not yet accustomed myself to the English value of a peach, since they had grown like blackberries in our garden at home, but I did at least know that here in London they were very precious. Judge of my astonishment, therefore, when our host suddenly picked up a handful of peaches from the table, ran to the window and hurled them at certain occupants of the benches in the gardens beneath. "Nearly got him," he cried—and in a minute we were all throwing peaches at the passers-by, who received them with mixed emotions.

One celebrated man, whose name I do not dare to

divulge, had a passion for chicken, but only for certain portions of the chicken, namely, the oyster. He, therefore, whenever he gave a little dinner for, let us say, three people, had eight chickens killed and roasted, ordered the particular portion of their anatomy to be detached for his own use, and ate nothing else. He regarded himself, in doing so, as exercising considerable frugality.

Nor shall I ever forget the story that was going round London in those days about one of the Rothschilds, which may or may not be true, but which is at least an illustration of those patrician days. Like all the Rothschilds, he loved to surround himself with pomp and ceremony. One night towards the small hours of the morning, he returned to his house in Park Lane with a friend. As he walked up the steps the door was flung open, revealing four footmen who had been waiting there for hours. "What!" he said, "only four of you to let me in. What's the meaning of it? Where are the others?"

He was tactfully informed that they had departed to bed.

"Then fetch them down again," he cried.

I am glad to say that his innate kindliness triumphed over his desire for pomp, and that the footmen were allowed to slumber in peace.

Most lavish of all, however, were the great balls. Oh! those brilliant dances at Stafford House, where Millicent Sutherland used to look so superbly beautiful at the top of the great staircase; at Devonshire House, where the staircases were massed with orchids, where the stream of people glided up and down like a glistening, many-coloured snake, where the whole of the great families of Europe seemed to be gathered together—Bourbons, Marlboroughs, Romanoffs, Rothschilds—in one immense procession of magnificence.

It needed a full year, not only of English but of French metropolitan life, before I really felt that, after all, I was part of this great procession and not merely a spectator of it. And perhaps the greatest compliment which I received at this time was when I was commanded to sing before Queen Victoria at Windsor, in company with Tosti, and Jean and Edouard de Reszke.

The date, if I remember rightly, was July 4th, 1890. We all set off merrily from the station at three o'clock, by a train that was due to arrive at Windsor at half-past three. Jean and Edouard were both in high spirits. Tosti had on his long cape, which always seemed to arouse the curiosity of the crowd.

I felt strangely excited by the idea of singing to Queen Victoria and to the German Empress. I looked out of the window, drummed my fingers on the window pane, and cleared my throat.

"*Poof! ma chère,*" said Tosti, "*qu'est ce que tu fais? Tu n'as pas peur, Toi?*"

No, I was not afraid. But I should not have been an artist if I had not been, as I say, excited.

There must have been some mistake about the train we were to take, as there was no carriage to meet us at the station and so we were forced to ascend to the castle in a rickety old cab. The driver hesitated for some time.

He took us to the right entrance, and it was nearly four when we were eventually shown into a little room in the castle.

The performance had been commanded for four o'clock, but by a quarter past four nobody had appeared to take us to the presence. "I hope they know that I am singing at Covent Garden to-night," I said, and resumed my contemplation of the room.

It was half-past four before a courier arrived to tell us that the delay was due to the non-appearance of the German Empress who had gone for a walk. She had not returned, but we were to go in to Queen Victoria, who would receive us alone.

As we entered the room a tiny figure in black, attended by her ladies in waiting, took a step towards us. I realized that this was Queen Victoria and that in this frame dwelt the spirit that for over half a century, through storm and stress, had dominated the hearts of countless million subjects. She shook hands with us one by one, looking us straight in the eyes as she did so. I had a dim sense of a picture come to life, so like was she to her portraits—the smooth silvery hair, the heavy eyelids.

The Queen asked us various questions about our careers, and then there was a long pause, during which I distinctly heard the glass-cased clock on the mantelpiece ticking out the precious seconds. It was now nearly a quarter to five, and thinking of Covent Garden, I began to grow anxious.

Queen Victoria broke the silence. "The Empress," she said, "is very late. I think we will begin." And without any more ado she returned slowly to her chair, sat down, and waited.

We sang, and sang. There were solos, duets, more solos and finally (or, as we thought, finally) the trio from the last act of *Faust*.

It was growing dark, and the clock on the mantelpiece struck half-past five. I could almost hear, in imagination, the crowd shuffling outside the Gallery at Covent Garden. It was only too evident that they had forgotten to inform Her Majesty that I was singing at Covent Garden in the evening. She would certainly have been the last to ask us to continue had she known. As it was, she was probably prolonging the performance until the arrival of the Empress.

At that moment there was a bustle outside, the door opened and the Empress came into the room. She was rosy from her walk. " Now," I thought to myself, " at last we shall be allowed to go." But, to my horror, Queen Victoria smiled graciously at the Empress and said: " What a treat you have missed. We must have more for you! "

It was on the tip of my tongue to tell her that I was singing at eight, but Jean nudged me, and with a sinking heart we returned to the piano. Once again we went through the programme, only I fear that this time was a hurried affair, and the trio from *Faust* must have sounded almost like rag-time.

And then I felt so absolutely desperate that in spite of a fear that I might be doing quite the wrong thing, I managed to whisper to Miss Minnie Cochran that I was worried to death about getting back to London, and wondered if it would be possible for us to be dismissed. Evidently this message was conveyed to Her Majesty, for after a few gracious words and the offer of refreshments in another room, we *were* dismissed.

Before we departed from the castle, Miss Cochran handed us each a little parcel, which we hurriedly accepted, and then, with mingled emotions, we were all driving down the road, this time in the royal carriage, to the station.

By a miracle of fortune we caught a train just as it was steaming out of Windsor Station. There would be no time to eat, and little to dress, but with good luck I should just be able to appear.

Meanwhile, we were longing to know what was in our parcels.

"You show yours first," said Tosti to me.

"No, you show yours," said Jean to Tosti.

Finally, we compromised by all undoing them together. There were disclosed:

Myself: A little brooch of pearls and rubies.

Jean: Gold links.

Tosti: Gold pencil.

Edouard: Gold and platinum links.

When I reached Covent Garden, the first act was in progress. Mr. Harris was tearing his hair, and behind the scenes there was pandemonium. Disregarding all questions, I ran to my room, dressed feverishly, dabbed some make-up on my face, and positively ran on the stage. I had delayed them only fifteen minutes, which all things considered, was not bad.

But it was a very hungry Gilda who was singing to the great audience that night!

CHAPTER VI

MERRY JESTS—LORD AND LADY LYTTON

PARIS now became for me my chief *pied à terre.* I had been so much of a wanderer in the last two years that I was indeed happy to have a place that I could call home, and to have friends who would be more than mere acquaintances.

Many faces drift before me as I write of those friends, some who have long ago vanished, others who are still alive. Perhaps the most typical of all the delightful figures of that epoch in Paris was the Prince de Sagan. He was one's *beau idéal* of a gallant of Paris, with his exquisite clothes, his perpetually fresh buttonhole, his perfectly waxed moustache. What a grace there was about him and his kind! Many is the morning that I remember opening the boxes of orchids which he sent me, and then setting off with him in a dog-cart to drive in the Bois, which Boni de Castellane now tells me he borrowed from a friend!

One met everybody who was at all prominent in social or artistic Paris in the Prince's lovely apartment in the Place de la Concorde—Madame Alfonse de Rothschild, Meissonier, Boni de Castellane (then a young man with no designs on American millionairesses), Princesse Murat, la Comtesse de Chevigny, la Comtesse de Greffulhe and many others.

At the risk of appearing divergent I must tell the little

story of which the Comtesse de Greffulhe, who is now, of course, the Comtesse Jean de Castellane, reminded me only the other day. It occurred at a party given by Sir William Gordon Cumming. Amongst those present were the Prince of Wales, Soveral, Lady de Grey, and the Duchess of Manchester. During lunch a message arrived asking me if I could possibly manage to sing at Covent Garden that night. I said "Certainly not."

And then the Prince, with his wonderful smile, looked across and said, "I am going to Covent Garden myself to-night, so please, Madame Melba, send back another answer."

Naturally, I was honoured to do so. But I went on eating my lunch, just the same!

But none of the personalities whom one met *chez* Sagan was more amusing than that of Herman Bemberg. I could write pages about *him*. I had often heard Jean de Reszke speak of this brilliant young man, who was one of the most amusing figures in the society of Paris, which is amused by brains rather than by birth, and although in both these qualities Bemberg was irreproachable, it was, I must confess, his brains that most appealed to my democratic Australian character, and more than anything his bubbling irresistible sense of humour. He treated life as an immense fantastic joke. He was like some faun dancing mischievously down the Champs Elysées, piping cheerfully to those who would follow his folly. And I was perfectly prepared to follow it.

The very method in which he introduced himself to me was characteristic of him. I was sitting in my little *salon* in the Avenue Victor Hugo, when very slowly and softly the door opened. I could not imagine what it was, and I was just going to shut it, when through the crack there was pushed a magnificent bouquet of orchids.

This was decidedly intriguing.

"*Qui êtes vous?*" I cried.

The door opened, and I saw a very handsome young man, who advanced towards me, precipitating himself on his knees, and said:

"Only Bemberg."

I began to laugh. It was then noon, and I went on laughing the whole afternoon and most of the evening until midnight. That was the effect that Bemberg had on me!

If Bemberg had not been a rich man, he would have made an imperishable name for himself either as a composer or as a clown. For the moment I must confine myself to the humorous side of his character. I remember one day when I was staying with his mother and father at Meudon, he proposed that we should go out for a drive in his father's dog-cart. I assented gladly, and soon we were bowling down the long straight roads, I driving, towards the village of Meudon. Bemberg had behaved admirably up till this point; but as soon as we began to meet the local population he began to take off his hat. He took off his hat to everybody—to the old women carrying baskets, to haughty village belles lounging at the corners of the streets, to venerable clerics padding through the dust, and each time he took off his hat he swept a low bow as though to acknowledge some salute which they had paid him. I bore this for some time, but after about ten minutes I handed him the reins so that he could not continue. There are limits even to Bemberg's humour.

He was utterly irrepressible. During the rehearsals at Covent Garden of his beautiful opera *Elaine,* in which I played the leading rôle, I saw so much of him that he began to regard my dressing-room as his cloak room, and developed the habit of leaving his coat and his hat, and any other of his miscellaneous belongings, in my room during the performance. There is never much room in a dressing-room, even for one's own clothes, and I found this habit somewhat inconvenient. And so on the second night of the Opera, when I came down after the First Act and discovered, as usual, Bemberg's hat, coat and umbrella, calmly usurping the only chair in the room, I decided that I would teach him a lesson.

I cut his hat almost completely around the brim, covered the inside of it with black grease paint, cut his umbrella so that it would fall to pieces when it was opened, and put two eggs in his overcoat pocket.

At the end of the Third Act, Bemberg rushed round for his hat and other belongings, telling me that he had to hurry to Lady de Grey's box, where there was a particularly august assembly of persons waiting for him.

"*Eh bien!*" I said, "I hope you enjoy yourself."

I do not know whether Bemberg did enjoy himself, but Gladys de Grey told me afterwards that he arrived in her box with a face like a nigger, and that when he took off his hat it fell down at her feet.

Nobody enjoyed my little prank more than did Bemberg himself. He never seemed to mind his appearance. For instance, one day when I had a house at Maidenhead I asked Bemberg down, telling him that as we should be spending a great deal of time on the river, he need not bother to wear any town clothes. He arrived in a glaring blazer which he informed us was typical of the sporting Englishman, and which he wore with ready-made trousers—so ready-made indeed that after a few hours of Maidenhead they split all up the back, so that we had to pin him up with safety pins.

Friends, and art! The more I write of this book, the

more clearly do I see that those are the two things that have made life worth living. Some people, I know, would tell you that the artist must be sparing of his or her friends, that art is so stern a mistress as to brook no rivals. I have not found it so. The more I have sung, the more I have made friends, and the better the friends, the better, I hope, has been the singing. What, for instance, could have been more wonderfully encouraging than the little note which Jean de Reszke wrote in my autograph book at about this time?

"Nature," he wrote, "has endowed you with a voice of gold, undoubtedly the most lovely of our age. You are also a musician, and a charming woman. All those qualities can be appreciated by the public. But what I know, as well, is that you are the best of comrades, and that I shall keep eternally the memory of our relations in art and friendship. Count always on your devoted—Jean de Reszke."

He wrote these words, I remember, soon after I had appeared for the first and last time in my life at the Opera Comique. It was a matinée of *Carmen* given on December 11th, 1890, to raise funds for a statue to be erected to the memory of Bizet. I sang the tiny rôle of Michaela, and I could not understand the astonishment which everybody round me expressed when they heard I was going to sing it. "It was not a star's rôle," they said. "No great prima donna had ever sung it before. I should be eclipsed. People would be amazed. I was stupid to attempt it," etc., etc.

Why on earth a prima donna should not sometimes sing small and secondary rôles, I could not see then, and I am no nearer to seeing to-day. I hate the artistic snobbery of it. The part of Michaela has some exquisite music in it which I loved singing, and I sang it later on

JEAN DE RESZKE

EDOUARD DE RESZKE

at Covent Garden with Calvé, and again in America, with Zelie de Lussan, and other prima donnas following my example. And, anyway, my singing the part at the Opera Comique did not seem to interfere with the receipts, which amounted to the exceptional sum of 42,000 francs.

Everything seemed *couleur de rose*. I had a flat in the Champs Elysées, and I really think that those days were among the happiest that I ever spent: certainly they were among the most inconsequent. A sort of Spring madness seemed to have seized Paris that season. It was in the very air, and it particularly affected le Comte Charles de Mornay. Charles was of course a scion of one of the oldest families in France, and it was a grief to many of us when he died, shortly afterwards, of consumption. But, in spite of his delicacy, whenever he came in contact with a wild spirit like Herman Bemberg he seemed to become even wilder than Bemberg himself.

Of all the mad days I have ever known, that first April Fools' Day in Paris was the maddest, and it was all the fault of Charles. When I woke up in the morning my maid brought in a tray bearing at least twenty letters. The letters were in Russian, in Spanish, in German, in English—in fact, in every language I had ever heard of, even Chinese—they bore the most elaborate coronets, the most ridiculous crests—and occasionally they were written on the cheapest note paper. All these letters were proposals of marriage from various legendary noblemen, including Charles himself. In the afternoon I went out for a drive, and when I returned I saw a huge box reposing in my bedroom. I had rather forgotten the episode of the morning and it had not occurred to me that this would be another practical joke. Impatiently I opened it, and as I did so there was a piercing noise from inside the box, and one of the largest turkeys I had ever seen pushed out its head, and tried to bite me. I had hardly recovered from this shock when a little later another box arrived.

As I was about to open this box the Baron de Saint Imand was announced. He bowed low and advanced with a charming smile across the room. I thought that possibly he would be a useful person to open the box, and as the Baron was an exceedingly gallant man he said he would be delighted. After a great deal of breathlessness and energy the lid was opened, and out jumped a large rabbit, and settled on the top, regarding the Baron with quivering nostrils. The Baron was absolutely horrified because, at the same time as the rabbit, his own card fell out of the box.

"Ma carte—c'est une infamie!" I tried to explain to him that it was only a practical joke, but he was so obsessed by the insult that he would not listen to reason and vanished in a cloud of indignation.

The day was not yet over, for the two chief conspirators were coming to dine with me that night, that is to say, Charles and Herman Bemberg themselves as well as Gladys de Grey. I wondered if possibly some new trick would be played upon me, but I determined to say nothing to them about having noticed anything unusual in the day's proceedings. As soon as we had settled down to dine, a servant entered and said to me:

"I regret, Madame, that I have no more room to place the cakes, nor have I any more money to pay for them—and every minute they still arrive."

I treated this as if it were the most natural thing in the world.

"Put them anywhere," I said. "On the floor, in the cupboard, and do not bother about paying for them."

A few minutes later he came in again. "The cakes, Madame," he said. "They still arrive. There is no more room on the floor. They are piled up almost to the ceiling. What shall I do?"

I was intensely intrigued, and was longing to see what had happened, but I was determined that Charles and Herman Bemberg should not see me betray the slightest interest. So I turned to the servant and I said:

"Give them to the *concierge*, and when he has had enough give them to another *concierge*. There are plenty of *concierges* in Paris."

Well, that finished the dinner, but the evening was not yet over. We were going to the theatre, and so soon as we arrived in our *loge* I was greeted by the *ouvreuse*, who was almost in tears.

"Madame, there are a dozen oranges in the front of the box. What on earth am I to do with them?"

"They're yours," I said. And there *that* little matter ended.

The next day I received payment for the cakes. It was not a cheque, it was not even a money order; it was a huge sticky mass of one centime stamps, so large that I could have almost papered my bathroom with it.

The year went by, and on the next April Fools' Day I determined that I would have my revenge. As you may be aware, it is still the custom in Paris, where baths are not such common luxuries as in England or America, for those in need of a bath to hire it.

Here, I thought, was my revenge on Bemberg. And so I ordered him to be sent these baths once every quarter of an hour, beginning at 8 o'clock in the morning, and going on till midday. The fact that he was an exceedingly *chic* young man, whose toilette was regarded by the *jeunesse dorée* of Paris with an emotion almost of veneration only lent colour to the joke.

But I was not going to let him off as easily as all that. I therefore arranged that at midday a Professeur de Memoire, who I hoped would be a gentleman of exceedingly determined disposition, should call upon him. The Professor arrived, and demanded that he should teach Bemberg the first lesson without delay. Bemberg swore that he had never sent for him. The Professor expostulated.

What, Monsieur Bemberg had even forgotten that he had sent for the Professor! That only showed how much he needed him!

Bemberg repeated with emphasis that he had not sent for him. The Professor continued to insist.

How he got rid of him eventually I do not know: but soon after lunch he arrived at my flat almost in tears. He said that his clothes were ruined, that the Professor was an idiot, that he had been put to a great expense, that he was absolutely disgusted.

"Well, Herman," I said, "it is your fault. You began it. I didn't."

And that was the last of practical jokes between us for some time. I may add that I did not pay either for the baths or for the Professor.

In order that this chapter may not seem too entirely frivolous, I feel that a rather more sober character should be introduced. I am thinking of Lord Lytton, who was then, of course, our French Ambassador.

Although he was a very quiet and reserved man, he always filled me with a certain feeling of awe. Perhaps that was due to the fact that I had not read his books. Whatever the reason, he was, to say the least of it, an impressive man, a man of an old-world courtesy which was rather rare even in those days. I am afraid that my chief recollection of him was of the occasions (which were very frequent) when he took snuff.

He would take from his pocket a little gold snuff-box with an enamelled miniature on its lid, carefully dip his fingers into it, lift his eyes to the ceiling, and then, very slowly and very delicately, sniff it up his nose, with an air of infinite relish. But that was not all. When the snuff had procured for him its utmost sensation, he would flick his fingers and take from his breast pocket a large red handkerchief, which with infinite precision he would apply to his nose. Then he would say "Ah!" clasp his hands behind his back, and walk with a happy smile towards the window. It made me feel that there must be something very attractive about his particular brand of snuff.

Lady Lytton, whom I loved, was a twin sister of Lady Locke, whose husband was Governor of Victoria, and who had given me a letter to her when I left Australia. I shall never forget a practical joke which they played on me one day when I was asked to tea at the Embassy. I arrived, to find Lady Lytton (as I imagined) sitting in a chair by the fire, and we immediately began to talk. I asked her a great many questions about her life in Paris, for I had not seen her for some months, and as the conversation took its course I could not help wondering why Lady Lytton was constantly smiling so secretively. And then the mystery was solved, for from behind a screen the real Lady Lytton emerged, and I discovered that I had been talking all the time to Lady Locke. The likeness was, I think, the most amazing that I have ever known.

CHAPTER VII

TOSTI—LANDON RONALD

It was not till the autumn of 1892, when I made my début in *Aïda* at Covent Garden, that I first really got to know Tosti. As a matter of fact, it was at Lady Randolph Churchill's that we first met, but only when I had studied *Aïda* with him did I come to appreciate him to the full.

Tosti was a little man with a great personality, full of funny stories, some of them somewhat too *risqué* for publication. He too had an abounding sense of humour. He was always one of my first visitors when I got back to London from abroad; and so when on one occasion I returned, and days went by without a visit from Tosti, I wondered what had happened to him, and thought I would go round and see what was the matter.

I went. I arrived at his house, and was greeted by Berthe his wife, who seemed in a state of great agitation.

"Where is Tosti?" I said. "Why has he not been to see me?"

"*Ma chère*," she said, "*c'est épouvantable!* Tosti has lost his teeth. He wishes to see nobody at all."

"Teeth or no teeth," I said, "I am going to see my Tosti. Where is he?"

She shrugged her shoulders and pointed to the door much as though he was in the last stages of a fatal illness.

A Melba

souvenir affectueux

TOSTI, 1902

I went upstairs, and found him crouched in a chair, looking very miserable.

"Tosti, Tosti!" I said. "What is this about your teeth? Why have you not been to see me?"

"I can't see my friends," he cried. "I have no teeth."

"Well—why don't you put in your nice false ones?"

"Je ne peux pas! Je ne peux pas!" he repeated. *"Cela me donne la fièvre."*

All arguments, all blandishments, all mockeries even, were of no avail in the task of persuading him to put in his teeth, and so after a short time I departed, trusting that he would eventually get over his indisposition.

I went abroad again for several months, and when I came back I wondered what had happened to Tosti and his teeth. I had no need to wonder, for I had hardly been in my room an hour before the door was flung open and Signor Tosti was announced. He advanced towards me grinning like a Cheshire cat and showing all his teeth, with a cigar stuck between his lips. The tragedy was over, and we sang songs for hours together.

There were moments when I would willingly have slapped Tosti—moments in which he was like a naughty child. Now that I am on the subject of Tosti, I cannot help recalling one night at Covent Garden when he nearly caused Caruso and myself to disgrace ourselves. The opera was *La Bohême,* and as soon as I came on to the stage I noticed that Tosti was sitting in the front row. For the first act, all went well, and he behaved perfectly. But in Act II, where we neither of us have very much to do, Caruso suddenly whispered to me, "For heaven's sake, look at Tosti." In a rash moment I looked. He presented such an amazing appearance that it was only by exercising an almost superhuman self-control that I was able to keep my face. He had taken a white handkerchief from his pocket, and attached it to his mouth so that it looked exactly like a very long and particularly ludicrous white moustache. Nor was he content with this. He puffed out his cheeks, pushed his head forward, and stared at us with great goggle eyes, an expression of the utmost solemnity on his face. You know how infinitely funnier every incident of that nature seems when one is in such a position that it would be fatal to laugh, so you may imagine the plight I was in for the rest of that act.

Although English people are, at least, as musical as any nation in the world, they never seem quite to *abandon* themselves to music like some other peoples. If an Italian or a German hears a piece of music or a singer that he loves, he goes mad with joy, no matter what it is he hears, or where he hears it. Not so the Englishman. He wants to know what he is applauding. He is "ca' canny" in his emotions.

Two pictures are in my mind when I write this—one of Venice, one of the Thames. What a difference!

One night, in Venice, where I had gone for a brief holiday after a strenuous season in Milan, Tosti and I decided that we would go out on the Grand Canal and give a little concert. It was a marvellous night, with the moonlight silvering the roof of the palaces—the sort of night in which one felt that even the dullest of souls must be moved to some sort of poetry.

Thrilled with excitement, we borrowed a harmonium, which was sweet and in tune, though it had seen better days, and guided by Ambroggio, my faithful gondolier, we pushed off from the steps of the hotel, the prow of the gondola plashing alluringly in the still water.

Then I began to sing. I forget what it was I sang

first—Tosti's *Matinata,* I believe, or his *Serenata.* At least, I know that it was something of Tosti's own composition. Never shall I forget the marvellous feeling that I had as my voice echoed over the water in that city of dreams. I can see, at this moment, the little gondolas drifting in on us from all sides, out of the dark canals, curving round corners with lanterns gleaming faintly. And I can still hear the cries of "*Bravo, bravo, Tosti!*" "*Bravo, Melba!*" which burst out when I had finished.

In ten minutes we had drawn a crowd. We started to go slowly up the canal, while I sang another song. More and more gondolas followed, until the whole canal was thick with them. We turned down the side canal. The chain of gondolas followed, like a black serpent with a hundred eyes. Soon it seemed that half Venice must be listening to me. The moon rose higher in the sky, windows were opened and dark heads pushed silently out, pattering footsteps echoed down all the side streets. Still the gondolas followed, and still I sang. It was not till nearly twelve o'clock that I returned to my hotel, having learnt exactly what it must feel like to be the Pied Piper of Hamelin.

When we were next in England together, at Henley, Tosti suggested that we should try the experiment again, only this time with the English setting of the Thames. I was a little doubtful, for I knew the English temperament, and Tosti didn't. However, the night was so glorious—one of those warm nights in June that linger between the freshness of spring and the heat of summer —that I agreed.

We went out in two punts tied together, again with a little harmonium, and steered for that part of the river where the punts lay thickest. I sang—again enjoying myself intensely. The last notes died away. Silence.

Not a cheer, not even a clap from the assembled punts. I could not understand. I thought of how half Venice had come out to hear me, and this apathy was chilling. I whispered to Tosti:

"What's the matter with them? Am I singing badly?"

"Cara Melba," he whispered back, "you have never sung more divinely."

We tried another song, drifting, at the same time, to another part of the river. No punt followed us, and when I had finished there was the same silence, broken only by the ripple of water in the reeds.

"Very well," I said to Tosti. "As they don't realize that they're hearing a *prima donna* for nothing, I shall remind them. Give me your hat."

He gave me his hat, and we punted round, thrusting the hat under the noses of the most attached couples we could spy out. After twenty minutes' hard work we had collected four and eightpence.

"What shall we do with this?" I said in disgust, giving Tosti back his hat.

"What can one do with four and eightpence, unless to buy a bun?" he said.

A few days later a great friend of mine came up to me and said, "Were you singing on the Thames the other night?"

I nodded.

"I knew it," she said. "The people were absolutely entranced."

I thought of my four and eightpence, and held my peace.

Apart from musical self-consciousness, which is bad enough, there is also in England a really astounding ignorance of the work of new composers. We hear of things in London ten or fifteen years after they have been known, and known well, on the Continent.

This ignorance is not confined to the masses, but characterizes even some of our most celebrated musicians. I cannot help thinking, in this connection, of a famous English musician, whom I will call Z. I was staying with Lady Charles Beresford in her house at Brighton. As she was not very well at the time, she had her bed taken into the drawing-room, and in the afternoon she asked me to come and sing to her.

"Of course," I said. And a divine concert we had. In particular, I sang a great many new French songs by composers who had already made a great name abroad.

In the evening, Z, who was also staying in the same house, came up to me in, perhaps, not the best of tempers.

"You disturbed me terribly this afternoon," he said; "I couldn't write my letters."

I looked at him with a certain amount of surprise.

"Really?" was all I thought the occasion called for.

"And what *was* it that you were singing?" he asked.

"Oh, some French classics—Chausson, Ravel, etc."

"Never heard of him," said Z, and turned on his heel, leaving me to ponder the strange ways of this land of hope and glory.

It was at this time that I first met a young man with beautiful eyes, curly hair and a long nose, who was afterwards to play a considerable part in my career, and was to be known to the world in general as one of the best musicians of our time—Sir Landon Ronald.

I was singing *Faust* at Covent Garden, and during one of the performances I noticed that wherever I went I was followed by the slight shuffling figure of this young man. He stood in the wings while I sang, he even clambered doggedly after me up the stairs when I went to my dressing-room, always fixing me with those immense luminous eyes that shone out of his pale face like stars.

Eventually I could not bear it any longer, and when I saw him trotting after me in one of the corridors I turned round sharply and said to him:

"I wonder who you are? And why do you follow me like this?"

He gave a pull to his tie, smiled shyly and said:

"I'm Landon Ronald."

"And who may that be?" I asked, slightly mollified by the smile.

Another pull to the tie, and he replied in a husky voice:

"I've just been engaged as *répétiteur* here."

He paused and looked at me pathetically. I said: "Are you any good?"

There was something attractive about him, and I thought I would give him a chance. I was then studying Massenet's opera *Manon,* and I wanted somebody to play the rôle for me. Why not the youth who stood before me?

And so I said, "Do you know *Manon?*"

Very quickly he said, "Yes."

"Very well. Come to my hotel to-morrow at twelve o'clock, and I'll see what you're made of."

He turned up at my hotel the next day at twelve o'clock, still with the same shabby suit, and sitting down at the piano, he played the opening bars of *Manon,* without the music.

"Here," I said, "not so fast. You have studied this. I haven't. I want the book."

He smiled, waiting for me to find my place, and then played on. We went through the whole of the first act without a pause, and when we had finished I said, "You play beautifully, and you seem to have a wonderful memory. Have you studied *Manon* for long?"

He shook his head diffidently. "No," he replied. "I borrowed the score after the performance, and sat up learning it all last night. I had never seen it before."

And that is why Landon Ronald is Landon Ronald!

I was so impressed with his playing that shortly afterwards I took him to America as my accompanist and conductor. We went all over the States, and gradually I noticed his art becoming more and more finished, his interpretations more and more sympathetic. But he was still, musically speaking, a beginner, and he was not always quite sure of his orchestra.

One night, he underwent a terrible ordeal—the sort of ordeal that must come to all conductors as their worst nightmare. Campanari was singing before a vast audience, and after a few moments of the song it was evident that Landon was in trouble with his orchestra. He had not mastered the accompaniment, and in spite of feverish efforts he could not bring the singer and the orchestra into accord.

Suddenly Campanari stopped singing. There was a deathly silence in which I heard Landon put down his baton with a little tap on the desk. Campanari smiled gently and in a sympathetic voice he said, "I think we'll begin again."

They did begin again, and this time all was well, and the applause for the young conductor at the end of the song was as great as for the singer himself.

I always think, if anything goes wrong on the stage (so wrong, that is to say, that it is impossible to disguise it from the audience), that it is far better to own up frankly, and to start again, than to blunder on from bad to worse, until all the audience are put in a state of nervousness and suspense.

Once, for example, I was singing at Blackpool with Landon Ronald, and one of the encores was his own song, "Away on the Hill." He began to play the accompaniment, and at once I noticed something unfamiliar. I began to croak the few first bars, and then I stopped. I turned to him and said: "Landon, Landon, please try the other key. I'm not a contralto yet!"

It afterwards transpired that he had been playing the song for a contralto the night before, and had begun the accompaniment mechanically, without thinking.

I need hardly say that every audience adores a little scene like that!

CHAPTER VIII

ST. PETERSBURG—PALERMO—NICE

A REPUTATION is a curious thing. Like a snowball running downhill, it grows with uncanny speed, and like a snowball, too, it melts away in a moment unless it is solidly moulded. Certainly, at this time, my own reputation was spreading beyond the limits of my wildest dreams. I was receiving offers of engagements from every part of the world—engagements which I was forced to refuse on account of existing contracts.

However, when, in February, 1891, I was invited, in company with Jean and Edouard de Reszke, to visit St. Petersburg in order to sing before the Tsar Alexander III, I felt that this rare privilege was in the nature of a command, and I approached the directors of the Paris Opera in order to obtain a temporary release.

It was not the habit of those directors to give such "leaves," but they gave one to me. Whether I was particularly Scotch and obstinate, or whether they felt that the Tsar's wish ought to be granted, I don't know. Suffice it to say that I was given six weeks' leave of absence, in the middle of the season.

The Tsar had expressed a particular desire to hear *Romeo et Juliette,* and here, at the outset, was a difficulty. By immemorial tradition no language but Russian could be sung in the Imperial Theatre. What Romeo would sound like in Russian, even if any poet could be found sufficiently heroic to write it, I do not know. I know only that neither Jean nor Edouard nor I could attempt to sing it in anything but French. And so, after a good deal of negotiation, it was decided that for the first time in the history of the Tsar's Theatre, we were to be allowed to sing in that language.

What a strange journey it was from Paris to St. Petersburg, even in those days when Europe was tranquil, before the storm had broken! All went well, however, until we got to the Russian frontier, when I found that, by some mischance, my name had not been mentioned to the authorities, although I was travelling as one of the Tsar's artists.

I had been sleeping, and in the late afternoon I awoke to see the light gradually fading from the snow-bound, untidy-looking frontier station. I wondered why we were waiting so long, and then realized that it was because of the searching examinations of passengers' luggage by the dark, fiery-eyed customs officers who were stamping their feet in the snow outside. A closer inspection revealed to my horror, an exquisite cloak which I had brought especially for *Lohengrin,* lying on the ground, perilously near the soldier's feet. I dashed outside and tried to explain, in a mixture of four languages, that the cloak was for the Opera, that it was a very beautiful thing, and that on no account must it be spoilt. All was useless. They merely gazed at me with silent indifference. What would have happened had I not discovered a Russian friend on the train, I do not know. However, a few words from him soon put matters right, and instead of indifference, the soldiers escorted me back to the train with many apologies. I did not care for their apologies, but I cared intensely for my cloak, now safely reposing in my trunk.

How can I describe my impressions of St. Petersburg

in those days? It seemed a city of ineffable sadness, given over to a strange silence, broken only by the cold, monotonous jingle of sleigh bells. Dusk was falling when we arrived but the universal mantle of snow gave to the fine buildings a look of shadowed brightness, as though they were clothed in a light that never shone on land or sea. I felt melancholy, and very, very far away from all my friends. And I remember (so strange are the images which the mind retains!) that the first thing I saw was a man who was rubbing snow on his ear in order to prevent him having frost-bite.

But melancholy was soon swept away by a series of the most magnificent and glittering entertainments of which the whole, semi-barbarous hospitality of old Russia was capable. I was staying at the Hotel de France, and on the next morning when I woke up, a message was waiting for me on my table summoning me to a dinner given by the Grand Duke Alexis, the Tsar's eldest brother. Having heard a little of the sumptuousness of Russian entertainments, I decided to wear my most resplendent frock, with the few jewels which I possessed in those days.

Dinner was at eight, at the Grand Duke Alexis' own palace, and he greeted us with charming courtesy, speaking, to my relief, perfect English. We were conducted to a magnificent room, and were more or less formally presented to those charming Russians, of whom, alas! so few can now be surviving.

Now, I did not know anything about Russian habits. And when we all moved to an immense table, on which reposed a dazzling array of dishes, although I thought it strange that we should be expected to dine standing up, I took it as part of the local colour, and started to make a very hearty meal. The appetite of those around me, however, seemed curiously small, for most of them only toyed with a small portion of caviare or nibbled a savoury biscuit. And then the explanation was made clear to me, for the great doors were swung open, another hall was revealed, glittering with gold plate, and dinner was announced. I had been endeavouring to make a meal off *hors d'œuvres!*

What a greedy little monster I must have seemed, I thought, as we went in. However, after the dinner had been progressing for what seemed an interminable time, I no longer felt greedy. My own appetite was quite put to shame by that of the Russians.

How gorgeous everything was! When a Russian entertains, he puts his whole heart and soul into his hospitality, as though his reputation were at stake. Nor does his generosity stop with a mere dinner. There is always some little favour left at one's house the next morning and sometimes these favours take the shape of the most wonderful gifts. I know that after that party at the Grand Duke Alexis', at which I had merely sung a few songs with Jean and Edouard, there arrived the most exquisite bracelet of diamonds and sapphires—"as a little souvenir." And the Emperor himself, before my departure, presented me with another bracelet which seemed to me so typically Russian in its design that I always wore it afterwards as a mascot. It was composed of engraved diamond cubes and large, irregular pearls, strung together on a slender chain of platinum and gold.

But most redolent of all the semi-barbarity and gorgeous colouring of Old Russia seemed to me my first sight of Russian ballet. We are so satiated with Russian ballet nowadays that there seems nothing sensational, nothing particularly remarkable about it. But then, when the ballet had never moved from St. Petersburg, to look on it for the first time was an unforgettable experience. Our Western eyes had been trained to regard ballet as merely a conventional monotonous affair of toe-dancing, white ballet skirts and occasional gymnastics. Ballet for us had little colour, little thrill, practically no contact with life. And when I sat back in my box, and saw the curtain rise on a stage of marvellous colour, listened to the fierce fiery music, marvelled at the superb grouping and choreography of it all, I felt that I had discovered a new art.

I turned to Edouard de Reszke, who was sitting by my side, and said, "Think how amazed they would be by this ballet in Paris or in London."

"Yes," he agreed. "But how would you get it over? They would never believe you if you told them how beautiful it is."

Edouard was quite right. When I returned to Paris, I raved about the ballet to everybody I met. I told them that it was like nothing we had ever seen or ever could see, and I told them, too, something of the training of the dancers which I had witnessed over there, how they were taken as small children, and trained day in and day out for their life's work—so different from the half-hearted, amateurish methods which were all we knew in those days. But did they listen to me? Not at all! They merely laughed and said that they already had all the ballet they wanted. I often wonder what would have been the result on British dancing if I could only have persuaded people to listen to me thirty years ago.

It was a strange contrast amid all these gorgeous ceremonies to go one day to a small room in the Conservatoire in the suburbs of St. Petersburg to sing to a little old man with a determined face, long white hands, and quick bright eyes, who was too ill to venture outside.

The little old man was Rubinstein, and I had gone to him in response to a letter which, alas! I did not keep, saying:

Dear Madame Melba,

I am old and ill, and dare not venture out into the chill winds. But I feel, though it seems presumption as I write it, that I cannot let you leave St. Petersburg without asking if you would pay a great honour to an old man. Can you come for a few minutes to sing me just one song?

ANTON RUBINSTEIN.

I went to him, and I sang him a good deal more than one song. He accompanied me in songs which he had never seen before without a moment's hesitation, and when, after I had sung to him, he sat down without a word of preparation and began to play an elaborate *Concerto* of Liszt's, I marvelled at the spirit of genius which could so dominate a worn-out body that it gave it the force and strength of a young man.

It was not, however, till I left Russia that I realized to the full the amazing fire and abandon of the Russian temperament. On the last night I had to take so many curtains that finally, in a state bordering on exhaustion, I sent for a chair to be placed in the wings to allow me to rest between times. I remember that in the last curtain of all I was suddenly startled by seeing what seemed to be an immense white sheet let down from the gallery. It was only a chain of scores of handkerchiefs which the students had tied together, and were waving frenziedly to and fro.

But there was more in store. They swarmed round me when I tried to get to my carriage, shouting and gesticulating, their breath showing white and misty in the cold northern air. The pencil with which I was vainly endeavouring to sign a hundred programmes at once was taken from me by a young man, bitten to pieces with a single crunch of strong white teeth, and distributed to his chosen friends, who received it with a reverence and an excitement which, I should imagine, must have compared favourably with that of the mediæval peasants who scrambled for the so-called sacred relics which were the stock-in-trade of wandering preachers.

And finally, when I eventually succeeded in reaching my carriage, it was only by walking over the coats of my admirers who like so many young Raleighs had cheerfully thrown them indiscriminately into the snow and slush. As a *finale* I discovered that my carriage was crammed with orchids. And I must confess that my gratitude was mingled with a feeling almost of relief when after endless delays I eventually managed to drive away.

Writing of the frozen North has made me feel a longing to return, in memory at least, to the sunlight, and though after Russia, seasons at Paris and London intervened, there was nothing very eventful about them and I cannot resist shifting the scene, with a writer's privilege, to Sicily, where during the Spring of 1892 I appeared in *Traviata* at the Opera House at Palermo.

As a matter of fact, now I come to recall that time in detail, the crossing from Naples to Sicily had been anything but sunny and spring-like. It had been one of the worst crossings conceivable, and when I arrived at Palermo in the early morning, I went straight to my room and told my maid that on no account was I to be disturbed. And had it not been for a strange coincidence I suppose that I should have slept for many hours.

I had just fallen into a sound sleep when suddenly I woke up. For a moment I could not recall where I was and lay in a sort of doze, wondering what had disturbed me. And then I realized that in the next room, somebody was playing with exquisite feeling the *Serenata* of Braga on a violoncello, whose tones echoed clearly through the thin wooden walls. The situation was so unreal and so deliciously fantastic that I sat up and joined in, as I happened to know it.

The music stopped suddenly.

"*Chi è la?*" The voice was that of an old man, but there was a catch in it as though he were laughing.

I laughed back.

"*Chi è la?*" I repeated.

"*Sono Braga.*"

"*Sono Melba.*"

There was a sound as of the violoncello being rapidly precipitated to the floor, and then:

"I must see you. Let me come in quickly!"

"Not possible! I am in bed."

There was a sound of something suspiciously like a curse.

"What time may I come?"

I thought over the situation, and then said, trying to speak with an air of propriety which the situation did not seem to warrant: "At two o'clock."

And at two o'clock through the dazzling sunshine bearing a bouquet of flowers in his arms, Braga came to me. How delightful he was! We talked and talked. He played and I sang. That is all I remember, but I do know that those hours in Sicily were indeed golden.

From Sicily I went back to Paris, *en route,* as I thought, for America. But when I returned to Paris, it was to be greeted with the news that the Metropolitan Opera House had been burnt down. Henry Abbey and Maurice Grau came and told me that as there had been no clause in my contract concerning the question of delay, I should be legally justified in demanding the whole of my salary. I told them that as I hadn't sung, I didn't expect to be paid. They looked relieved.

And then, I suddenly realized that I was in a quandary. I had £200 in the bank, no prospect of an immediate engagement, nothing. So I said to myself:

"I'll gammon. Nobody shall know I'm hard-up. I shall go to Nice."

I went to Nice. I went with two maids instead of one, and took the best possible rooms in the best possible hotel. What would have happened but for a stroke of luck, I do not know. Probably I should have languished in a debtor's prison. But it happened that Mr. Grau was at Nice for a holiday, and said to me, "Would you like to sing here this season?"

With assumed indifference, I replied that I should not mind, but that I imagined all artists would already have been engaged.

"Oh, I'm sure they'll be delighted," he said, "and I can get you 4,000 francs a night." I waved him away. "I wouldn't dream of singing for less than 5,000," I said.

Well, I was given my 5,000. And I often think that it was 5,000 francs' worth of bluff.

CHAPTER IX

TERROR AND TRIUMPH—KING OSCAR

Now I come to a time of terror; a time when for days I went about in fear of my life.

The place was Milan; the date, the early spring of 1893. I had arrived at Milan trembling with excitement at the thought of singing in the great Opera House of La Scala, which was (as I well knew) one of the most critical audiences in the world. But very soon I was trembling with another sort of excitement, for immediately I entered my hotel, I was handed a batch of letters in a strange spidery handwriting, which as soon as I opened them proved to be from anonymous enemies, all threatening me with various sorts of disaster unless I left Milan immediately.

I went up to my room and called my secretary, my beloved Louie Mason, whose like I have never since found in the whole world. I said to her, "Look at these!" and picking up a few at random I pressed them into her hands. She read them carefully, and I walked to the window to look out on to the bustling streets while I awaited her verdict. It seemed so horrible that in this brilliant sunshine, in this city of music and of art, there should lurk such poisonous people as the writers of these letters. The sunshine seemed tarnished; there was a shadow over the bright roofs, and even the faces of the people whom I could see below seemed to be distorted and suspicious.

"Well," I said, turning to her, "what do you think of them?"

She tossed them impetuously on the table.

"Of course they are horrible," she said, "but take no notice."

I nodded. "We will wait and see," I said.

The next day there were more anonymous letters, not only sent by post, but delivered by hand. All my inquiries as to the senders led nowhere, and even the hall porter seemed to have no recollection of the kind of man or woman who had delivered the notes. They were even worse than the day before. I was told in one that poison would be put in my food unless I gave up the idea of singing at La Scala; in another I was warned that if I attempted to enter the lift, it would break and I should crash to pieces on the floor below. In another I was told that were I to go out at night there would be a stiletto waiting for me in more than one dark corner of the streets.

Perhaps I was foolish to read these letters, but when one is young and inexperienced, and when, in addition, one is faced with an ordeal so nerve-racking as a first appearance at La Scala in an opera like *Lucia,* which has been the testing ground of every *prima donna* for years before my time, it is hardly to be wondered at that I was in a state of acute anxiety. Every mouthful of food I took seemed likely to poison me. I would not go even downstairs, let alone out of doors.

The day before the performance, after still more threats of an even deadlier nature, I called my secretary, and I said to her:

"I cannot stand it any longer. I think I had better go. Even if I were to come through alive, the ordeal would be so terrible that I should not give my best."

She stood in front of me and put her hands in mine.

" You can't go, Nellie," she said. " It would not be you. You have got to stay and face the music."

I drew away from her and began to pace the room.

" I don't mind the music," I said. " It is these terrible letters."

She argued, she entreated. And so helpful was she, so utterly unflinching in her determination, that I should go through with the ordeal, that I took her advice and I stayed. I honestly believe that had it not been for Louie Mason I should not ever have sung at the Scala, and I think I may say that if I had not done so, I should have missed one of the greatest triumphs of my life.

You will remember that in the opera of *Lucia* some twenty minutes of action takes place before the first notes echo behind the scenes telling of Lucia's arrival on the stage. How well I remember standing behind the wings listening to the harp playing Lucia's solo, my heart throbbing, my hand clutching Louie Mason's, and wondering if when I had sung these notes they should prove to be my last. And then when I walked on to the stage, unlike my usual custom, I allowed my eyes to wander anxiously in the direction of the audience. And immediately I had done so I noticed a curious phenomenon. It seemed to me that the whole of the vast audience were turned away from me, so that I could only see their backs! So startling was this that I almost forgot the phrase I was singing. And then the beauty of the music caught me by the heart and I sang the opening melody as I had rarely sung it before. And as I was singing I saw the audience turning, turning, gradually, in my direction, which my quickened imagination distorted into something ominous. As you may be aware, the boxes at the Scala are so built that many of the seats of the occupants are actually turned away from the stage. I had forgotten this fact. And when I remarked it from the stage, it seemed to me that the audience, or at any rate the box holders, had turned away from me simply because they were determined not to listen to my singing!

How I ever sang my initial *recitatif* I do not know to this day. It was a terrible ordeal. But it was also a very brief one. For before I had finished, an immense "Brava! Brava!" echoed all over the theatre. The rest of the performance, though I say it myself, was a crescendo of triumph, and I am told that after the Mad Scene the applause went on for ten minutes.

And when, finally, the curtain fell, and I stepped back, worn out, to my dressing-room, I thanked God and Louie Mason that I had stayed to face the music.

The Scala was a remarkable institution in those days. One could see some of the most wonderful performances of opera in the world, and yet, at the same time, one was constantly shocked by customs which seemed utterly out of keeping with the general artistic tradition.

Never shall I forget a night not long after this when one of these customs was suddenly made known to me without any warning. I was again singing *Lucia,* and was in the middle of one of the most impassioned love duets with Edgardo, when all at once the music ceased. Edgardo turned swiftly away, and with hardly a second's pause the orchestra blared out the national anthem in another key. For a moment I remained with outstretched hands, wondering if I had gone quite mad. And then it dawned on me that the Queen had just made her entry into the Royal Box and that this was the Italian method of doing homage to her.

How utterly inartistic! I do not mind the fact that I

was made to look like a complete fool: I certainly *felt* one—but I do resent—and any artist worthy of the name would agree with me—being stopped for several minutes in the middle of a very tense scene and then being expected to continue where one left off as though nothing had happened. One's operatic emotions may be fairly elastic, but they are not as elastic as all that. However, I hear that great musician Toscanini has put an end to this custom. And I should like to offer him my sincere congratulations on doing so.

But even this custom, which might at least claim the excuse that it was prompted by loyalty to the Throne, was not quite so distasteful to me as another, which, thank God, Toscanini has also stopped. When I first saw an example of it, I was sitting in a box with Puccini at a performance of *Tosca,* which, as it is hardly necessary to state, Puccini always considered one of the finest of his operas. To my horror, after the prayer, the *prima donna* stepped forward, with her hands to her heart, her face wreathed in smiles, and after repeated bows sang the whole *aria* over again.

For me, the whole act seemed spoilt, and I turned to Puccini indignantly. "Why do you allow that?" I asked him. "It's unforgivable."

Puccini shrugged his shoulders. "If there are no '*bis's*' in Italian opera," he said, with an air of resignation, "there is also no success."

I could not understand it, and I said to him:

"Why don't you take a lesson from the Germans? They don't expect applause even at the end of an act. They never lose their parts, and that is why their opera is the greatest in the world."

Puccini was an extremely simple man. I do not think that it is anything to his discredit to say that he was really a peasant of genius. He very rarely talked, except in short *staccato* sentences, while he sat shyly on the edge of a chair. The only time he ever really "got out of himself" was when he was sitting at the piano, either playing some extracts from his operas or improvising—a pastime of which he was extraordinarily fond. He would sit down sometimes and improvise a whole scene from an opera straight out of his head, and when asked: "What was that you were playing?" he would merely shrug his shoulders and say: "Nothing."

It was with Puccini himself that I had the priceless advantage of studying *Bohême.* Indeed, I went down to Lucca that summer and stayed for six weeks, while almost every day he came to my hotel, very often lunching, and marking my copy of the score in his neat little handwriting, to give me his personal impressions of how the opera should be sung.

How full Italy was then of great musicians! It was during those golden days in Milan that I first had the honour of meeting Verdi. He was then in the wonderful "Indian Summer" of his genius—the period which gave us *Othello* and which was finally to fade into the darkness with the strange swan-song of *Falstaff.*

I had no idea that I should ever know Verdi, until one night, after I had been singing *Rigoletto,* I learnt that the Maestro had been in the House, and that he was now outside my dressing-room waiting to see me.

I bounded to the door and said: "Maestro! what an honour! And they didn't tell me that you were here——"

He bowed, slowly, almost sternly. It was like a tree trying to bend. That was the impression he gave one, of some gnarled, wonderful, old tree. There was an impenetrable reserve about him which made one's conversation with him slightly stilted. And yet, he had bright eyes, like a boy's, and eager restless hands.

Greatly daring, I ventured on a suggestion.

"Maestro, I have a favour to ask of you." (I felt rather as though I were appealing to a judge.)

"Yes!" said Verdi.

"I want to sing to you your opera *Othello*."

Then very slowly he smiled.

"That, Madame, is not a favour," he said. And straight away we arranged that on the following day I should go round to his house and sing to him.

I shall always remember that lesson—the long cool room, with the sun streaming through the windows, and Verdi sitting down at the piano, and playing and playing until we had finished the whole opera. He was an inspiring master. He made one feel his phrases as he himself felt them, and he gave to each phrase an added loveliness.

When at last we had finished, and I had sung the few, halting high notes which mark the passing of poor Desdemona, he leant back, looked up at me with one of his rare smiles, and said:

"Tell me—with whom have you studied this rôle?"

"With Tosti," I told him.

"Ah!" He nodded. "*Caro* Tosti! I wondered. He is the only man who would have taught you to sing my opera like that."

We parted firm friends (I hugging a precious photograph), and his last words to me were that one day he would listen to me singing his opera in public. But, alas! I never did that, for not long afterwards he died. It was a terrible disappointment to me, but I feel that I may console myself by remembering that I sang his music as he himself told me it should be sung.

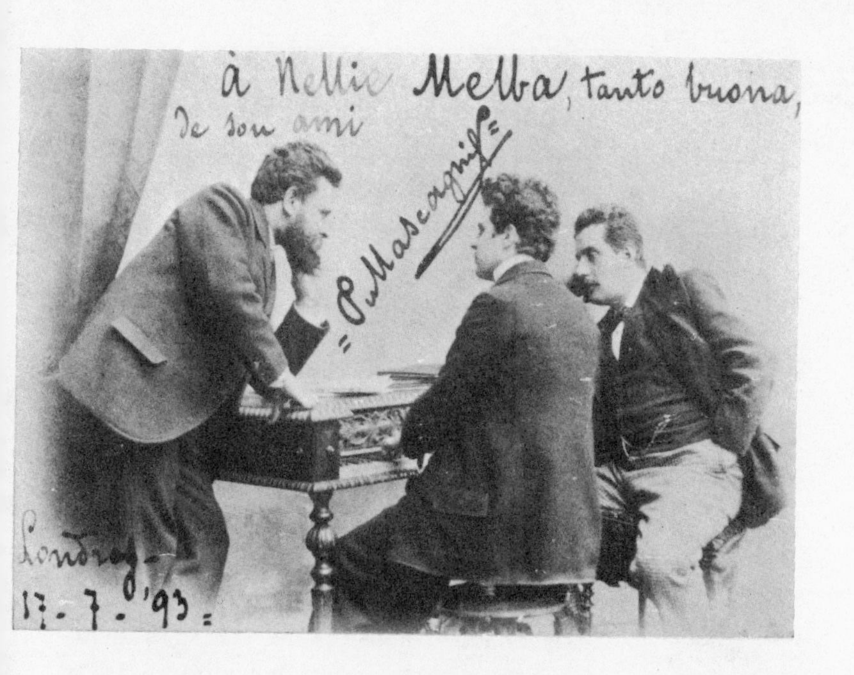

RANCHETTI, MASCAGNI AND PUCCINI

I never realized, till I began to write these memoirs, what a bird of passage I have been. Here, there, and everywhere—England, France, Russia, Italy—to keep track of oneself in those days is a bewildering task. I often wonder if those who listen to a singer remember that they are listening, in nine cases out of ten, to a woman with a home which she can hardly ever see. It might add a little sympathy to their thoughts of her if they did.

I must go quickly over the next short period, the spring of 1893, mentioning *en passant* that I reappeared at Covent Garden in *Lohengrin* on May 15th, and that four days after that I redeemed my promise to Leoncavallo by creating the rôle of Nedda in *Pagliacci,* which, by the way, is one of King George's favourite operas. His Majesty told me that he saw it ten times during this season alone. I want to pass on to the autumn which was set aside for a first tour of Sweden and Denmark.

Sweden and Sweden's King (Oscar) (who was the last King of both Norway and Sweden) will always be linked in my memory, for of all the kings I have ever had the honour of knowing, none was more genial or charming than this smiling giant. As a matter of fact, it was only by luck that I met him at all, for during the whole of my tour His Majesty was in Norway. And just as I had finished my engagements, and was on the point of sailing for America, a message arrived saying that His Majesty requested me, if possible, to remain a little longer in Stockholm in order that he might hear me.

With considerable difficulty I managed to arrange that I should open in America a fortnight later than I had anticipated, and I informed the King that I should be honoured to sing before him. I smiled when I read the programme that he had proposed, for it was about as arduous a selection as any singer could possibly undertake, embracing, as it did:

1. The Balcony Scene from *Romeo*.
2. The Second Act of *Lohengrin*.
3. The Third Act of *Lucia*.
4. The Fourth Act of *Faust*.

However, in those days, four of the most strenuous acts of four different operas deterred me not at all, and I felt inclined to congratulate the King on his good taste.

I was still more inclined to be grateful to him when I saw him at the Opera, for twice during the performance he rose of his own accord and bowed to me from the royal box. His gracious act was at once noticed by the audience who did not seem to know whether they should follow his example or remain seated. Some of them half stood, others sat still, wondering if they were infringing some rule of etiquette.

During the performance, a message was brought round by an A.D.C. to say that the King wished to see me at the Palace the next day, and as I had very little time, the audience was fixed for 11 o'clock. I arrived ten minutes before the time, and was ushered through endless suites of the exquisitely decorated drawing-rooms until eventually I arrived at a small room, furnished in the simplest possible style. Here I found the King waiting for me, with a single groom-in-waiting by his side. He greeted me in Italian, and for some time we talked in this language, until suddenly, finding I could not express myself freely, I said: "Perhaps Your Majesty does not know that I am an Australian."

The King: "Are you really? That's splendid. Then we'll talk Australian. But before we say anything else, I want to confer this decoration on you."

It was the decoration "Litteris et Artibus" and I

expressed my appreciation and honour with such sincerity that I made him laugh.

"But won't you pin it on for me, Sir?"

The King: "Of course I will. Lend me a pin."

Myself: "I'm afraid I have only a hat pin."

The King: "Fancy a woman without a pin!"

The gentleman-in-waiting supplied one, and His Majesty pinned it on my breast, where it has often reposed since.

The King: "But one ought never to give people pins. It's supposed to bring ill-feeling. I shall have to take your decoration off again."

Myself: "Oh, Sir, please don't do that."

The King: "Very well, then. I know a way of making that all right."

And he kissed me on both cheeks, explaining that, by doing so, he was taking away any evil spell. After that he took me to see the Crown Prince—the present King—and came down to put me into my carriage.

I left Stockholm a proud woman, not only because of the King's graciousness but also because, when I arrived at the station, I found a crowd of five thousand people to see me off, all singing their divine Swedish folk tunes. It was one of those tunes which Christine Nilsson introduced as a solo in *Hamlet*.

It was three years before I was again to have the honour of seeing the King of Norway and Sweden, and this time it was in the most unorthodox way. I was sitting one afternoon in my flat in Paris when my butler rushed in, very agitated, crying:

"Madame—Madame—there is a lunatic at the front door." I prepared to fly, when he added: "An enormous man, of a height incredible. He demands to see you, and he pretends he is the King of Sweden!"

I gasped with relief and anxiety, for while I was glad to escape from the mythical lunatic, I was not at all sure how the King would like the reception which my butler appeared to have given him. However, when he entered, his face was wreathed with smiles, and he greeted me with all his old cordiality.

"I've come to have tea with you," he said; "I'm absolutely dying for a cup of tea."

After tea, he sprang to his feet, saying, "Now let's sing." And he went to the piano and dragged out half a dozen operas, opening at random at the duet in the second act of *Lohengrin*.

"You will be Melba," he said, "and I shall be Jean de Reszke." We sang duet after duet, and I was delighted to find that he had a fresh, sweet tenor voice. And so enjoyable were our duets that it was nearly seven o'clock before he bade me good-bye.

CHAPTER X

NEW YORK—KING EDWARD VII

COBBLESTONES and jolting cabs! That is my first memory of New York, where I landed in the winter of 1893. There is nothing much left either of the cobblestones or the cabs nowadays, and the contrast between Fifth Avenue then and now makes one realize with a shock the amazing rate at which America has progressed.

To-day the traveller from London who arrives for the first time in New York is struck by an impression that he has landed in a city of infinite size, infinite efficiency and almost excessive speed. Everything seems bigger, quicker and more mechanical. And I suppose, to some people, everything seems uglier. I must admit, *en passant,* that I do not understand those people, for to me there has always been a very real and inspiring beauty about the soaring skyscrapers, with their clean line and their masculine grace. And I look forward to the day when, as is bound to happen, we shall have them in every country.

But everything was very different in 1893. At least, so it struck me as I made my miserable journey over those interminable cobblestones. I contrasted it with the smooth London streets, and the quick canter of the hansom cabs. And I am afraid America suffered in the contrast.

From the artist's point of view, also, New York in

those days was a very different place from New York of 1925. In London, if an artist made a great success, he or she was received on a footing of absolute equality with the most "exalted" people in the Capital. Not so in New York. An artist was an artist, and although she might be the subject of amazing hospitality, though innumerable kindnesses might be showered upon her, there was always a subtle difference between her and the rest of society.

However, I was too much interested in my work to bother much about anything so material as the Four Hundred seemed to my youthful imagination, and even if there had not been my work, there would have been the fascination of a new country, still in those days in a somewhat raw state of civilization as compared with the cities which I had left behind.

I stayed at the Waldorf Hotel. We had had a blizzard crossing the Atlantic, and for the first day I decided that unlike my usual custom, I would rest in my room instead of trotting round to see the sights. And when the night came and I went to bed, I shall never forget the gradual feeling of suffocation which came over me as my lungs endeavoured to cope with the amazingly efficient steam heat for which American hotels are famous. I lay there panting, wondering if perhaps there had been a fire downstairs, or if I were being overcome by some subtle form of asphyxiation. Feeling I could bear it no longer, I got out of bed and began to walk to the bedroom of my secretary. There was a sitting-room between the two rooms, and as I opened the door I saw her coming towards me.

"What is it all about?" I said. "Can't you breathe, either?"

She shook her head and laughed.

"No. I am absolutely suffocated."

And so we went round and, not caring what happened to the carpets, we opened those windows, which I am sure had not been opened for several years, and then we went back to sleep in healthy English fashion.

The conditions under which I first sang at the Metropolitan were not altogether ideal. Apart from the arduous year which I had already spent and the exceptionally bad crossing, from which I took longer to recover than I had expected, I was told that I had made a mistake in selecting *Lucia* for my début. People said that it was a Patti opera—and indeed, Madame Patti was at that very time making a farewell tour of the United States. Then again, on the eve of my appearance, one of the principals suddenly fell a victim to laryngitis, and I had to act with an Enrico who had not even once rehearsed the part. In addition, there had been no Grand Opera in New York the last season, owing to the fire at the Metropolitan, which had necessitated extensive building alterations. A new house, a new audience, a new country—it was not unnatural that I felt nervous.

How I conquered that nervousness is, I think, best told in the words of the critics:

> "The temptation is strong to say that in vocal equipment she surpasses all her rivals. In finish of vocalization she is the finest example heard on the local stage since Sembrich made her début here ten years ago. Her voice is charmingly fresh and exquisitely beautiful, and the tone production is more natural and more spontaneous than that of the marvellous woman (Patti) who so long upheld the standard of *bel canto* throughout the world."
>
> *New York Tribune,* Dec. 5th, 1893.

However, in spite of criticisms such as this I realize now that *Lucia* was not the ideal opera in which to have made my début. It was not, in fact, until the production of *Romeo and Juliet* that I considered I really established myself.

The Metropolitan Opera House is such a national institution in America that I trust it will not cause any undue heart-burns if I remark that its acoustics have never seemed to me to be nearly as good as either those of Covent Garden, the Auditorium in Chicago, or La Scala, and last but not least, the Manhattan. I do not know the reason for this—in fact the science of acoustics is still so little understood that probably nobody could tell me. The fact remains that the perfect conditions which obtain at Covent Garden, and the other theatres I mentioned in which singing is a sheer joy, are not to be found at the Metropolitan.

But whatever I might think of the Opera House, there could be no two opinions as to the audiences. American audiences are among the most intelligent in the world. I do not know how much mere dollars have to do with this, for one cannot help remembering that they have always had the money to pay for what they wanted, and have always been able to afford the best. The fact remains that they know what is good and that they will never put up with a "second best." And they judge for themselves without waiting for the critics.

In particular, I adored singing for the "matinée" girls, as they were called. I don't think they exist in any other country. I wish they did. These girls were the débutantes of New York. They turned up at all the matinées, wearing huge posies of flowers at their waists, and when the performance was over they would stream down the gangway and throw the flowers to me, over the heads of the orchestra, on to the stage.

And then gradually New York society, who did not regard artists as of sufficient importance to warrant their inclusion in their habitual amusements, began to wonder who was this Madame Melba who was having so great a success, and wondered if perhaps after all it might be interesting to make her acquaintance. I had not the faintest objection to allowing them to do so. I have always been perfectly happy whether my host is a millionaire or a bootmaker, provided that he possessed, whatever his profession, a sense of humour and a sprinkling of brains. And just about now I met a great many people, who, like the lady in *Romance,* possessed "just bunches of character."

One of the first women with whom I dined was that volatile and amusing old lady, Mrs. Paran Stevens, whose daughter was Lady Paget. Like many other delightful people whom I have known, she was also entirely vague. She called at my hotel one day and after asking me to dinner left her card on my bureau, saying, "That is the address, and dinner will be at 8 o'clock."

On the appointed day at about a quarter to eight, I set out, and told my driver to go to the address which Mrs. Paran Stevens had given me. It was right at the other end of the town, and when we eventually drew up in front of the house, I noticed to my surprise that the house was empty. This seemed to me very odd, but after a number of inquiries I discovered the explanation of the mystery. It was Mrs. Stevens' old house, which she had left a full year past. But while she had changed her address, she had apparently forgotten to change her cards, and so it was that I arrived half an hour late for dinner.

However, Mrs. Stevens was so entertaining that a little extra drive seemed worth while. I remember that after dinner when we had gone upstairs, she stood in front of the mantelpiece and addressing the other women who were present, said in her husky voice:

"People all say that because I wear a wig I have no hair underneath. It is a lie—an abominable lie! Just look at this!"

And with one energetic tug she pulled off her wig, disclosing underneath a sufficiently plentiful crop of greyish hair.

We agreed with her that it was abominable, that people should say such things about her, and rather hastily suggested that she should put her wig on again, as the men might be up at any moment.

After a certain amount of difficulty she did begin to put it on, and then to our horror, it stuck. And it was only just as the door opened and the men began to troop in that with a final gurgle of relief Mrs. Stevens' wig was pulled on to her head again.

I had not been singing long in New York before I made one of the greatest friends whom I have ever had, the novelist, Marion Crawford. The first time he came to see me I was staying at the Savoy Hotel, and it was not long before I discovered that he himself had a most appealing tenor voice. In fact, we often used to sing Faust and Romeo together, and I think I may honestly say that there have been some Fausts and some Romeos whom I would gladly sacrifice for a little of Marion Crawford's artistry.

He was, more than almost any man I have ever known, acutely sensitive to beauty—so much so that when he was emotionally affected he would throw absolutely all restraint to the winds and bring out the deepest secrets from his heart. One afternoon when he had come to see me and I had sung to him, I noticed that when I had finished, the tears were streaming down his face. I felt embarrassed at the sight of a brilliant man like Crawford in such a state, and so, in order to give him time to recover, I suggested lightly that perhaps he might care to write in my autograph book. He looked at me strangely for a moment and then said:

"I wonder if you would understand what I should like to write."

"Let me see," I said. And as I bent over his shoulder I saw that he had written:

"Credo in resurrectum mortuorum."

(I believe in the resurrection of the dead.)

He laid down the pen, folded his hands and looking straight in front of him told me the following story:

Years ago, when he was quite a young man he had fallen deeply in love with a girl who, at first, seemed to return his love. And then one day he discovered that she was untrue to him. The shock of this discovery was so great that instead of breaking his heart it seemed to kill it. "I became hard," he said, "and absolutely without feeling. In fact, I had lost faith in all women."

"But," he added, turning to me with a smile, "you have made me live again."

I don't think I have been more thankful for my gift of song than on that occasion.

It seems difficult to speak of John Jacob Astor in the same breath as Marion Crawford, but I feel I must do so because it was at about the same time that I met both these men. Tall, with a metallic voice which seemed to snip his sentences rather than to say them—he was a strange character, a mixture of kindness and a quality which might perhaps best be described as indifference.

Astor's parties were of course magnificent, from the orchids on the tables to the pictures on the walls, everything was almost overwhelmingly superb. And yet, in spite of his wealth, there were moments when one felt that the epithet "Scotch" would be almost too generous to give him.

I cannot help saying though it does not come into this part of the story, that if it takes an American to be really generous, there have been moments when I have come to the conclusion that it takes an American to be really mean. I shall never forget an occasion when Jean de Reszke, Edouard de Reszke, Calvé, Plançon, Coquelin and myself were crossing the Atlantic in the same ship as an immensely rich American millionaire some time later. We had learned indirectly that the Seamen's Charities had been doing very badly that year, and so we got together and decided that we would give a concert as a benefit for them. I think you will agree that apart from any services which I might be regarded as rendering, the caste of the concert was such as one would rarely have the opportunity of hearing on land.

We arranged the programme, and when we had all decided what we would sing, we began to collect for the seats, and as a little beginning we each put £20 into the bag as our own contribution. I went round the ship with the subscription list, and was delighted with the generosity with which I was greeted. When I showed the list to Jean, he said:

"*Toi, tu connais*——? Ask him how much he will give."

"Of course," I said. "I had forgotten him"—and I started off to the other end of the deck, where the multi-millionaire was sitting in an arm-chair well wrapped up with rugs.

"How much are the seats?" was his first question. I told him.

He drew a long reflective puff at his cigar, and then said, somewhat grudgingly:

"I will give you 250 francs (£8 os. od.) on condition that my wife and I have front seats."

I admit I was somewhat crestfallen at the result of my request, and I was also a little hurt by being treated as a sort of concert agent whose business is to put blue crosses in black squares. And so I told him that he must see M. Coquelin about the position of the seats, that I hoped he would enjoy the concert, that I was sure he deserved to do so in view of his generosity, and with that I left him.

We were then about two days out from New York. And some years later, in almost exactly the same locality, that multi-millionaire met his death in "The Titantic."

What delightful memories I have of these New York hostesses. Mrs. Ogden Mills, the mother of Lady Granard, Mrs. Whitelaw Reid, whose husband was later Ambassador in London, and Mrs. W. K. Vanderbilt. Although in those days these families were newer than they are to-day, the rush and clatter which makes New York society now-a-days a sort of arduous battleground was not nearly so much in evidence. I remember that W. K. Vanderbilt's house, which was full of divine treasures, was then in a part of New York which was regarded as quiet and secluded. I said to him one day:

"Won't it be a pity if this neighbourhood becomes noisy and overbuilt? If you look out of the window now" (and I glanced out at the comparatively sleepy

Fifth Avenue) "you might almost imagine that you were in some sleepy part of London."

Vanderbilt laughed. "Oh, this will never get busy," he said. "Not for a generation or two, at any rate. We grow fast in New York, but we don't grow as fast as all that."

And yet to-day the Vanderbilt residence is of course in the very centre of the capital.

And then there was Mrs. Ogden Goelet, whose daughter was afterwards Duchess of Roxburghe, whom I picture moving gracefully among the lovely things in her house off Fifth Avenue, arranging the most delightful parties, and taking me to her box at the Opera. And while I am talking of Mrs. Goelet I cannot help recalling the *dénouement* to a rather dramatic incident in my life, which occurred a little later at her house in London.

Because the story illustrates so well not only the trials of a *prima donna,* but the tact of that wonderful gentleman who was afterwards Edward VII, I shall tell it in full.

I had been commanded to sing before Queen Victoria at Buckingham Palace. I was naturally honoured by the command, and when the day before the performance I contracted laryngitis and was forced to go to bed, you can imagine that I was bitterly disappointed. But this disappointment would have been nothing, had it not been for the disastrous interpretation which was put on my illness to the Prince of Wales by one of his friends.

It was at Gladys de Grey's party, about a week later, that I suddenly realized I was in disgrace. I was standing in a corner talking to Charles Beresford when His Royal Highness was announced. After his fashion, he looked all round the room, bowing to his friends one by one; but when his eyes reached my corner, he glanced at me coldly for a moment and then looked away. Not a shadow of a smile, not even a hint of recognition, crossed his face. I felt absolutely miserable, and thinking that everybody had noticed the slight, I sat down on the sofa, wishing that I could sink through the floor. Had it not been for the fact that the Princess of Wales herself sent for me and talked to me for several minutes, I believe that I should have died.

The next morning I rushed round to Lady de Grey's. I said to her: "The Prince of Wales cut me last night. Can you possibly explain what it means?"

Gladys took my hand, and then with a queer apologetic little smile she said:

"Well, Nellie, I am afraid that the Prince has heard that you were enjoying yourself on the Thames on the very night when you should have been singing at Buckingham Palace, and he is naturally very angry about it."

I drew back in astonishment. "It is an utter lie," I said. "A disgusting invention! I was ill in bed. I could hardly talk."

I walked round the room for a moment fuming with anger.

"Can you prove it?" said Gladys.

"Of course," I answered. "Dr. Semon was attending me and will give me a certificate to say that what I tell you is the truth. But what use is that? What am I to do?"

Gladys smiled. "Don't worry," she said. "Leave it to me."

I did leave it to her, and I thanked my good fortune that I had so staunch a friend. Audiences with the Prince of Wales cannot be had for the mere asking, even when the person who desires the audience is in good favour. And when he is not! . . . However, Lady de Grey managed it for me. And at four o'clock one afternoon I drove to Marlborough House and was shown into the Prince's suite.

He stood up and bowed stiffly. "You wish to see me?"

"Yes, Sir. I am terribly unhappy. You cut me at Lady de Grey's the other night."

He looked away and frowned; then: "Why didn't you sing at Buckingham Palace?"

"I was ill, Sir."

"Are you quite sure?"

For answer I drew out my certificate and held it before him. The Prince looked at me for a moment, and then slowly a smile hovered on his lips. "Oh, I don't want to read that," he said.

I told him how ill I had been, how I was lying in bed with laryngitis: how I was hardly able to speak: and I added, "Surely, Sir, you could not imagine that I would do such a terrible thing, having had the honour to be asked to sing at Buckingham Palace?"

The Prince then smiled his wonderful smile, and I knew all was well. He shook me warmly by the hand, and I took my leave.

And it was two nights later, at Mrs. Ogden Goelet's house, that this tragic little comedy was finished. The scene was at dinner, and the Prince honoured me by asking that I should sit at his table. There was a moment's pause in the conversation, and looking at me with his wonderful smile, and with a little glance at his hostess, he lifted his glass and said:

"Madame and I have had a little misunderstanding. But we have made it up now, and we are going to be great friends again. Madame Melba, I drink to you."

Side by side with American millionaires, I was having a good taste of American democracy. My first real experience of that debatable quality occurred one Sunday afternoon outside the door of the Metropolitan, just before one of the Sunday Evening concerts which I had the pleasure of helping to success. It was snowing heavily, and as there was no cover over the artists' entrance, I decided that I would go in by the subscribers' entrance. I was stopped in the doorway by a tall man in livery, who said in a gruff voice:

"Where's your ticket?"

"Please let me pass," I said, hardly looking at him, and endeavouring to walk past.

A brawny arm shot out in front of me. "No one passes here without a ticket," said the man.

I looked him straight in the face. "Surely you know who I am? I am Madame Melba."

"I don't care who you are," he replied. "You're not going to pass without a ticket."

A man behind offered me his ticket. "No, thank you," I said. "If I can't get in without a ticket, I shan't get in at all."

Had it not been for the advent of Henry Abbey, one of the Directors, who was summoned by somebody who witnessed this scene, and who arrived in frantic haste, I do not know what would have happened. It is quite possible that the thousands of people who were waiting inside that hall would have gone away disappointed. However, when he did arrive and had escorted me through, I said to him:

"Don't you think that man ought to apologize to me?"

"I surely do."

He came round. By then my blood had cooled a

little. Still I looked at him sternly and said: "You know, you ought to go down on your knees and beg my pardon."

The man shuffled his feet. "You can't blame me, mum," he answered. "I was only doing my dooty, I might have got the sack if I hadn't."

I could not help smiling, and told him that I supposed he was right. But if it ever happened again, I added, he *would* have to go down on his knees. However, it never did happen again, and after that he was one of my most loyal servants.

CHAPTER XI

FURTHER AMERICAN EXPERIENCES

HAVE you ever noticed how some of the most charming people have also little vices which seem quite incompatible with the rest of their character? I have known delightful women who spoiled their lives (and other people's) by unreasoning jealousy, and otherwise splendid men who bored one because of petty conceit. Take the case of Tamagno, who was at this time in New York. Here was a great tenor who, I suppose, will always be remembered. They used to say that his voice was so powerful that his top C's caused the chandeliers at Covent Garden actually to rattle.

But in spite of his big position and the great sums of money he made, he suffered from occasional fits of meanness which made him positively ridiculous.

I shall always remember one amazing example of the trait. It occurred at a dinner given to us, just about this time, by the Millionaires' Club in New York. Jean de Reszke was sitting next to me, and almost immediately opposite us was Tamagno, sitting on the right of the Italian Ambassador's wife. I had already been informed of Tamagno's little weakness, and I was so amused and so anxious not to miss any evidence of it that might occur during dinner that I fear I must have been a dull conversationalist.

However, I had not long to wait. A mysterious thing happened. Tamagno had spread out a table napkin on his knees, and was glancing round him with avaricious eyes. I whispered to Jean:

"What *is* he doing?"

"I don't know, but it looks very odd."

It *was* odd, odder than we thought. For Tamagno began to pop some crystallized fruits into his napkin, quite calmly, as though he were doing the most natural thing in the world. The crystallized fruits were shortly joined by salted almonds, and chocolates, all of which were carefully laid in Tamagno's hoard.

What the wife of the Italian Ambassador must have thought throughout that dinner, I tremble to think. But worse was to come.

The time arrived for the women to leave the table. My eyes were so glued to Tamagno that I hardly realized where I was. But in a sort of dream I saw him rise to his feet, take up one of the beautiful bunches of orchids with which we had all been presented, bow gracefully and say:

"E permesso, signora? E per la mia figlia chi e ammalata a l'albergo." (Will you allow me, signora? It is for my daughter, who is ill at the hotel.)

The poor woman was so astonished that she could only smile artificially and murmur that of course it was permitted to take them. If Tamagno had also calmly stuffed his pockets with knives and forks she would probably, in her bewildered condition, have murmured the same thing. Anyway, Tamagno took them. And then, to my undying amazement, he rose from the table, clutching his bundle tightly, and went out with the women, leaving the men to themselves.

Poor Tamagno! I knew what to expect from him after that dinner. But even so I was not prepared for another singular incident which occurred when Mancinelli gave a little luncheon to some of us at an Italian restaurant in New York. It was a very excellent little luncheon, I remember, and among the dishes were *côtelettes de veau à la Milanaise.* We all devoured our cutlets, but at the end of the course several still happened to be left. This was too much for Tamagno.

Leaning over the table, with a side glance at the cutlets, he said to Mancinelli: "What are you going to do with those?"

"Do with them?" replied the bewildered Mancinelli. "Nothing."

"Ah," Tamagno sighed with satisfaction. In his resonant tones he summoned a waiter. "*Date mi un giornale*" (Give me a newspaper), he cried.

The newspaper was brought, and then, with the utmost deliberation, Tamagno proceeded to wrap the cutlets up, one by one, in the newspaper. Suddenly pausing, and sensing that an explanation was required, he said: "You see, my little dog—he loves *côtelettes de veau.*"

The sequel to this story is worthy of note. On the next day Mancinelli called at Tamagno's private suite at about 12 o'clock. He and his daughter were just sitting down to lunch. Need I tell you what was the dish in the centre of the table?

The time has come for me to leave New York and to journey to Boston. I should probably not have visited Boston so early—the spring of 1894—had it not been for the enormous success of the New York season, which prompted Mr. Abbey to arrange this special tour. But I shall never be sufficiently thankful that I did go, for it was to be my introduction to the world's finest body of musicians—the Boston Symphony Orchestra.

I wonder if the average reader to whom an orchestra

is just an orchestra, a collection of instruments, and nothing more, can realize the great soul which animated that superb institution. I grew to love that orchestra almost as though it had been a single human being instead of a collection. And from the very first moment I admired and venerated its patron and inspirer, Major Higginson.

Major Higginson is one of the unknown heroes of musical history. Even in America, he is comparatively unhonoured. And yet, had it not been for him, the Boston Symphony Orchestra, even if it had managed to survive, would not have attained anything like the same degree of excellence.

Major Higginson was one of the very finest types of American. The type that says to himself: "I want the best. I am going to have the best. And I don't care how much I pay for it." He would suddenly say to his directors: "I have heard that there is a little man in the orchestra in Madrid who plays the flute like an angel. We have got to have him. Send him a cablegram. Go over if necessary. Kidnap him if the worst comes to the worst. But get him."

For thirty-seven years, Major Higginson fought for his orchestra, day in and day out, as though it were some beloved child. It was, of course, a non-union body—a fact that I have always thought particularly significant. And nobody, however exalted their position in the world of music or society, could ever engage the Boston Symphony for extra performances.

The actual engagements were always carried out by his manager, Mr. Charles A. Ellis, who was given *carte blanche* whenever he went to Europe, and so nobody seemed to realize that it was Higginson whom they had to thank.

How much they had to thank him for! He would allow pupils and students into the great hall for the nominal price of twenty-five cents, and many is the time that I have seen them standing in long queues outside the building, having waited from five o'clock in the morning, in rain and cold, to obtain admission. So much for those who say that America is not a music-loving country.

An absurd memory occurs to me while I write of the Boston Symphony Orchestra. One of the trombone players—a superb performer—became so inflated with his prowess that he decided that his wife was not a fit companion for his genius, and applied for a maintenance order. When the case came to court, the Judge said to him, "Don't you care for your wife any more?"

"No," replied the man. "I have become an eagle. She has remained a sparrow. You can't expect us to live together any more."

"Eagle or no eagle," replied the judge dryly, "you have got to keep her, whether you live together or not."

When I first sang with the Boston Symphony Orchestra, although I knew after five minutes that I had never sung to such a marvellous accompaniment, I did not fully realize the prestige which the Orchestra had in the eyes of all good Americans. It was a prestige so exceptional that most foreign artists were rather awed by it, and never dared even the smallest criticism. I suppose I must have been different.

One day we were rehearsing the *Allegro ed il Penseroso* of Handel, with flute *obbligato*. In an important part one of the instruments played a C natural instead of a C sharp.

"C sharp—C sharp," I shouted, turning round and pointing at the man who had made the mistake.

There was a dead silence. Then they all burst out laughing. And I realized that I had created a record as far as the Boston Symphony Orchestra was concerned. Nobody had dared to criticize them like that since the time of their formation.

Yes—Boston knew the best in music, and it has always had it. Indeed, all American audiences are audiences before which it is a delight to sing. Their praise is worth as much, if not more, than that of any audience in the world.

It was in Boston that I first met the man with whom I was to be associated under the happiest circumstances for many years, Mr. Charles Ellis. Mr. Ellis at that time was a young man with a comparatively small reputation. I was under contract with Abbey and Grau, but he arranged a concert for me in Boston, which was so perfectly staged and managed that I decided I would get him to do some work for me. He came to see me one morning, and as soon as I saw him and had talked to him I appreciated his brilliant sense of organization and business acumen, and within twenty minutes of his entering the room we had arranged that in future he should be the sole manager in America for Nellie Melba.

What is there about Boston that makes its society so charming, with the same quiet appeal which one finds among one's friends in England? There is a quality about the social life of Boston totally different from that of most great American cities, a quality which can best be described as one of repose. Certainly, at least, I can imagine no other American city capable of producing that unique figure, Mrs. Jack Gardner.

Mrs. Jack Gardner was, in many ways, my *beau idéal*

of what a rich woman should be. I don't know how many millions Mrs. Gardner had—probably she did not know herself—but whatever her fortune, it was spent in the service of beauty. To some extent Mrs. Gardner occupied the position in the United States which Lady de Grey held in London, and certainly no other woman in America could possibly have conceived the stupendous plan of bringing over from Europe an entire Venetian Palace and setting it up, stone by stone, in Boston, Massachusetts.

She was in the middle of this vast enterprise when I met her, and she was naturally full of excitement. Every stone of the palace had to be numbered and checked. Every precious piece of carving had to be packed in shavings and preserved from careless hands. Even the Italian plants in their original pots, filled with Italian earth, made that perilous journey across the Atlantic and arrived, by some miracle, to flower under a foreign sun.

Of course I was longing to see "It" as she always described her palace, but "It" was sternly guarded from all prying eyes until it was finished. Nobody, not even the President of the United States, would have been allowed to enter. Everything, inside and out, had to be perfect before Mrs. Gardner would share her treasure with the world. Meanwhile we had to be content with rumours of what was going on inside, of which one of the most prevalent was that a certain Italian prince was lingering in prison for allowing one of his pictures to be smuggled out of Italy on consideration of £40,000.

Then one day the summons came. Mrs. Gardner rang me up on the telephone. "It's finished," she said, a note of triumph in her voice, "and you're going to be one of the first people to see it. May I call for you in my brougham this afternoon at three o'clock?" Needless to say, I accepted.

It was a bitterly cold afternoon when we set out for the palace, with a blizzard blowing at sixty miles an hour. Imagine therefore my delight when we arrived, and two tall Italian servants opened the door, to admit us to an exquisite garden full of spring flowers. For the courtyard of the Palazzo had all been roofed in with glass so that, even in winter, one could have Italian flowers and a very fair counterfeit of Southern warmth.

A room which she called the "Van Dyck" room was one which immediately captured my attention. It was of immense size, with a tall roof which even in the daytime was shrouded in shadow. At night it was lit with hundreds of candles, and the first effect one had on entering it was that of darkness so thick that none of the pictures could be seen. However, one had not been in that room five minutes before every picture became clearly visible in its smallest detail.

People talked about Mrs. Gardner, of course, as they talk about anybody who takes the trouble to undertake a really big job. They said for example that it was affectation for her to carry her passion for detail so far as to insist on the letters being handed up in a basket each morning, as is done in Venice. Finding that she did not in the least mind this criticism they went farther, and when they heard of her marvellous painted ceilings, said that the pictures on them were so improper that she had been forced to hide them in the roof.

But she took no notice—this great little woman—but went on her way with the true fervour of the æsthete (that much abused word). One picture of her will always linger in my memory—that of the little ceremony with which she always preluded her dinner parties. Imagine a long Italian gallery, dimly lighted, with white statues glimmering on either side, and a hint of marvellous pictures in the dusk. We all gather at one end of the gallery and then Mrs. Gardner—a tiny figure in white draperies—lights a taper. Very slowly she walks down the gallery in silence, while we wait, past the statues into the distance, and then we see her gravely light two little candles in front of an altar at the far end.

It was an unforgettable sight, and naturally enough people used to talk about Mrs. Gardner, and try to make out that her place was a failure. I wish they could have seen her, as I did, sitting in her music room, on a big throne, surrounded by all the most interesting people in the America of her day. They did not come to her (as is often the fate of art persons) for gifts, though she was certainly the most generous of women, as I am reminded by a beautiful yellow diamond which she gave me. Her method of presenting it was indeed characteristic. She came to see me one day at my hotel, stayed talking for a while, and just as she was about to depart, drew a little parcel wrapped in white tissue paper from her bag, saying, "I have brought a little souvenir that I thought you might like." The little souvenir was the yellow diamond. One cannot help wondering how some other people of one's acquaintance, if they had so far forgotten themselves as to part with a yellow diamond at all, would have given it.

But Mrs. Gardner was loved, not for her gifts, but for herself, for the wonderful spirit of fine culture which seemed to radiate from her. Sargent, for example, loved staying with her more than with anyone else in the States, and once he got inside the palace, nothing would drag him out. He painted a very beautiful portrait of his hostess, and another of his most famous pictures, that of a Spanish dancing girl, hangs in a long gallery at the palace, and we used to sit and watch it as we drank our coffee after dinner.

Chicago was in those days an even greater contrast to Boston and New York. In fact, all my early memories of Chicago were rather turbulent. I shall never forget an evening when I was singing with Jean de Reszke in *Romeo and Juliet*. It seemed to me as the performance progressed that we were not holding the audience as we usually did, and that somewhere in the back of the hall there was a disturbance brewing. And then there was a commotion, a general rising, a few startled screams, a confusion in the orchestra, and before I knew what had happened I saw clambering up over the footlights a man with staring eyes and the face of a lunatic, coming towards me.

It *was* a lunatic, a man who had in some way or other escaped from his asylum and had obtained entry to the house. For a moment everybody was paralyzed. And then Jean came to the rescue. He ran forward, drawing his stage sword from its sheath and waving it fiercely in the man's face. The man looked as though he might give fight—and if he had done so I don't know what would have happened, for he was a powerful fellow and a theatrical sword is not a very good weapon against the strength of a maniac.

However, just as things began to look serious, a party of men from the wings rushed on to the scene and dragged him off.

It was not very easy to play Juliet after that little *fracas!*

I have always regretted that Washington was a

comparatively bad place for business, because it has always been a city of such happy days for me. I remember one night when I sang at the house of Mrs. Leiter (whose daughter was afterwards Lady Curzon of Kedleston). I had forgotten that she had been a pupil of Madame Marchesi in Paris. And so when I saw her coming down the stairs I had to close my eyes for a moment before I could remember where we had first met. And then what a strange contrast it all seemed! It was only a few years ago and yet, in those days I had been just starting, timidly and almost diffidently, on my career, and had seen few girls so lovely as this young daughter of America, as she then was, in her sable coat and her evening gown. At that time I thought her the most beautiful of women. And though I have seen countless beautiful women since, the impression of her fresh loveliness remains.

But for me, of course, Washington will always be inseparably connected with Mrs. Nicholas Longworth, the vivacious, impulsive, and altogether delightful daughter of President Roosevelt. It is impossible to be in the company of Alice Roosevelt (as one cannot help calling her) without feeling that one is living far more quickly and intensely than usual. As I write I can feel her hand clutching my arm in her excitement at a great event which we recently witnessed together.

The event was President Wilson's declaration of war on Austria. We had gone to the Senate House together, and even before our arrival at the scene of action, I had been so worked up by Alice's enthusiasm that I felt almost exhausted. But our emotions were to be still more harassed when we took our seats in the gallery and the President, in his calm, deliberate tones, began to expound the situation. If you have read that famous speech, you will remember that for a very long time Wilson did not disclose his intentions. In fact, the first part of the speech seems all to point to a continuation of neutrality.

That, at least, was the impression that Alice received. As the minutes rolled on, and the President's voice echoed up to us in passionless monotony, her agony of apprehension increased. " He's not going to! He's not going to!" she whispered, feverishly gripping my hand to steady herself. And when, in particular, Wilson said, " Austria is our friend," or words to that effect, I am sure that it was as much as Alice could do to prevent herself from jumping over the gallery and protesting to the House. Had Wilson not declared war I tremble to think of the consequences.

Well, of course, he *did* declare war. And of all those shouts that made the roof of the Senate House ring, and ring again, none shouted louder than Alice Roosevelt, unless (I must add in self-defence) it was myself.

And then after Washington, Philadelphia, where I found more charming friends. Outside Philadelphia lived a little old lady who was like one of those pictures of early Dutch masters, of wrinkled faces and quiet smiles, and long, slender hands. This was Mrs. Griscom —perhaps my ideal type of mother. I shall never forget the occasion when her great son, Mr. Lloyd Griscom (who was afterwards Ambassador in Rome) returned home after a long trip abroad. He was very tall, and she was very small, and as he bent down to kiss her he said in his deep Quaker voice:

" How is thee, little Mother?" and she replied, looking up: " So well now, my son."

When I got back to New York I was so thoroughly infected with the American spirit of getting things done in the briefest possible time that I nearly let myself in for an artistic disaster. One Saturday morning when I was breakfasting I took up the *New York Herald* and saw that on the following Friday, January 29th, 1894, I was announced to sing Elizabeth in *Tannhäuser*. That was my first intimation, and had it not been for some spirit of adventure in the New York air, I should probably have rushed down to the theatre and made them cancel the performance. Instead of that, I sent a special messenger down to the Opera for the *répétiteur*, said to him, "I begin learning Elizabeth with you this morning," put him down at the piano, and started singing before he had been in the room five minutes. I learned that part in three days, and though I really did not know it, I sang it on Friday, and I got good notices.

But here comes the warning to all young artists, not to do likewise. For though I got through the performance on Friday, though I even sang it again without a mistake on the following Tuesday, the next performance, which took place in Philadelphia, found me out. It was a horrible evening. I forgot some of my words in the Prayer, and several times the orchestra had to go without me. So nerve racking was the ordeal that I felt a wreck for several days afterwards, and when I got back to New York I sent for the *répétiteur* again, and said: "This time I really am going to learn Elizabeth."

CHAPTER XII

LONDON AGAIN

WHEN I returned to Covent Garden in 1895, my position was very different from that of a year ago. It was not only that I was a star. It was not only that I had made many wonderful friends. Perhaps I can best explain it, if it does not sound too conceited to do so, that the name of Melba was now almost common property.

This was due, not so much to any social success, as to the actual homage which I was honoured to receive from the leaders of the musical world themselves. Arthur Nikisch, for example, the famous conductor, with whom I sang at an orchestral concert in the Queen's Hall in the height of the season, had done me the signal honour on one occasion of putting down his baton and stepping on to the platform, to accompany me himself.

Whenever I think of Nikisch, I think of that lovely phrase in *Faust,* when Marguerite appears at the height of the revels, and the music slows down and softens while she sings:

"*Non, monsieur! Je ne suis demoiselle, ni belle,*
Et je n'ai pas besoin qu'on me donne la main."

It was at Covent Garden that I first sang this phrase to Nikisch, who had never heard me, and to my astonishment, as soon as I had finished that act, in which I have no other phrase to sing, he came round, kissed my hand and said:

JULES MASSENET

"Madame Melba—I know from your rendering of those few bars what a great artist you are."

"*Non, monsieur, je ne suis demoiselle* . . ." how often I have sung those words, I do not know. But never has the melody of them, so soaring and yet so simple, failed to thrill me with something of the wonder which Marguerite herself must have felt.

What a genius Nikisch was! He had one little vanity by which I shall always remember him; his beautiful hands. They were always white and supple, and throughout the winter they were encased in long fur gloves. It was, after all, a pardonable enough vanity, for Nikisch's hands were his fortune. He did many little things to draw attention to them, and I have heard that his long white shirt-cuffs, which I remember waving in front of me on many occasions, were specially designed to set them off.

Speaking of that one phrase which Nikisch heard me sing makes me think of dear Reggie Lister, for he also was captivated by a phrase. It was that which I sing in the second act of *Traviata,* pianissimo, with my back to the audience:

Dite alla Giovane si bella e pura.

Reggie used to tell me that he often had come over from Paris, especially to hear that one phrase.

Reggie Lister was an artist in life. His *joie de vivre* amounted to genius. One felt his bright presence in a room even when he was silent. He radiated youth and charm, and all who knew him loved him. What wonderful evenings of music we used to have in his apartment in Paris—just Reggie and Emily Yznaga and Gladys de Grey and I . . . I playing my own accompaniments, and I fear, often thumping wrong notes.

Hélas! Tempi passati! When Reggie Lister died

it was as though a light in the world had been dimmed. I am thankful that after his death George Graham (who is now our ambassador at Brussels) became a friend of mine, and helped me to bear his death.

During this summer I was often in Paris, preparing Massenet's *Manon Lescaut,* under the direction of the composer. Massenet was a charming, oldish man with a passion for flowers, and a habit of coining very pretty phrases. He used to call me Madame Stradivarius (as indeed did Joachim too) since a Stradivarius is small in a small room and swells as the room increases in size, yet still retains its quality. But what a devil he was for work! If he was not such a great man, I should be inclined to call him pernickety. He never let anything pass, however slight; and if he did not like my singing of a phrase, he would go over it a hundred times.

One of the first places to which we went together was to an amusing American woman, Mrs. Ayer. Mrs. Ayer was quite a character, and had the most extraordinary ideas about dress. For instance, she came up to me one day after having seen me in Ophelia, and asked me where I had obtained the pretty wig I wore in the first act. I could not remember where I had got it, but I told her to ask Jean Worth, which she promptly did, giving him orders to make one exactly like it for herself. She then wore it in the street, and a very extraordinary figure she made, with the masses of false curls, a highly painted face, and marvellous jewels.

Speaking of Worth makes me feel that I must pay to him some of the debt I owe for the constant help and advice he gave me, in making me realize how important it was to look as well as I sang. Jean Worth was rather a unique figure. He himself gave one the impression, with his little beard and his polished manners, of being a complete Frenchman, and it was difficult to realize that his father had been, I believe, a Manchester boy with a broad North Country accent. His father in those days had more or less retired from the business, and was only to be seen wandering about the great *salons* of the Rue de la Paix, wearing a black skull-cap and making occasional suggestions to his brilliant son, but Jean himself was a greater designer than his father had ever been. All the women in London used to flock to see him, and had he ever written his memoirs, I should imagine that he would have had some very sensational things to tell. I can see him now, placing the tips of his fingers together and half closing his eyes as he examined critically the figure of some woman in need of clothes. He would only look at her for some thirty seconds, but he always knew after that brief investigation exactly what dress she ought to wear.

Some of the dresses which Worth made for me were dreams of beauty. In particular, there was an exquisite coat of cloth of gold, hand-painted and sewn with jewels, which I wore in *Lohengrin.* It was so lovely that when I appeared in Russia before the Tsar and Tsaritsa they sent for me after the second act, and one of the first actions of the Tsaritsa was to bend over my cloak and take it in her hands and to stroke it, saying: "How perfectly lovely this is!"

I always felt very smart when I came back from Paris with a new collection of Worth dresses, although when I look at the rather faded photographs of myself in those days I can hardly help laughing at the fantastic fashions which we used to think beautiful.

On one of these return visits from Paris I felt tired and depressed, and decided that I would spend as much of my spare time as possible on the river, and it was at about this time that I took for the season a very pretty house at Marlow, shaded by immense trees and with the splash of the water within sounding distance of my bedroom. This little cottage soon became the *rendezvous* for a good many interesting characters, but my first memory of it is of another description.

One of my first excursions was from Marlow to Stoke Poges churchyard, which I need hardly remind you was the scene of Gray's *Elegy,* and where Gray himself is buried. As soon as I entered the churchyard I was struck by the quiet, lazy, English beauty of it all, the rooks cawing in the elms, the moss-covered grave stones, and most of all the little church; and I decided on the spur of the moment that it would be an ideal adventure to enter the church and to sing to the organ. I looked round for a caretaker, and I saw a little old charwoman surveying me with bright eyes from the doorway.

I asked her where I could get the key of the church, and she told me that the Vicar had one; whereupon Mr. Bernard Rolt, a young composer and great friend, who was staying with me, trudged away through the long grass to approach the Vicar.

He was gone rather a longer time than seemed necessary, and when he came back there was a broad smile on his face.

"What are you laughing at?" I asked him. He said:

"I asked the Vicar for the key of the church, and he seemed rather unwilling to give it to me. So I thought I had better tell him that it was for Madame Melba, and that she wanted to sing at his organ. 'And who is Madame Melba?' he said. 'I never heard of her.'"

I laughed, for it really was rather remarkable that the Vicar of Stoke Poges, which is only twelve miles or so from London, should not have heard of Madame Melba. However, I soon forgot the incident after I had groped through the shadows to sit at the organ, while the old woman with much wheezing of breath blew for me. I remember that I sang Gounod's *Ave Maria* and some other sacred compositions, finishing up with "God Save the Queen," and when I took my departure I asked the old woman if she had liked the little concert. She nodded and said: "Yes, it was very nice. But 'God Save the Queen' was the best."

But I am afraid that my rests at Marlow were few and far between, for when I was not singing in London I was either in America or making lightning trips to Paris, and to the Continent. In the autumn of 1897, Joachim and I and other artists appeared at Bergamo for the festival in honour of the centenary of Donizetti. Nor shall I ever forget wandering with Joachim down the Exhibition to see on the wall a few sheets of Wagner's MSS.—not his own MSS., but the copies which in order to make a few pounds he had done of Donizetti, a composer so infinitely far below him in genius. I sat there looking at those copies with Joachim, wishing I had known Wagner in those days.

Among the artists who were also singing at Bergamo was a soprano, called Alva. She was quite a capable singer, but her voice was not of the quality which would ever arouse superlative enthusiasm. Her name was not, therefore, mentioned in the reports which were sent back to London, and I am afraid that the majority of those reports were devoted to Joachim and to myself. Madame Alva therefore wrote to Joseph Bennett, the Musical Director of the *Daily Telegraph,* whom I had never met, a letter which ran like this (I am quoting from memory):

"Dear Mr. Bennett,

"I cannot understand why you have made no mention of my name in your reports of the Bergamo Festival, and have devoted so much space to Madame Melba. I had as much success, if not more, than Madame Melba, and it is a gross injustice that you should persist in ignoring me. I should like to know your reason."

Imagine Madame Alva's horror when Mr. Bennett, who apparently was not used to receiving letters of this description, calmly printed Madame Alva's letter in full in the *Daily Telegraph,* with the simple comment: "We thought that perhaps the readers of the *Daily Telegraph* would like to know Madame Alva's opinion of herself." Needless to say, I was at once accused of having organized this exposure myself; and needless also to say, I knew nothing about it before it was sent to me in the form of a press cutting. But I was exceedingly sorry for the unfortunate woman who had been so misguided as to run her head against the critics.

CHAPTER XIII

MY ADVENTURES IN CALIFORNIA

I WONDERED when, in 1894, I set off for another tour of the United States, whether I would have to make all my friends in America over again, and if they would quite have forgotten me. But I had no sooner set foot in America than I found not only that my rooms were full of flowers from all those friends I had left behind, but also that there were orchids and roses and lilies and violets from people whom I had never met at all.

Among the most gorgeous bouquets that I found awaiting me was one from the Marquis de Castellane, commonly known as Boni. I had met him very often in the apartment of the Prince de Sagan, his uncle, in the Place Vendôme, and he had struck me as such a fascinating, unusual character that I wanted to meet him again.

And when Boni came to see me in my hotel it was like a breath of the Boulevards on Broadway. Among the straightforward, essentially simple American men by whom he was surrounded, he seemed indeed worthy of the nickname of "Powder Puff," which he used himself to quote with a tolerant smile. His exquisite clothes, his glistening cane, his elaborate buttonholes, and the air he always had of holding all the riches of the East in fee, even when he was hard put to it to pay his hotel bill—all combined to heighten this impression. He was a most charming companion.

It was more or less of an open secret that Boni de Castellane, in coming over to New York, would not be altogether averse from the idea of marrying an heiress. In fact he was so open about it that any doubts that one might have had about his intentions were completely removed. He would discuss it as openly as if he had come over to make an investment or to buy a house and he would laughingly say that after all it was not as though he had nothing to bargain with, for apart from his charming person, the name of Castellane was not one which could be bought for a mere song.

Needless to say, everybody in New York was wondering whom Boni would eventually choose to share his title. I had a shrewd suspicion that he was going to marry a certain very charming lady with a great deal of money, to whom I knew that he was very much attached. And when the news was suddenly sprung on us that he had proposed to Anna Gould and had been accepted by her, I was exceedingly surprised. A few days after the engagement was announced, Boni came round to see me, and going over to the looking-glass and giving a little pat to the orchid in his buttonhole, he turned to me with his infectious laugh and asked me what I had to say about it.

For some reason or other, I did not feel inclined to say very much at that moment. I thought for a moment before I answered him, and then said:

"I do not know Miss Gould, Boni, but if you love her, then of course there is nothing more to say. But I would like just to ask you one question. Do you think that French and American marriages are really successful? I do beg of you and pray you to go home and think it over once again, and really to look before you leap."

MELBA AS NEDDA IN PAGLIACCI

MELBA AS ROSINA IN THE BARBER OF SEVILLE

However, he only laughed and went away, and the next time I saw him he was married. And I think Boni's own very frank confessions will tell you that that marriage was never a success.

We have heard a great deal just lately of Boni's extravagances, of his ostentatiousness, and there seems to me to have been a desire in certain quarters to paint him as rather heartless, rather vulgar, a man whose one idea was to spend money. I do not know if those who have spread this legend have any justification for their assertions; but certainly Boni de Castellane never showed me that side of his character. It is true that he loved display and gorgeousness, but he was also one of the finest connoisseurs in Europe, and if he spent £2,000 on a picture, a tapestry or a piece of furniture, you may be pretty sure that the £2,000 was well spent. In fact, if he may have spent a fortune of Anna Gould's money in the curiosity shops of London and Paris and Rome, it is equally certain that he made her another fortune by his exquisite taste. Boni was never wrong. He had an unerring instinct for what was good. I have seen him go into a shop, discover some picture, or piece of furniture, and buy it in less time than it would have taken the average man to consider it at all. And yet these swift purchases of his were dictated by knowledge and not by a mere whim. Some of the things for which Boni paid £1,000 during his married life are worth £10,000 to-day.

I do not think I can finish this little sketch of Boni de Castellane better than by saying that whenever he has asked me to sing for him I have always done so. He has his enemies and he has his detractors; but I believe that his name will live long after they have been forgotten.

It was during my friendship with Boni that I also met a very different type of figure—Archbishop Corrigan. I first came in contact with him through the marriage of my secretary, Louie Bennett, to Mr. Kenyon Mason, at the Archbishop's house adjoining St. Patrick's Cathedral, on January 14th, 1896. The Archbishop was one of the most broad-minded men I have ever met, but even I was surprised when he accepted an invitation to a party I gave afterwards, and turned up saying that he would eat like an ogre. And he said, apropos of a mauve dress that I was wearing during the ceremony, which toned most beautifully with his archiepiscopal purple, that he had never seen Heaven and Earth so charmingly blended before.

The Archbishop lived very simply in an austere house behind the Cathedral, and there I would sometimes visit him, to sit in his quiet study while he talked to me of America and all that he hoped it might become.

As a slight return for the trouble he had taken about my secretary's wedding, I asked if I might sing the *Ave Maria* in the Cathedral, and I shall never forget the feeling, almost of awe, which I experienced as my voice floated out to the immense congregation.

Grave and gay—how varied was life just then. My next memory is of a party, with Jean and Edouard and Ysaye, who was just then starting to electrify America with his Stradivarius. Suddenly Ysaye, jumping to his feet, rushed over to the little orchestra, took hold of the 'cello, hoisted it on his shoulder and began to play it like a fiddle. It was ludicrous of course—but even so he made it sound beautiful. How we all roared!

I am afraid I am dwelling too much on the light side

of things. I am afraid too, that I may be giving too much the impression that my career was absolutely untarnished by any hint of failure. It is true that as a rule I did not have to worry much about such a word, but there now occurred a performance which I certainly cannot call anything but disastrous. I had long wanted to sing the rôle of Brunhilde in *Siegfried,* in German. In Paris I had mentioned to Madame Marchesi this desire, always to be met with a horrified expression and great fluttering of the hands, as though I had threatened to cut my throat. I was well aware that Brunhilde was not by any means an ideal rôle for me, but I thought that Madame Marchesi's horror was exaggerated, and much against her wish, I had asked Herr Kniese over to Paris to coach me in the part.

But as the day approached for the first performance, which took place at the Metropolitan Opera House, New York, in December, 1896, I began to grow more and more nervous. And from the moment when the curtain went up and I began to sing, I knew that Madame Marchesi had been right and I had been wrong. The music was too much for me. I felt as though I were struggling with something beyond my strength. I had a sensation almost of suffocation of battling with some immense monster—a very different feeling from the usual exaltation which I had experienced in my other rôles. How I got through the performance I do not know, but when it was all over I threw a dressing-gown round my shoulders and sent for my manager.

He came in and as soon as he had sat down, I closed the door and said:

"Tell the critics that I am never going to do that again. It is beyond me. I have been a fool."

He went out and told them, and they departed.

But one of them, and a very famous critic, whom I met a few days later, came up to me and said:

"You were quite right, Madame Melba, to make that decision. Your voice is like a piece of Dresden china. Please, please don't smash it."

I learned my lesson. But it was an expensive one, for even this one performance did very great harm to my voice, and though I was able to appear once or twice after it, I gradually found that I was not singing at my best, and I was told that if I went on without a rest, I might never be able to sing again. And so in the middle of the season I threw up all my engagements, and went back to Paris, where I kept an enforced silence for nearly three months more. And may I, having told this story, implore young singers not to attempt to sing rôles which are beyond their power.

"Madame—look! look! We're in Paradise!"

I rubbed my eyes, and found my little maid Caroline standing by the window of my sleeping compartment, *en route* for California. I followed her gaze, and for a moment indeed, I felt inclined to believe that we *were* in Paradise. We had left behind the dreary snows and clouds of the eastern States, but here, like a dream, lay orchards of peach blossom, glittering in the sunshine, and green fields and the full beauty of spring.

That vision has always remained with me, and whenever I am depressed I close my eyes and call it up again. There is something so amazingly happy about Californians and all my friends there seemed to have perpetual smiles upon their faces. Memories of many parties crowd in on me, one which was given at the Bohemian Club by Mr. Walter Martin, with a peach tree buried in the floor and climbing over the table, and others which were given at the house of Mrs. W. H. Crocker, where I was staying. I also stayed with Mr. Dick Tobin at San Mateo, where we would go up after lunch to the veranda and watch the polo matches. Nor can I forget Mr. Bowie, who had been American Minister in Japan, and came back with all the skill of the Japanese in his finger-tips, painting divine little sketches which he hung all over the house.

The houses of the Californians were amazing. You could see in California in those days, even as you can see now, a house that might have come straight out of an old English village; a palazzo that might have been lifted bodily from Florence, a villa that made you think that you were in the Riviera. After a time I became more or less used to these shocks, but most English people took a good time to realize that the house they were visiting was not actually a French house or an Italian palazzo, but was entirely American. When Sir Johnston Forbes-Robertson was touring in California, he went to have tea with a Mr. and Mrs. Kohl, who were renowned for their hospitality, and as he entered the hall, with its clustering old oak beams, and its quaint lattice windows, he turned to his hostess and said:

"What an exquisite old house you have! Do you mind telling me how old it is?"

"Exactly ten days," said Mrs. Kohl calmly. So that was that.

One of the very kindest people in California was Mr. John Mackay, the moving spirit and financial genius of the great system of commercial cables which were stretching from America to the other world. When I arrived he sent me a huge box of orchids, and inside the box a letter telling me of a characteristic gift, viz., that any cables that I wished to send I was to accept as a gift from him with his homage. It so happened that a few days afterwards at a party given by Mrs. de Young I sat down on a settee in the middle of the floor which had one of its casters missing. As I sat down the settee tipped slowly to one side and knocked down a big bronze bust which was just behind me, grazing my head and rendering me unconscious for several minutes. It was an unplea ant enough experience, and the news of it spread like wildfire, not only in California, but to England and to France and Australia. It was rumoured that I was killed, that I was seriously ill, and sometimes even that I was buried; and cables began to pour in on me asking for news. Naturally, I had to reply to them, and it was then that I remembered Mr. Mackay's promise. I felt that I could not possibly avail myself of his offer in view of the extraordinary number of cables that I would have to send, and I wrote and told him so. He wired back saying, "If you don't I shall never speak to you again."

It was in California, too, that I first met that fine artist, Madame Schumann-Heink. Madame Schumann-Heink had a face which was possibly more interesting for character than remarkable for beauty, and I am afraid that she did not at that time pay very much attention to her dress. And I always think that it is a very remarkable tribute to her art that in spite of these difficulties, she has held audiences spell-bound all over the world.

At that time Madame Schumann-Heink had not yet made so great a reputation as she was later to have, and when I went to hear her in Paris afterwards, I was interested to know what the French people would think about her. As soon as she came on to the stage my heart sank, and I bit my lips with pain at the fear of what the French people would think of her, for it was an afternoon concert, and Madame Schumann-Heink was in evening-dress—and presented an appearance which the Parisians evidently considered very odd.

Knowing the hypercritical attitude of the Parisian public, I trembled for her. And then she began to sing, and before she had finished her *recitatif* in the Mozart *Aria,* the whole house rose to their feet and cheered her. They had forgotten everything but her artistry.

When I arrived at San Francisco, it was to find a city in the grip of the fever of war. The crisis which had long brooded between Spain and the United States was reaching its climax. Great headlines denouncing the Spanish policy flared across the tops of the newspapers, demonstrations were held in the streets, and the question on all men's lips was "When will war be declared?"

I could not have chosen any part of the States more inopportune for the commencement of an opera season than San Francisco, because as you are probably aware, this city was the centre of Spanish settlement in days gone by, and even at that time many descendants of Castilian pioneers still lived in the city. However, that was not what troubled me. The most agitating problem before me was the fact that I was due to open in *The Barber of Seville*—to sing the leading rôle of an intensely Spanish opera in a city where the very name of Spain was anathema.

What should I do? Would there be a public demonstration against me? Would there—even worse—be a demonstration of Spaniards in favour of their national ideals? I sat in my hotel, sent wires right and left to try and alter the performance, saw my manager, held conferences with the leading artists—all to no purpose. It was too late. *The Barber* had been announced, and we must go through with it.

War was declared. In the harbour of the Golden Gate itself we heard something of the echo of the strife. All day and all night there was marching and counter marching in the streets. It seemed incredible that I should ever sing the rôle of Rosina without some untoward event.

However, I shrugged my shoulders and hoped for the best. "After all," I said to myself, "I am not a politician or a diplomat. I am an artist. Music is international, and this opera shall be one in which no echo of the war shall be heard."

How little I anticipated what actually happened when I said these words! How little I looked forward to the extraordinary scene in which I was about to play a leading part!

If you are acquainted with *The Barber of Seville,* you will of course remember that in the second act occurs a scene in which Rosina, the heroine, is being given a singing lesson. Rossini, the composer, with his well-known laziness, left this scene a blank, leaving it to the discretion of the *prima donna* to sing whatever song she chose during the lesson. It was rather a charming innovation in opera, and in the part I had often left the song I was going to sing till the last minute, choosing "Mattinata," "Still wie die Nacht," or even the Mad Scene from *Lucia,* as the mood suited me.

I was still undecided as to the song I should sing during the Lesson Scene when I went on the stage. I was too preoccupied with the mentality of the audience. An uncanny silence hung over the vast auditorium, crammed though it was to capacity. All the artists were nervous. I felt—I know not how—that instead of the usual electric chain of sympathy which I had been used to creating between the audience and myself, there was a cloud of sullen hostility, which needed only the most trivial incident to cause it to break.

The first act passed by without any serious trouble, but every minute the atmosphere was becoming more electric. As the curtain rose on the second act, I stood in the wings, in my gawdy Spanish dress, thinking furiously. Was there any means by which I could stop the demonstration that was looming all too clearly ahead?

The cue for my entrance was played and with a heavy heart I went on to the stage. Mechanically I sang the music that precedes the lesson scene, noticing as I did so, that the audience was becoming more and more restive. Suddenly I remembered that I had not yet decided which song I should sing during the lesson. I bit my lip with vexation, and quickly ran through in my mind a selection of songs that might be suitable on this most disastrous of nights.

Suddenly, at the very moment when I had to walk to the piano, an idea flashed through my mind. Whether it was right or wrong, I know not, but I determined to put it into practice. Trembling with emotion, I found my way to the piano, sat down, and instead of the *Aria* which the audience were expecting, I played the opening bars of the "Star Spangled Banner."

The effect was miraculous. As my voice floated out I could hear the sound of the vast gathering rising to their feet. By the end of the first few lines every man and woman in the audience was shouting their National Anthem, and my own voice was drowned and inaudible. But indeed, in any case, I should have been unable to go on. For once in a way, my voice would not obey me.

Excitements, like misfortunes, never seem to come singly, and the theatre at San Francisco was, not long afterwards, to provide me with yet another thrill of the first order. I was singing separate acts of opera, and during the whole of the first part of the evening it seemed to me that some sort of commotion was going on in the theatre which I could not understand. There was a strange knocking underneath the stage, and a certain restiveness among the audience, which thoroughly got on my nerves.

And then—it happened! I was just going on for the Mad Scene in *Lucia,* when suddenly I saw a long flame burst through one of the gallery windows, as quickly as the thrust of a knife. There was a scream of "Fire! Fire!"—a scuffle, and for a moment it seemed that there might be a panic. I looked up at the boxes. The occupants, women as well as men, were sitting there, quite calmly and quietly without any attempt to move. I breathed a silent prayer of thanks to them, for their example had communicated itself to the audience.

I stepped forward, moved by a sudden impulse. "Please . . . *please,*" I cried, "go out quietly. There is no danger." I am afraid I was telling a lie, because there *was* danger—however the lie was in a good cause.

Then I noticed a figure hastily endeavouring to scramble up out of the orchestra on to the stage. It proved to be Bimboni, the *chef d'orchestre*. I was so furious with him that I said sharply: "Stay where you are, Bimboni." And as he continued to climb up, I leant forward and gave him a resounding crack on the head. I shall never forget the indignant expression on his face as he sank back on to his seat.

Well, that theatre was burnt to the ground. And the

total damage to human life was exactly one sprained ankle, and one lost coat. I always think that is a wonderful tribute to American discipline. But I thought it an equally wonderful tribute to American energy to discover, on leaving the theatre, that the newspapers had already brought out a special edition about the fire, containing a great deal more information than we knew ourselves.

And so—home to our hotels in all our war paint—some as Mefistofeles, some as Lucia, some as courtiers, some as soldiers. But all of us must have looked clowns.

CHAPTER XIV

IN GERMANY AND AUSTRIA

I HAVE almost finished with the nineteenth century. The date is the winter of 1899. The place Holland, and a very long time ago it all seems. But I do not wish to linger in those last days of 1899, for my time in Holland, though eminently successful, was not altogether an agreeable one. The Boer War was in full swing, feeling ran high, and though everybody was kindness itself to me, I could not help feeling an awkwardness inseparable from the state of affairs. And I was glad when a letter arrived from Herr Wolff, the well-known agent, asking me if I would undertake a season of opera in Berlin.

I wrote back saying that I was delighted, and in an incredibly short time, the matter was arranged. Even in those days, German efficiency was highly developed.

Although I made my début in Berlin at the Philharmonic Hall, with Joachim playing my obbligato in Mozart's *Il Re Pastore,* it is of the Opera House that I retain the most vivid impressions, not because it was here that I first met the Kaiser, but because I first sang under the conductorship of Dr. Karl Muck.

Muck—what an artist he is! If there was any one characteristic which distinguished him as a conductor from his contemporaries, it was his extraordinary precision. Under his baton the orchestra played as one man. Everything was perfect, and his genius was even the more remarkable when one remembers that he would conduct such totally different operas as *Lucia* and the *Walkyrie* on consecutive nights without turning a hair.

And now I am writing of Muck I think it my duty to throw a little light on an episode in his career which occurred in the United States during the war, and which must have caused him a very great deal of distress. For many years, of course, Muck had not been able to leave the Imperial Opera House, although I know for a fact that Maurice Grau had offered him $1,000 a week to conduct at the Metropolitan in New York. But when he eventually did go, as conductor of the Boston Symphony Orchestra, he was a striking success.

Then the war came, and even in neutral America, Muck, although he lived entirely for his art, must have suffered for his nationality. However, all seemed to go well until the rumour was suddenly spread abroad that at a very important concert at Providence he had been asked to conduct the "Star Spangled Banner," and had refused.

Muck denied that he had refused, said that there was no particular reason why the national anthem *should* have been played at that concert and that he had never been asked to play it at all. Many people, because Muck was a German, did not believe him.

But Muck was speaking the truth. For my manager, Mr. Charles A. Ellis, himself told me that a telegram had arrived before the concert asking that the "Star Spangled Banner" should be played, that he had opened it himself, and that Muck knew nothing about it, because Mr. Ellis thought it unnecessary to give it at a classical concert.

I know that you may say it is no business of mine. But I cannot bear to hear a false rumour without endeavouring to scotch it.

My début in the Imperial Opera House in Berlin was made in *Lucia,* but it was not till one night towards the end of the initial season that the Kaiser came to hear me. On that night when I reached the theatre there was a great feeling of tension and excitement in everybody I met, for it was a gala night and the Emperor and Empress were to be present. I caught something of the thrill, too, though apparently I should have been more impressed than I was, for I did not then realize the extraordinary halo of dignity and importance that hung round the Kaiser's head.

However, I was soon made to realize it, for as soon as I had entered my dressing-room, the manager made his appearance and speaking with evident excitement informed me that I should be summoned to the Imperial Box after the third act.

I expressed myself duly gratified. And then suddenly the manager turned and said, very gravely:

"Have you any scent on your handkerchief?"

I laughed, and replied: "I don't know. Why do you ask?"

"Because His Majesty intensely dislikes perfume," he answered. "Please remember that most distinctly." It struck me as very odd. However, as I shared the Kaiser's dislike of too strong a perfume, it did not cause me any great trepidation.

And then at the close of the Third Act, with my hair still dishevelled from the mad scene, I threw a cloak over my shoulders and was conducted to the Imperial Box. Here I discovered the Emperor standing up, a glitter of ribbons and medals, and indeed a very imposing sight.

If I had known all that was in store for the world at the Kaiser's bidding, perhaps I should have felt differently. Perhaps I should have noted him more keenly, tried to find out more about this strange personality from my own point of view. But in any case an extraordinary incident now occurred which would have probably made further investigation impossible.

We had been talking for several moments—the Kaiser spoke perfect English—and I remember that he had just been discussing with considerable ability the performance he had witnessed. Then, bidding me good evening, he walked abruptly to the door.

I had apparently committed some *faux pas*. Perhaps I had not shown sufficient homage, perhaps I had not said "Sir" sufficiently often. Whatever the reason, he appeared offended. The Empress, who seemed a charming and most sympathetic woman, remained talking to me. But our conversation was interrupted behind by a strange clicking noise.

I looked round, and saw the Kaiser standing in the doorway flicking his fingers impatiently to signal to the Empress to follow him. I turned back to the Empress and saw that there was a look of unspoken apology on her tired face. However, she followed obediently—I could not help thinking rather in the manner of a puppy dog—and I never saw either of them again.

The next few weeks were among the fullest I have ever spent. From Berlin I went to sing at the Leipzig Gewandhaus, with Nikisch, who conducted for me, and insisted on playing my accompaniments; from Leipzig to Dresden and Cologne, and then back to Berlin again, where incidentally I cannot help recalling, with a smile, my satisfaction that on my return visit I was paid exactly double the fees which I received on my first appearance.

One of the greatest pleasures of my Berlin visit was my re-discovery of Fritz Muller, a little Australian boy whom my family had helped to go to Germany. One often hears of the unhealthy life which infant prodigies lead and the way in which they are segregated from the rest of their fellows; and when I learned something of Fritz Muller's life, my heart bled for him. He was then studying the pianoforte at the Hochschule, and I went over there to see his professors and to ask him how he was getting on. How grim and stern they were, those professors! They seemed to regard him not so much as an Australian boy with blood in his veins as a sort of automaton to be made to work day in and day out.

I saw that Fritz was rather pale, and I said to the chief professor, who was a generously-proportioned man with large white side-whiskers:

"Don't you see that he gets any exercise? He looks to me as though he were being worked too hard."

The Professor blew out his cheeks and shrugged his shoulders.

"He has an extraordinary desire," he said, "to play cricket and football."

"Well, don't you let him?"

"Heavens, no!" he said. "What might happen to his fingers? But"—and here he patted Fritz with an elephantine gesture on the back—"we allow him in the summer to catch butterflies with his professor."

Poor little Fritz! I am afraid he did not much relish the catching of butterflies, even in the most learned surroundings, for he was rather like a butterfly himself, and a few months afterwards he did actually fly away from school, but where he went I have no idea. But before he had gone, he came to see me one morning after hearing me sing the Mad Scene from *Lucia* the night before. And he left a little note on my table, with my own elaborate *cadenza* beautifully written out in full—a feat of memory which greatly astonished me.

MELBA, 1895

Incidentally, this *cadenza,* which has now been printed, was composed by Madame Marchesi and Taffanel during my student days in Paris. Many were the hours we spent in perfecting it, and I always think that it is one of the most bird-like passages ever written for the human voice, with its trills and its runs and its lightning arpeggios.

Berlin was full of interesting personalities just then, and among the most vivid was Herr von Mendelssohn, a nephew of the great Mendelssohn, and himself a fine musician, who used to play in the Joachim quartette. Mendelssohn was a very rich man indeed, so rich that his house was like a palace and even his stables were magnificent. In fact, they were less like stables than some form of banqueting hall—and often after dinner at his house he and Joachim and I and a few others would take our coffee in the stables, and pat the horses' heads before we went.

One night, in Berlin, I dined in company with Joachim and a few friends at Mendelssohn's house. There was music afterwards, and I sang. After I had sung, Mendelssohn came up to me and kissed my hand. "I am going to give you a little souvenir of the wonderful pleasure you have given me to-night," he said.

I was delighted. "Do tell me what it is!"

He shook his head. "No, you will receive it to-morrow. I hope you will like it."

The next morning I was sitting in my salon at the hotel when a courier entered and handed me a small parcel "from Herr von Mendelssohn." I undid it, and found a beautiful little box of white satin. I opened the box, and there I found "the souvenir."

It was one of the most exquisite pearls I have ever seen. I lifted it out, and held it in my hand. It was of unusual size, absolutely round, and of a flawless lustre which seemed to radiate light.

A few weeks later, I returned to Paris, and one of my first actions was to take the pearl to a great firm of jewellers to have it set. As I produced it I saw a look of astonishment come over the assistant's face. He bent over it and called another expert. Soon there were half a dozen of them all marvelling at my pearl.

"Excuse me, Madame," said the manager, "but would you tell us where this pearl came from?"'

I told him that it was a present, and that I had no idea of its history.

"It would be most interesting to find out," he said, "because it is unique. I am certain of one thing, however, it has not been on the market for years, or we should have known of its existence."

I wrote soon afterwards to Mendelssohn, asking him if he would tell me about the pearl. He wrote back a charming letter. "The pearl," he said, "belonged to my mother. You must not thank me so much. I wished you to have something that belonged to her."

And now I have done with the nineteenth century, and find myself on January 8th, 1900, standing before an immense audience at Vienna. Writing of these constant changes of place and circumstance makes me wonder why I sometimes did not feel the strangeness of living like a bird of passage, always seeing fresh faces, and driving down alien streets. Yet it seemed all part of the day's work, and I suppose that when one is young and happy one can face anything that comes along.

But if I had only known in those days the tragic fate that was in store for Austria, how different life in Vienna would have seemed. But there was nothing to tell me.

Vienna was a fairy city—so gay, so beautiful, so festive. And at night it intoxicated me with its brilliant illuminations and the constant echo of music—always music.

I gave two concerts at Vienna, and at the end of the second concert, Prince von Lichtenstein came round to see me and said:

"I have come to tell you how much the Emperor regrets that as this is not an Imperial House, it has been impossible for him to come to hear you. But he invites you to sing at his opera in any rôle you may choose."

I hesitated. "But does His Majesty know that I don't sing in German?" I asked, for I knew that only the national language was allowed in the Imperial Opera House.

Prince von Lichtenstein smiled. "Yes," he said. "He knows, and he says you may sing in any language you please."

It was a charming compliment, and learning that the Emperor wished to hear *Traviata* and the Mad Scene from *Lucia,* I made arrangements accordingly.

But I was a little nervous about it, for since I had to go to Buda-Pesth at once, to return only on the day of the performance, I should be forced to sing without any rehearsal. When I came back from Buda-Pesth, I found Richter, the conductor, waiting for me at my hotel with a broad smile on his face.

"You look cheerful," I said; "I'm not. How would *you* like to sing without a note of rehearsal?"

"Don't be afraid. I'm not afraid of you. And I hope you're not afraid of me. In any case I do know this—that you will sing what the composer wrote. You won't sing Melba-Verdi. You will sing Verdi."

I thanked him for saying that because it has always

been one of the golden rules of my artistic creed that a composer's score is sacred. I would not add a single cadenza to Verdi.

Richter asked me a few things about certain passages in the Mad Scene, whether I made a pause here or an accelerando there, and then departed saying that "It will be all right."

I cannot sum up the performance better than saying that it *was* "all right" in every sense of the word. Prince von Lichtenstein bustled into my dressing-room after the performance with some flowers in his hand, and as he gave them to me he said, "More honours for Melba."

"What is it now?" I asked.

"The Emperor has commanded me to say that he has conferred on you the honour of 'Chamber Singer to the Imperial Court.'"

"How I am spoilt in your country," I laughed.

I asked for an audience to thank the Emperor and was informed that he would receive me on the following morning at eleven o'clock.

With my usual deadly punctuality, which some of my artistic friends seem to find so irritating, I arrived at the Palace at a quarter to eleven. The quarter of an hour extra was none too much, for I was led through so many ante-rooms, so many gilt corridors, so many immense saloons that by the time the journey was over I was quite tired. However, eventually we reached the door of a small room which was flung open, and I was in the presence of the Emperor.

I saw an old man in a black coat standing very erect with his hands behind his back, and the whole room seemed filled with sadness. It is true that he smiled at me, an extraordinarily appealing smile, but as soon as one saw him one knew that here was a man who had endured terrible suffering.

He advanced to meet me, and after he had given me the medal, he said:

" You have done a great deal for me, Madame Melba."

" I am honoured, Sir. But how?"

" Don't you know that I have not been to a theatre for years?"

I told him that I did not know, and then, after a pause, he said:

" No—not since the Empress was assassinated."

I felt so deeply moved that I was at a loss to know how to reply, but he added:

" You have sung me out of my retirement. I shall never forget that. It was a very great effort—but I am glad I made it."

CHAPTER XV

PRACTICAL JOKES

ONE of the drawbacks of Fame is that one can never escape from it. People have often said to me: "How wonderful it must be never to have to explain yourself—to be known wherever you go"; but they do not seem to realize that there are a great many moments in life where you would give anything to be "nobody." To be one of the crowd, to share its joys and its griefs, that is a stimulation which only too often is denied to those who have made any sort of name for themselves.

So at least I found in the summer of 1900, when I set off to Ireland to sing at a great charity concert in the Royal University Hall at Dublin. I was the guest of the then Lord Lieutenant, Lord Cadogan, and among those staying at the Viceregal Lodge at this time was Lord Coventry. We very soon found ourselves drawn together by a common passion for old curiosity shops. Whenever we found it possible to escape, we would go off together into the less respectable parts of Dublin and spend a delightful hour of "bibelot" hunting.

The only trouble was that we were too well known. Most of the people had seen my photograph in the papers and immediately concluded that, since I was a *prima donna,* I must also be fabulously rich. It was the same with Lord Coventry. As soon as they saw the Viceregal carriage draw up at the door they all thought "Here's a millionaire," and the prices of the grandfather clocks and old china suddenly leapt to ridiculous heights.

One day, therefore, we decided that we would put on

old clothes, dispense with the Viceregal carriage, and go out incognito. We set out from the lodge on foot, and after we had been walking for a few minutes, summoned a jaunting-car, told the driver to go to a certain address, and leant back, congratulating ourselves on our clever idea, and dreaming of all sorts of bargains that we were going to pick up.

Suddenly the driver, who was a cheery, red-faced individual, looked over his shoulder.

"Fine afternoon, m'lord," he said.

Lord Coventry glanced at me uneasily.

The driver immediately turned his head round again, and this time addressed me, saying:

"That's a grand concert you'll be givin' to-morrow, Madam."

I thanked him for the compliment.

"Yes," he continued. "Sure, I'd give the world to be able to hear your honour, and to take the wife, too."

We could not help laughing at this development. Here we had come out, blissfully thinking that nobody knew who we were, and now I found myself being asked for tickets for my concert from a jaunty driver whom I had never seen before.

I gave him a pass for the concert, and we alighted, choosing a place situated about a hundred yards from the shop we were bound for.

"Here at least we shan't be known," said Lord Coventry.

"The shop is dark inside and it's difficult enough to see the bibelots, let alone the customers."

We entered, and the proprietor advanced towards us. For a moment he peered at us in the gloom and then said:

"Well, your Lordship, it's glad I am that you've brought Madame Melba, too."

At that, we gave it up. Unless we both disguised ourselves completely, it seemed that we must be content to be known.

The funniest part of this story, however, comes at the end. It was dusk when we got back, and as we alighted at the gates, Lord Coventry said to me:

"For the life of me, I can't remember the password."

"I can't either," I said. "But does it matter? The sentry knows who we are."

We advanced to the sentry, only to find that apparently the sentry was the one man in Dublin who did *not* know who we were, or even if he did know, was quite determined not to let us in until we had given the password. It seemed as though we should have to stand there for ever outside the gates, and it was only the fortunate arrival of an *aide-de-camp* that at length made it possible for us to enter.

I do not know whether, with the opening of the reign of King Edward and the close of the Victorian age, a new era was born. We are rather too apt, I think, to mark off our historical eras too abruptly.

But certainly it is perfectly true that at about this time one noticed a change in Society. Queen Victoria had so cast her spell over the century which had gone that she seemed to act as a link between ourselves and an age with which we had got out of touch. And my impression of the change, viewed in perspective, is that, somehow or other England became more *youthful.* We had a new century, a King full of vitality and *bonhomie,* and a whole army of new hostesses.

You have only to look through the volumes of *Punch*

to gain an appreciation of this change. The caricatures of the "Too utter" young man had given place to the first satires on the woman smoker and the modern girl. No longer was the same importance attached to minute points of social etiquette (although of course etiquette at Court was very rigidly observed) and there were many riotous house parties in which everybody seemed to live in a permanent state of high spirits.

The practical joke was the symbol of the new age. It was a form of outlet for a boisterousness which had long been bottled up and denied any outlet. It broke out in the most unexpected places and some of the forms it took were highly amusing.

My next memory of Ireland is when I went to stay at Baronscourt with the Duke and Duchess of Abercorn. Baronscourt was one of the finest places in all Ireland, set among green hills far away from the whirl of "civilization." I was very tired and a little on edge when I arrived, and I remember that the first thing I saw as soon as I was shown into the drawing-room was the Duchess, and Lady Hamilton (the Duke's daughter-in-law), the three children, and the governess, all solemnly knitting. The flash of the needles was so persistent that before I said, "How do you do," I cried out, "For heaven's sake stop knitting or I shall go mad."

However, the beauties of Baronscourt very soon calmed me down, and after the first day I found myself thoroughly enjoying life. By now, I should imagine, everybody must have heard of the rage for practical jokes at Baronscourt, and needless to say the Duke—who was a most kindly host and indulgent father—was the target at which all the family aimed in this form of amusement.

The favourite joke we used to play on the Duke had its origin in his passion for a particular chair in the dining-room. It was a very comfortable chair (though I doubt if it was much more comfortable than any of the others) and he used to insist that it was the only chair in which he could possibly sit. As it was rather difficult to distinguish this particular chair from its fellows, he hit upon the brilliant idea of tying a little piece of red ribbon to the back.

Of course, you can guess what the family used to do. They used to change the red ribbon whenever his back was turned. The Duke would come in, look for the ribbon, sit down in the new chair, and say:

"Ah! This is the best chair in the house!"

After this had palled, we went to the village, bought several yards of red ribbon, and tied a precisely similar bow to the back of every chair in the room. I shall never forget the Duke's discomfiture when he was confronted with a dozen chairs, all with his particular mark of approbation tied on to them.

Breakfast of course offered endless opportunities for practical jokes in which the Duchess herself used to join. We sent to London for a whole set of those maddening instruments of torture which were just coming on the market—sneezing powder, and tubes that one put under people's plates, pressing them and causing the plate to rock as though an earthquake were in progress. When these were exhausted, we fell back on the more primeval habit of attaching a table napkin to the Duke's coat by means of a safety pin.

One day we all tramped out for a shoot on the moors. I forget whether we had good sport, but I do remember that just before lunch a real Irish downpour set in, with the result that everybody, including myself, was drenched to the skin before we could reach shelter. The Duke was in an agony of apprehension. What could he possibly do? I might catch cold. I might not be able to sing again. Why had he brought me out like this? And he looked up at the sky as though he himself were responsible for the elements.

"Please don't bother," I said; "I want to forget I'm a *prima donna* to-day, and merely remember that I'm an Australian."

And very soon, when we were devouring the most delicious Irish stew which had been brought out on to the moors, I only remembered that I was very hungry.

I had not been with the Abercorns long before I too was made a target for practical jokes. At first Lady Phyllis, who was the ringleader in these proceedings, had been a little shy about experimenting on me, but one day suggested that we should all go down to the lake and row out to a beautiful little island which lay in the centre. I rather suspected that some plot was on foot, and so I took the pains to inform myself what it was before we started. I discovered that the plan was to row me out to the island, maroon me there, row back and refuse to rescue me till I had sung them a song. I was not "having any" of this plan, and so when we got to the island I kept a strict watch on the boat, refused to be lured away, and clambered hurriedly in as soon as I saw any signal of departure.

So that on the whole I was let off very lightly. There was nothing worse than a pillow fight over the banisters on my last evening, and an apple-pie bed to finish up with.

Now that I am on the subject of practical jokes, it is a little difficult to stop, so vast was the outbreak of them just then. One of the most incurable practical jokers I have ever met was Lord Hardwicke's second son, Bernard Yorke. In later days he came out to stay with me in Australia, and he was always concocting some fresh scheme. The climax occurred on Christmas Day.

We all turned up to see the Christmas tree which he informed us he had prepared in our honour, and were delighted to find, fastened to the branches, innumerable presents, which one by one, we untied. There seemed something vaguely familiar about my own present, which, if I remember rightly, was a piece of Sheffield plate. Growing suspicious, I glanced at some of the others. And then I realized what had happened. He had calmly gone round the house appropriating anything that he could conveniently tie up. What fun it was!

Perpetually I was reminded during this Irish tour of the days, years before, when I had first gone as an unknown and struggling singer to Ireland to visit my husband's relations. In those days I had been to them merely "Charles's wife," a strange and wild colonial girl who needed a certain amount of explaining in so proud a family as the Armstrongs. And another memory I had was of singing in the open square on a drizzly afternoon at a concert in Birr and being well routed in popular favour by the village belle, a strapping lass with red ribbons in her hair. Even in those days Ireland had made a very great appeal to me, but now it was very different. I suppose it must be that some unconventional strain in my Australian nature responded to the cheery open humour of the Irish people. I loved them. At any rate, I know that I was the only one who laughed when during a procession of the Viceregal party at Leopardstown, a drunken man shouted from the ranks of the crowd:

"Well, you're a poor-looking lot, anyway!"

But I must be leaving Ireland for fresh fields and pastures new.

CHAPTER XVI

MONTE CARLO

It was at Monte Carlo in the Opera Season of February, 1902, that I first began my artistic association with Caruso, a partnership which was never clouded for an instant, and of which I have the happiest memories. I had already sung with Caruso in London, but I had never really known him as a man, never fully understood what a simple, lovable creature he was. It may be a surprise to those who have thought of Caruso merely as the fierce temperamental artist to learn that he was full of practical jokes, and that his bubbling sense of humour was so irrepressible that he would make fun even in the middle of the most poignant of scenes, such as the last Act in *La Bohême* where Mimi is dying on the bed. Never shall I forget one night at Monte Carlo, before an immense audience "thick" with Grand Dukes and Princesses and Marchesas, how I was suddenly startled in the middle of the death scene by a strange squeaking noise which seemed to come from Caruso as he bent over me. I went on singing, but I could not help wondering at the time if Caruso was ill, for his face was drawn and solemn, and every time he bent down there was this same extraordinary noise of squeaking. And then with a gulp which almost made me forget my part, I realized that he had a little rubber toy in his hand, which at the most pathetic phrases he was pressing in my ear. You know how difficult it is to stop laughing when you are supposed to be solemn; but when you are supposed to be dying the temptation is almost too much to be borne.

The *première* at Monte Carlo, which took place in February, 1902, when we gave *La Bohême* was a great success. Caruso absolutely captivated Monte Carlo. As a voice—pure and simple—his was the most wonderful tenor I have ever heard. It rolled out like an organ. It had a magnificent ease, and a truly golden richness. But though his singing was spontaneous and natural, I do not think that in those days he was so fine an artist as later on, when perhaps his voice was not so wonderful. It makes me sad to think that the culmination of his art should not have coincided with the greatest years of his voice.

Renaud was adored too—and what an artist he was. His phrasing was perfection, his acting superb. He was a consummate musician. Indeed, I think that Monte Carlo had no reason to complain for lack of artistry that season.

Speaking of Renaud reminds me of how I once asked him why he did not go to Paris and sing at the Opera there.

He looked at me curiously for a moment, and then said:

"*Je ne peux pas. Je suis deserteur.*"

I was distressed at the time, but I am happy to think that he was afterwards forgiven. And for the wonderful work he did in the Great War he well deserved the Legion of Honour.

Santos Dumont, the great airship pioneer, was one of the most vivid figures at Monte Carlo just then. He was a tiny little man who always seemed to me to be walking on tiptoe, as if at any moment he might fly away into the air like a bird. However, there was nothing at all unstable about his mind. He had one of the quickest, most flashing intellects of any with which I have come in contact.

One glorious day when the sky was blue and the wind was soft I met Santos Dumont as I was setting out for Cap Martin, and I said to him, in a moment of impulse:

"Why don't you come over and meet me in your airship?"

I fully expected him to say no, but he consented with alacrity, and said he would certainly come over.

Well, I waited and waited, until I could wait no longer. Still there were no signs of Santos Dumont, so I had to set off for home, on earth and not in the sky. However, on my way back, when I arrived at the Bay of Monaco, I was very vividly reminded of Santos Dumont's promise, for there, in the middle of the water, I saw what I took to be a huge tent, with a little man struggling in it. This was Santos Dumont. In spite of the ideal day, something had gone wrong with his machine and he had been forced to descend into the water. But he was not in the least depressed when I saw him a few hours later at the hotel, for he had saved his engine, and was only waiting for an opportunity to try again.

Some people were in the habit of making fun of Santos Dumont in those days at Monte Carlo. In fact, when he took General Arthur Paget and Miss Bridget Bulkeley, now Mrs. Benjamin Guinness, to see him start on one of his exhibitions, all General Paget said was, "It's like a hundred Maxim guns going off." But I always stood up for him and respected him, and I think that after events have justified me in my trust.

When I write of Monte Carlo, as it used to be, a flash of colour seems to swim before my eyes, an echo of distant music, a scent of orange blossoms—all mixed in a wonderful kaleidoscope, and tinged with a glory, a brilliance, which, alas, has departed. The orange blossom is still there, the ball still rolls at the Casino, but the Monte Carlo of to-day is only a poor relation of the wonder city that was.

Perhaps the tragedy of Russia is a little responsible for this. The Russians used to strike such a vivid note of colour in the *tout ensemble* of Monte Carlo. Everywhere one used to see these Russian Grand Dukes, mythically wealthy, with that proud carriage, that innate nobility of which a fine Russian is the classic example. There was something superb in the way in which they would stroll out of the Casino, after making a fortune, or losing it, at the tables, and walk down the steps as though they had not a care in the world.

In those days everybody used to dine at the Grand Hotel, the Grand Dukes included, and there, sitting at the open windows, they would throw coins into the street to the vagrant singers who had been serenading them from the pavements.

On one of my first nights "off," Lady de Grey, who adored Monte Carlo quite as much as I did, strolled with me into the Casino.

When we reached the table, there were two vacant places, separated by a large, bearded Frenchman, and as he showed no sign of shifting his seat to allow us to sit together, we seated ourselves on either side of him, and soon became absorbed in the game. I had quite good luck, but it was very soon evident from the fierce snorts and ejaculations that came from the Frenchman, that his luck was decidedly out. Every louis he put on the table "went west," and to my surprise, he kept on glancing angrily, first at Lady de Grey, then at myself, as though we were in some way responsible for his misfortunes.

Suddenly he rose to his feet, glared at us, and cried, in a voice that I could hear with piercing clarity:

"What can I expect? Sitting between two *cocottes*."

I looked at him in astonishment, hardly realizing at first that *we* were the *cocottes*. And then I caught Lady de Grey's eye. She was roaring with laughter, and as she leant across to me she said:

"Please don't say anything to him. I've never been so flattered in my life!"

What a gallery of portraits, some grave, some sad, come back to me as I write of these days! One of the most striking was that of Arthur Sullivan, who adored gambling almost as much as he adored writing those sparkling tunes which seem destined to take a permanent place in English light music. He was, of course, an old man in those days, and once seen, he was never forgotten. He used to bend over the table, the light shining on his wrinkled forehead, and stretch out a hand crammed full with gold pieces. The extraordinary thing about him was that his hand was so shaky that sometimes the coins fell on the wrong numbers. However, the croupier was very kind to him and allowed him plenty of time while his trembling fingers pushed the coin into place.

Then again, of course, there was the old Duchess of Devonshire, of whom I used to see a great deal. The Duchess was an example of one of those players who become so excited by the game that they quite forget their usually sweet manners.

The Duchess always used to go in alone, and people very soon discovered that she intensely disliked people to speak to her while she was playing. I believe she used to think that it brought her bad luck. Whatever the reason those who were sufficiently ill-advised to attempt to engage her in conversation never received any reply.

I very soon noticed, after a little experience of the Casino, that it was usually the people with most money who gambled most carefully. William K. Vanderbilt, for example. Not only did he scrutinize the table with an eagle eye, but he kept a careful check of all his winnings or losings. He used always to put his money on one table, planting down the big gold plaques on an assortment of numbers, and then he would walk to another table and put money on exactly the same numbers there. And win or lose, he was always smiling.

Another friend of mine, Anthony Drexel, or "Tony" as we all called him, was a methodical gambler in spite of his millions. I shall never forget being with him one day at the Casino, when we had both lost heavily and neither of us had a franc in our pockets. "I'll borrow some," said Tony, and so we started to make a tour of the halls, seeking some kind friend who would lend us money to burn. Not one did we find. They knew who I was, they knew who he was; but there seems to be a sort of suspicion against lending money in Monte Carlo, and it was not till I discovered my old solicitor, Mr. W. F. Fladgate, that we were able to go on with our game.

I learnt soon afterwards one of the reasons why people are not too eager to lend money to would-be players. One of the most prominent figures in Monte Carlo at this time was Baron Hirsch, and one night I had been playing fairly heavily, with atrocious luck, and completely ran out of funds. I saw Baron Hirsch, whom I knew fairly well, standing near by, and I went up to him and said:

"Baron Hirsch, I want to throw good money after bad, but I haven't got any. Will you lend me a thousand francs?"

Instead of at once diving into his pockets, as most of

one's friends would have done, he frowned, hesitated, and only after a considerable display of reluctance, produced a thousand francs which he handed to me.

I was rather surprised by this behaviour from a usually generous man. However, I thought no more about it, and the next day sent him a cheque for the amount I had borrowed with my sincere thanks.

Two days later, a little package arrived at my hotel. I opened it, and discovered a charming diamond brooch, accompanied by a letter from Baron Hirsch himself. In it he said:

Dear Madame Melba,

You are the first woman who has ever paid me back money which she has borrowed. I am so touched that I have taken the liberty of buying you the enclosed little brooch, which I hope you will accept as a token of my admiration.

I understood, after that, the "superstition" against lending money to stranded women, and I took care never to have to borrow again. It was not a superstition. It was hard common-sense.

However, Monte Carlo abounded in superstitions. Everybody has his favourite numbers. One of the most pathetic sights I ever saw was an oldish woman, none too well off, who pinned her faith to the number five. All one afternoon she sat opposite to me, placing louis after louis on five, and every time she lost. Suddenly she ran out of funds. Turning quickly to the croupier, she said:

"You know who I am. I've got some more money in my trunk. Please give me a louis to put on five."

And she began to cry.

The wheel started to spin, and in an agony of suspense the little woman waited for her money. It was too late.

The ball stopped rolling, and the number that turned up was—five! I shall never forget the look of despair on that woman's face as she walked unsteadily from the room.

I often think that the people who gamble without caring whether they win or lose come out best in the end. I remember once, after I had been gambling, and losing, looking at my watch, seeing that it was time for rehearsal, and hurrying to the doors of the theatre, which of course adjoined the Casino. For some reason or other the door-keeper would not let me in. I was so annoyed that I said to him: "Very well. Tell Mr. Gunsbourg that as you won't let me in, there won't be any rehearsal." And with that I went back to the tables. When, only a few minutes later, Mr. Gunsbourg bustled in, full of apologies, I had already won 20,000 francs.

Monte Carlo had its funny side as well as its tragic. There was the fascination of the place. I was once sitting, playing idly with Lady de Grey, when an old woman bustled in, and with much *éclat,* put two francs on the red, and five francs on the black. "*Voilà?*" she said, solemnly. "At least I shall get one of them back!" But she did not. The ball turned up zero.

For me the small gamblers were just as interesting as those who showered gold on a dozen numbers at once. However, it was thrilling to see, as I saw, a man like Ephrussi, who broke the bank twice, in one evening —but it was equally thrilling to see Christine Nilsson gambling modestly, for hers was so vivid a personality. How well I remember her—a woman still beautiful, with steely blue eyes, in a bonnet with big ribbons covering her ears. She would throw her money on the table, in a haphazard sort of way, and one could never tell whether she won or lost. But I don't think either her winnings or her losings were very great, because she had known how hard money is to make. Monte Carlo was full of rumours in those days. Most of them did not interest me, but I should like to know if there was any truth in one—namely, that she had papered her bathroom with all her American hotel bills.

To turn to musical matters. It was at this time that I created the opera *Hélène* by Saint Saens, and naturally I saw a great deal of the composer, who had come down from Paris to supervise the final arrangement. Saint Saens was one of the most amazingly youthful old men I have ever met, and he was still writing music of a vigour and freshness that he never surpassed. We used to trot about Monte Carlo together, he, usually rather taciturn, but sometimes letting loose a volley of observations on music, opera and life in general.

Saint Saens, like most great men, was eccentric. One evening, when we were going out to a party together, I arranged to call for him at his house, and punctually at a quarter to eight, I arrived in my carriage to bear him to our destination. Saint Saens appeared, a little grumpy at having to go, for he did not much care for parties, got into the carriage, folded his arms, and relapsed into silence.

Suddenly he cried: "Stop! I must return at once!"

"What is it?" I asked. "We can't go back now. We shall be late."

However, he insisted, so we went back; he entered the house again, and returned a few minutes later, putting a white object in his pocket as he got into the carriage.

"What had you forgotten?" I said.

"My toothbrush," he replied, gravely.

"Your what?"

Saint Saens shrugged his shoulders.

"I have no key. I find, from long practice, that my toothbrush opens the door. So I always carry it with me." And he produced the toothbrush from his pocket and patted it affectionately with his long, clever fingers.

He was one of the few men I have met who never made the faintest attempt to be agreeable to people for whom he did not care. I saw him once at a dinner party being approached by a very effusive woman who was anxious to get him to come to her house.

"*Cher maître,*" she said coaxingly, "will you not dine with me one evening next week?"

"I have no time," said Saint Saens, brusquely.

"But could you not be *very* nice, just for me?" she persisted.

"I don't want to be nice to you," he snapped. And there the matter ended.

He was a man absolutely without the conventional ideas of modern society. One day, while I was resting before dinner, I heard downstairs a sudden sound of the piano being played fortissimo. I could not think who it was, because there was nobody in the house, besides myself, who played the piano, and certainly I had never heard it played so loudly before (or so beautifully).

Needless to say, it was Saint Saens. He had come to call on me, and the footman had apparently been late in informing me. And so instead of ringing the bell, he chose this way of announcing his presence.

CHAPTER XVII

AUSTRALIA AGAIN—DAME RUMOUR

SIXTEEN years had passed since I left Australia, and though it may sound heartless, I had almost forgotten what my native land looked like. But now, at long last, it seemed that I should be able to return. And now, as soon as I began to talk about Australia, the very mention of the name made me long for the sight of the tall white gum-trees, for the flash of yellow wattle in the Bush, for the brilliant crystalline sunlight, for the great open spaces, and above all, for the sight of my Daddy.

And so, in November, 1901, I was able to send a cable to the Australian Press stating that I should throw up all my other engagements, and that I should arrive in Australia in the following September.

On August 22nd, I sailed from Vancouver in the *Miowera,* aptly called "The Weary Mary," due to arrive at Brisbane early on Sunday, September 14th. Never shall I forget that voyage. Four times in the middle of the sweltering Pacific we broke down and lay heaving on the burning waters for hours, and sometimes a whole night at a time. Those were before the days of wireless, and there was no means of letting my friends in Australia know that I was safe. Consequently, as I was to find on my arrival, the most alarming rumours spread all over the country—that we had been wrecked, that we had disappeared, that we had sunk. I should not have minded the delay and the discomfort had it not been for the fact that my father was an old man, and I feared that the agitation which this delay must be causing him was not only agonizing but dangerous.

However, all thoughts of that nature were for the moment set aside when, three days later, we eventually sailed into Brisbane Harbour. For how different was my home-coming to my departure. Then I had been an unknown girl, setting out on a lonely and arduous adventure; now they put red carpets down for me, they sent their mayors and their corporations, their officials, their leaders of art and literature and society to meet me, they pelted me with flowers.

But all the time, in the midst of the shouting and the triumph, I was thinking of my Daddy. He was due to meet me at Albury, some 200 miles from Melbourne, and when the next morning I started for the South, and the train stopped at every wayside station for the mayors of the little townships to come out to pay me their respects, I felt that I could hardly wait to receive the bouquets they offered me, so anxious was I to get on.

The train was due to arrive at seven o'clock the next morning, and at five o'clock I was up and dressing, taking great pains to look my best in my prettiest frock and my most becoming hat. I suppose that if I were to see myself now, as I looked then, I should think myself a pretty Judy cat, but it was all in a good cause. I am afraid I almost reduced my maid to tears with my exacting demands. Sixteen years is a long time, and when one has somebody whom one loves very much to meet at the end of the journey, one wants to look one's best.

A quarter to seven, ten minutes to seven, five minutes to seven, and then, punctually at seven, Albury was sighted. I leaned out of the window, not caring now whether I got the dust in my eyes and forgetting altogether about my hat. I saw the distant waving of flags and heard the rousing cheer from the crowd which had gathered at the station.

The train stopped. I fought my way through the crowd who surrounded me so closely that I was almost suffocated. I peered and looked round, but there was no Daddy.

"Where is my father?" I said. There was an inarticulate murmur. "My father," I repeated. "Why don't you take me to him?" And then they made a little gap in the crowd, and through it I saw a strange man dressed in black with a nurse at his side. Almost terrified, I walked towards him.

"Do *you* know anything?" I said. "Where is he?"

And then very quietly, with that surging crowd around me and the light of the early morning sun beating down on my face, the doctor (for he was a doctor) told me that my father was lying in a house near the station; that he had had a grave stroke, the day before, which had been brought about by my delay, and that though I might be allowed to see him, it was doubtful whether he would be able to recognize me or to speak a word.

Dumbly I looked round me at the crowd which stood there hushed and expectant; at the massed flowers with which they had decorated my carriage. All the triumph, all the glory, seemed to have vanished, to have turned to nothing, and I remember thinking bitterly: "What is the use of it all, now?" What did anything matter if the one person in the world whom I really loved could not share it all with me?

I followed the doctor out of the station, and as though by magic the crowd disappeared. We walked across a field, and arrived at a small house.

"He is here," said the doctor, "and you may go in and see him; but you must not say a word."

Mrs. Griffiths, whose house it was, met me at the door. She said: "He will recognize you." Without a word I entered and was shown into a darkened room.

There in a corner was my Daddy, lying in bed, very still. The nurse put her finger to her lips as we tiptoed towards him. I knelt down by his bed, and kissed his hand. And then very slowly, and with an air of infinite weariness, he opened his eyes; and as soon as he saw me the tired mouth twitched itself into a little smile. What I said to him, how long I stayed there, I do not know; but I do remember that when I told him that nothing would make me leave him, that the express must go on without me, and that I was going to stay there in that house and nurse him, he did manage to shake his head, putting even into that little gesture the air of unbreakable will which I remembered as a child, and from his lips there came the four words, repeated twice with infinite effort: "You must go on. You must go on." And then again, "Do not disappoint."

Well, I went on. How I did it I do not know. They kept the express waiting for me for a whole hour, and when I got back to it, I went straight to my carriage and I began to cry. But I went on. I kept my faith. And never have I had a task more difficult.

Always, too, I shall carry the memory of the kindness of those two friends—Mr. and Mrs. Griffiths.

How I got through the triumphal procession through Melbourne, I simply do not know, for my heart was full of my father. The whole of my being seemed still in that little darkened room beside the silent figure; but I remembered his wishes and I kept my promise. Every stick and stone of the place reminded me of memories of my girlhood. I remember passing Allan's music warehouse in Collins Street which had been specially draped in flags in my honour, and I thought how as a girl I had often walked up the narrow stairs and had gone into the dusty room for singing and piano lessons. Afterwards I passed one of the great buildings which had just been erected and remembered how in days gone by my grandmother had had a house near by, a quaint little rambling house, and that where now typewriters were clicking and offices were buzzing with activity, I had used to climb the wall to gather the ripening peaches which grew against it. But all the time I was thinking of my father, and I do not think that I really again took part in life until I received a telegram a little later saying that my visit seemed to have turned the tide, that he was rapidly regaining health, and that soon he would be able to return to Melbourne.

Of my first concert, with its marvellous reception and packed audience, I do not think it is necessary to speak, except to say that it was in some ways the greatest ordeal of any concert I have ever given, because no audience is so trying as that which consists of friends.

I gave five concerts in Melbourne and four in Sydney. May I be forgiven for saying that from those nine concerts I netted the sum of £21,000. I mention it because it was such a remarkable success in view of the drought which was then devastating Australia. You in England and America, to whom a drought merely means a temporary activity on the part of the garden hose, and a few brown patches on your lawns, can hardly realize the real horror of an Australian drought. All along the line from Brisbane to Melbourne I had noticed out of my window the carcases of sheep and cattle lying dead and rotting under the gum-trees whither they had crawled to eat the leaves. And when they could reach no more they had dropped dead. Everything was desolate with the desolation of the desert. Not a blade of grass.

And in spite of this they came, those country people, from the wilds of the Bush, from outlying hamlets, sometimes travelling for several days in acute discomfort, just to hear me sing. It was as wonderful a tribute as any artist had ever had.

But my return to Australia was not by any means an unmitigated time of delight. After having known all the luxuries and all the amenities of Europe, I was soon to discover that this country of my birth had a very great deal to learn about the things which go to make life comfortable. All the little crudities, all the little antiquated notions which in the old days I had naturally not noticed, now impressed themselves upon me, with overwhelming force, and though my love for the country was as strong as ever, there were moments when I felt like giving up the whole programme and going back to Europe.

I had my house in Toorak and my own staff of servants, and one day I decided to give a dinner party to a few old friends. I chose a Sunday, as it was the only free day I had, and on the day before the dinner I was informed that my cook would like to see me at once.

"Is it true that you intend giving a dinner on the Sabbath day?" she said to me.

I looked at her curiously. "Yes. Have you any objection?"

She folded her arms. "Objection! I should think I have an objection. I am not going to cook for you on the Sabbath."

"And why?" I asked her.

"Because I am not. And I should like to give a week's notice."

"You needn't do that," I replied; "you can go now."

It was very easy to say those words, but I did not realize at the time how exceedingly difficult it would be to get anybody else. Melbourne seemed to be absolutely devoid of cooks. I sent messages high and low, I set all the registry offices working, but no cook was to be had. I might as well have asked for a white elephant. And so in despair I went to my Daddy and asked him if he would lend me his. He said of course he would. But even then I found that there were extraordinary difficulties in the way. For in order to get that cook I had to go in person to the head of the Tramways in order that I might get her *fiancé* changed from the tram-line on which he was at present engaged to a tram-line nearer to my house! But eventually after infinite difficulties these important events were accomplished. It was worth it, for she was an excellent cook.

Nobody in England or America has any idea of the intensity of the servant problem in the Southern Hemisphere. What is a problem in Australia is even worse in Tasmania. I remember, now I am on this subject, that when I was last in Tasmania, I paid a visit to a man who may be described as the most important person on the island, and discovered when I got home that I had left my coat at his house.

So the next day I went round to fetch it, going on foot, as it was a divine afternoon. I rang the bell and waited. There was no answer. I rang the bell again and again, and still there was no answer. Wondering if there had perhaps been some accident, or if the house was shut up, I was turning to go, when a very dilapidated gardener emerged from the bushes and said:

"It's no use your ringing that bell. There's no one in the house."

I looked at him in astonishment.

"Are there no servants here?" I said.

The figure laughed hoarsely. "Servants!" he cried; "I am the only servant that I have ever heard of here." He paused and added, "Be you the lady what has called for a coat?"

I intimated that I was.

"I'll go and get it," he said. And as he shuffled through the door, emerging later bringing my coat in his grimy hands, I pondered on the extraordinary trials which one encounters in these remote regions of the South.

When all is said and done, however, these are but small things, after all. And in the long run they are wiped out of my memory by the generosity, the simplicity, and the openheartedness of my countrymen. In no country in the world is the hand so ready to give, the heart so ready to sympathize. But there are exceptions, and it is with some of those exceptions that I now find myself compelled to deal.

I am no believer in that method of writing an autobiography which dwells only on the sunny side—the writer, with a mistaken bravery, choosing to ignore the difficulties that have come his way, and to forget the darknesses through which he has passed. Everybody who has known fame has also known the agonies which fame has brought. And it is only fair, not only to myself, but to every boy and girl who is starting on the threshold of life, to reveal some of the bitterness which they are bound to experience in their struggle towards success, to tell them something, in fact, of the lies which will be told about them.

Dame Rumour has driven the last nail into many an artist's coffin. For the artist is of necessity a terribly sensitive being. He responds to praise as a flower opens to the sun, he shrinks from criticism as a sensitive plant. And when criticism gives place to falsehood, when his whole character is blackened, his most blameless action is interpreted as something vile—then that is for him "the very darkest hour of night." I know it, because I have been through it myself.

It was only to be expected that when I returned to Australia after sixteen years there would be at least a few scandalmongers to spread their gossip about me, and I wondered, from time to time, which particular rumour they would choose for my benefit. Would they say, for instance, that I took too much to drink—the favourite rumour which attaches to all politicians? I decided against that, because I concluded that nobody would be quite so imbecile as to imagine that a singer could keep her voice for a month under such circumstances. Would they discover that I was a morphia maniac? Looking at my exceedingly healthy face in the glass, I smiled *that* supposition away. I supposed, therefore, that they would content themselves by telling each other that I was in love with my tenors or my baritones or my conductors—it did not seem to matter very much which.

Well, to a certain extent I believe I came in for all of these rumours. And because I have seen the lives of so many men and women whom I revere and admire made miserable by similar stories, I want to set on record a tale which will, I believe, illustrate the way in which these rumours start, and may incline the credulous, not only now but in the future, to deal a little more kindly with the reputations of their public men and women, of whose inner lives they know nothing but hearsay.

When I had completed my tour of Australia, I yielded, although I was longing for peace and quiet, to the most urgent demands to pay a visit to Tasmania and New Zealand. A concert was arranged in Tasmania at Launceston, and a thousand pounds was guaranteed us by a Mr. Thompson, who at once started to make the necessary arrangements.

In those days, methods of communication between the mainland and the island were even more primitive than they are now, and at the last moment I found that, in order to keep all my engagements, I should have to cross in the next available boat, which was a little paddle-steamer. The discomfort of this would in any case have been bad enough, but to make matters worse there was a very heavy swell when we started, which gradually increased to a storm.

Never shall I forget the horror of that voyage. I am an exceptionally good sailor, but after an hour of tossing and buffeting in this tiny boat, with towering waves racing by us, drenching the decks with spray, I staggered down to my cabin. For another half-hour I struggled against it, and sat there alone, while the ship rolled and pitched with ever-increasing violence, until at last I was defeated.

For the rest of the voyage, I was a prey to the worst horrors of sea-sickness. I need not elaborate the subject. Suffice it to say that when eventually, by a miracle, we drew into Launceston harbour, I was prostrated, and my throat so torn and inflamed that I could hardly speak, let alone sing. Yet the concert was fixed for a few hours ahead.

In despair, I struggled up to my room at the hotel, and sent for the doctor. The cords of my throat were bleeding profusely. When the doctor arrived, he made

MELBA, HER STEP-DAUGHTER MRS. GEORGE ARMSTRONG AND HER GRANDAUGHTER PAMELA

an examination of my throat, told me that it would be madness for me even to attempt to sing for several days, and gave me a certificate to that effect.

It now remained to inform the people of Launceston that the concert would not take place. Had there been time to do so, I should have ordered special bills to be printed, explaining the whole circumstances, and regretting that, as it was necessary for me to catch the boat for New Zealand, I should have to leave the town at once, before the evening, in order to have a little rest.

However, I was not able to do this, and, for some reason or other, the arrangements miscarried, with the result that the people of Launceston were simply informed that Madame Melba was not going to give the concert after all, and had left the town by the first train after her arrival. Why? What was the reason? What was the matter with her? Those questions were on everybody's lips.

Dame Rumour quickly supplied the answer. I need not say how. You can guess the rest for yourself—the astounding stories that were told of my arrival, the legend that when I arrived at the hotel I called for a bottle of champagne and consumed it at one gulp—a feat which I should have imagined would have been physically impossible for any but a sword swallower. However, certain of the guests at the hotel described my arrival with additions which seemed to fit in with the malicious theory they had already concocted. The fact that a few disappointed and infuriated holders of tickets had come to hoot me as my train steamed out of Launceston station was magnified until it seemed as though the whole city had turned out to execrate me.

Now, that is a typical example of how a rumour starts. I have told it, not because it gives me the least pleasure to tell it, but simply because I think it is time that somebody had the courage to come out and meet the contemptible scandalmongers on their own ground. Just as the way to kill noxious germs is to expose them to the sunlight, so the way to kill this is to give publicity. And not only because of my own reputation to posterity, but as a means of helping others who have suffered I tell this story.

And now let me tell you how that legend was finally scotched. The years passed by, and in 1907, after a particularly strenuous season, I was ordered rest by my physicians, and I decided that I would take a sea voyage, and visit Australia to see my father. As soon as it was known that I was coming, requests poured in for concerts, and after communicating with my manager, Mr. John Lemmone, it was decided that I should visit, among other places, Launceston. I was particularly anxious to visit Launceston, because I had not fully realized the unfavourable impression that I had made, and my main wish in going there was to make up for the disappointment I had previously caused them.

The rest of the story centres round Mr. Lemmone—or, as it is far more natural for me to call him—John. Providentially my letter to him speaking of Tasmania arrived the day before he sailed for Launceston. For it contained in it a passage which, written with no ulterior motive, had the greatest effect in clearing my name. That passage read as follows:

> By the way, when you are arranging for a concert in Launceston, do fix it to coincide with the big steamers. Last time I went I had to cross in a paddle boat, and I was so utterly prostrated that I could not sing. Please do this, for I would not disappoint them again for worlds.

Armed with this letter, John arrived at Launceston. As soon as he mentioned the name of Melba, people sneered at him. "She'll be hooted out of the hall, if she comes," they said. "People will shout her down. She left us in the lurch before, and we know the reason why——"

Seeing how the land lay, John decided to go to the stronghold of prejudice, the local club, and attack the lion in his den. The scene that went on in that club-room deserves to become historic. John stood up in the centre of the room, facing the serried rows of self-satisfied faces around him.

"I hear that you're saying that if Madame Melba comes to this town, she'll be hooted out of the place," he began.

"We are," they said, "and it's perfectly true."

"May I ask why?" he asked quietly.

They started repeating the old charges, how I had left Thompson in the lurch, how I had lost him a lot of money, how I had calmly broken an engagement because it pleased me to do so, or worse, they hinted, because I was unable to do it owing to reasons which I have hinted above.

John interrupted them in the middle of this discourse.

"You're too damned provincial in this place," he cried. "You get up on your hind-legs and you deliver a lot of abuse against the greatest woman that Australia's produced, and you don't know one word of what you're talking about. Now," he said, putting his hand on the arm of the ringleader of my critics, "I'm going to ask *you* some questions."

"Fire away," said the latter, a little uneasily.

"Are you aware," he said, "that Madame Melba

compensated Mr. Thompson to the extent of £400, and all his expenses?"

No, they were not aware of it.

"Yet, he's in this town now, for his sins. Why didn't you ask him?"

There was silence.

"Are you also aware," he continued, "that Dr. Hogg, who is *also* still in this town, gave Madame Melba a certificate to the effect that, after the prostration caused by her sea voyage, it would be highly dangerous for her even to attempt to sing a note?"

This also had escaped their attention.

"You don't know much, do you?" said John. "Well, I'll tell you something more." And he drew from his pocket my letter which he read out. The words had an electrical effect.

"There," said John, when he had finished. "That's an honest letter, isn't it?"

And he showed them the postmark.

"What d'you say to that?"

They scratched their heads and muttered among themselves. One of them admitted, with none too good a grace, that perhaps, after all, they might have been mistaken.

"Mistaken?" he cried. "I should think you were mistaken. The trouble about all you people is that you're so provincial that you can't see farther than your own noses. You sit in this little island, year in and year out, and you just stagnate. Now it's about time you altered your ways. I'm going right round to the editors of your newspapers and I'm going to give them this letter. And then we'll see how you talk about Madame Melba."

He went round, saw the editors, and next day every

newspaper printed that letter, with an article attached to it. In an instant the whole atmosphere was cleared. Tasmania saw that it had made a fool of itself, and was eager and impatient to make amends.

And make amends it did. When I stepped on to the platform at Launceston, in a hall packed to suffocation, with thousands who had not been able to obtain admission standing outside, a roar of cheers broke out which was like the cry of a giant doing penance. At the end of the performance all the flowers of the island seemed to be heaped in front of me. They took the horses out of my carriage and fought to drag me through the streets. And when, eventually, I arrived, tired out, at my hotel, the street was overflowing with a sea of faces, and a universal song of welcome broke from the lips of all who were there.

It was a generous way of making amends for a lie, but it was not too generous, for through that lie I had suffered agonies of apprehension.

Of course, it would be absurd to say that every false rumour about oneself caused one pain. Some of them have been exceedingly amusing, and while I am on this subject I should like to share with the world some of the amusement I have gained from other stories of a higher nature, aimed at myself.

Not long ago, my great friend Mrs. Hwfa Williams was presented with a magpie. I do not know if this magpie bore any marked resemblance to myself, apart from the fact that it would never talk to order, but it was christened "Melba." One day, at a party where I was present, Mrs. Hwfa Williams entered the room saying to her guests "Poor Melba has been terribly sick. I think it is because she had been eating so many mice." Quite seriously the tale was spread round London that owing to my ravenous appetite for mice, my health had been impaired and I had been forced to stop singing.

However, experience has taught me how to regard stories like that, and one of my first teachers, whom I shall always remember with deep gratitude, was the late Lord Hardwicke, a great friend of King Edward, and the father of the present Lady Alington. I first met him during my début in London, when owing to my success in opera, the most extraordinary rumours began to be circulated against me. If they had been true, I should have been one of the vilest creatures on earth, and the fact that they were inventions did not make them any the less cruel.

I went to dine with the Hardwickes in York Terrace and, mentioning these rumours, said: "I am going to give up my career. When this season is over, I shall never sing again."

For answer, Lord Hardwicke left the room, to return a few minutes later bearing a book in which he had written my name. "Read that when you get home," he said.

And that night, in my own rooms, I opened the book, which was a volume of short biographies; began to read, and was still reading when the light of dawn crept through my windows. I read of the persecution of all those who had made a name in the world, from the discouragement of Galileo and the mockery of Columbus to the bitterness that was the lot of Shelley and the poverty that was Wagner's sole recompense for genius. I never complained of any lie, however gross, or however foolish; and that they are foolish, enough may be judged from some of the following examples:

1. That the reason that I can sing is that I have no roof to my mouth.

2. That I consume three raw eggs before each act of *Bohême.*

3. That I " show off " in church by singing psalms an octave higher than the rest of the congregation.

4. That I am a German Jewess whose father was born in Stuttgart.

5. That I am a Roman Catholic, a Nonconformist, a Christian Scientist, a Unitarian, a Theosophist, and a Spiritualist.

CHAPTER XVIII

NEW ZEALAND (A POETIC INTERLUDE)

THERE—I have written enough about rumours. Let me return to facts. I left off my narrative in Australia, the place being Melbourne, the date October, 1902. From Australia I proceeded to New Zealand, and here again I was, in spite of many delightful days, and charming people, to come in contact with a spirit of provincialism which at times made our tour anything but enjoyable.

We arrived in New Zealand after one of those crossings about which the less said the better, and the first person to meet us was a grim-looking gentleman who informed us that he had come from (I believe) the department for Inland Revenue.

"Very well," said John, "and what can we do for you?"

To our amazement, this official informed us that they had reckoned out exactly how much we were going to make during our tour, judged on the basis of full houses every night, and demanded that we should pay, in advance, full income tax on this sum, without allowing us anything for expenses.

The astonishing nature of this proposal so took my manager's breath away that some moments elapsed before he was able to say:

"But that is preposterous. We haven't any idea what

we shall make. There may be an earthquake. The audiences mayn't come. Anything might happen."

"Very well, then," said the official, "I shall have to come with you and watch your receipts."

We were perfectly willing that he should do so, though there was something not altogether agreeable—something slightly reminiscent of Prussianism—in the presence of a Government official sitting in our box office at every concert, watching the receipts to see that we did not cheat the revenue of half a crown. I am glad to say that after a time he apparently became persuaded that we were honest, and left us in peace.

Oh, yes, New Zealand was to provide us with many unrehearsed thrills. As you may be aware, parts of New Zealand, following the example of the old United States, are "dry," and parts are "wet." I happened, at Invercauld, to be on the prohibition side of the bridge, on the ground floor of my hotel. Within half an hour of my arrival it became only too evident to me that the other side of the bridge was anything but prohibition—in fact, all the night I was kept awake by drunken brawls.

Whether the fact that I was a singer had in any way prejudiced the manager of the hotel against me, I cannot say. But when on the day of my concert I went to him and told him that as I did not eat anything on my singing days I should be so much obliged if he would let me have a little supper when I returned, he looked at me askance and growled: "Supper? You won't get any supper. You've had the last meal you'll get to-day. My cook comes on at seven, and goes at seven, and she isn't going to stay up at night for anybody."

So that was that! Fortunately, I had a man-servant with me who descended to the kitchens when I returned, and prepared something for me himself.

That man-servant seemed to be regarded by some of the proprietors of the hotels which we visited as a form of grievance. At Wanganui, for example, when I had to send him down to fetch me some candles by which to dress for a concert—there being no other form of lighting available—I heard him being roundly abused. "The likes of you," growled the manager, "going out as a lady's maid. And what is she wanting candles for? She ain't a Roman Catholic, is she?"

It was my habit at most of the towns which I visited to sell my autographs for half a crown, and to give the proceeds to local charities. At one place, for some reason or other, only one autograph was sold, so John, naturally, said to me: "We can't very well send this half-crown to the charity. We'd better keep it for the next town we visit." To which I, innocently enough, agreed.

However, after we had left, an indignant letter arrived from the giver of the half-crown. "I'd like to know what you did with that half-crown I sent you," he wrote. "I didn't see it in the paper." Well, he has seen it in the papers now!

Still, in spite of everything, they came to the concerts, and that was all I cared about. In fact, they came in almost embarrassing numbers. At Wellington, the manager of the concert hall told us, by some mischance, that his hall held two hundred more people than it would actually accommodate, and I shall never forget John's efforts, with tape measures and much exercise of energy, in pushing off arms of chairs and packing the people tighter and tighter. However, we got them in. But I think that if it had not been for the fortunate chance that I possessed a bag of oxygen behind the scenes, with which I occasionally refreshed myself, the breath of huddled humanity would have proved overpowering.

The scene was now set for one of the most beautiful interludes in my life—a period of rich colour and loveliness which seemed, by its very profusion, to be sent as a sort of compensation for the trials and tribulations which had gone before. For the next few days I was to *live* poetry, to dwell in an atmosphere of peace that seems to come back as I write.

All our concerts were over, and we—that is to say, John and I—set out for the hot lakes. I had heard much of their beauty, but I was not prepared for the uncanny magnificence which greeted us the moment we arrived at the little station of Rotorua. It was dusk as we drove out of the station, and I noticed, all around me, a strange, subdued hissing, as though hundreds of snakes were in the fields. I learnt that this was the hissing of the steam, eternally escaping from the volcanic regions beneath. It is impossible to transcribe the extraordinary effect that this noise has upon one. It never ceases, although sometimes it is loud, sometimes soft, according to the violence of the disturbance.

Even stranger was the heavy scent which charged every breath of air one inhaled, for the air was thick with sulphur fumes. It was as though, in a rash moment, one had descended into the crater of a volcano, and indeed, there was little difference, for all around us were craters, and boiling springs, and seething mud.

At Rotorua there was, at this time, a famous woman guide who rejoiced in the name of Maggie Papakura. Now Maggie as soon as she knew that we were coming had got busy to prepare for us a welcome, with the result that long before we actually came the name of "Melba" was on every Maori's lips.

I had hoped to be allowed to come and go unnoticed, but I had not reckoned on the Maori sense of hospitality, for as we came in sight of the hotel there gathered round our carriage, mysteriously dark in the half-light, rows of dusky Maori faces. And I gathered from Maggie Papakura that the chiefs of every Maori tribe in the district had come out to pay me their respects. From behind the trees they came, silently regarding us, their spears in their hands, red flowers in their hair, war paint on their chests, the muscles of their arms and legs gleaming like satin in the flickering torchlight.

Then suddenly one of them leapt in the air, and in a piercing voice, and with a shaking spear, ran towards me, gabbling words which sounded like the most fearful curse that could fall on any human being.

I was terrified and put my hand in the arm of the ubiquitous Maggie.

"What have I done?" I said. "Why is he so angry?"

"Be calm, Madame," came her soothing voice; "he is not angry. He is saying, welcome, welcome, welcome."

I sighed with relief, only to start again as another chief sprang from the shadows.

"He is telling you," said Maggie, when he had finished, "that he is welcoming you as though you were the Queen of England."

And I realized, for not perhaps the first time, that royalty has its anxieties as well as its triumphs.

If an artist had been painting my arrival, his brush would have been stained with black and crimson. But on the second day he would have been prodigal with white and gold. For when we drove out, in the early morning, the sun was shining brightly and from time to time we would hear, from a neighbouring hillock, the sound of sweet singing. Looking up, I saw a group of native girls, clad in white, with wreaths of flowers in their hair, and echoing down to me, with the eternal accompaniment of the hissing steam:

Haere-mai, Madame Melba
Haere-mai, Madame Melba

And when they had finished singing, they threw to me, like fairy snow, heavy white blossoms from above.

I turned to Maggie Papakura, who again was standing by my side, in her gorgeous Maori costume:

"Tell me," I said, "what it is they are singing?"

"It is but a song of welcome, Madame," she replied, and at the same time she stepped out into the road and in a sweet crooning voice delivered one of the most charming little speeches I have ever heard. When it was over, we bid the Maori girls good-day, and went on to refresh ourselves from time to time with fruit, and a draught of the wonderful, slightly sulphur-flavoured water that bubbled up in endless streams.

If only I could transcribe some of the events of those days as I saw them, half the population of the world would take the next steamer to New Zealand.

On the third day, had any artist been travelling with us, he would have had to use every colour he possessed. The beauty of it all! We drove up through the mountains, immense ferns brushing the wheels of our coach, emerald mosses glistening in the shadows, until we reached the remains of the village of Wairoa, which was destroyed years ago by the eruption of Mount Tarwaera, which literally split in half, deluging the whole surrounding country in lava and boiling mud. And then we went on farther until we came to the most astounding sight of all—a lake of azure blue side by side with a lake of palest green. How or why these lakes, which are only flooded waters, should vary so in colour, since they are only separated by a few yards of earth, is a mystery to all scientists, and so I am not likely to be able to elucidate it. I only know that it filled me with a feeling of the deepest wonder.

CHAPTER XIX

ALFRED DE ROTHSCHILD AND OTHERS

HAVE Kings and Queens some special gift of memory which is denied to ordinary mortals? I have often wondered if that is the case, but never so much as on the day that I arrived from Australia, when I was summoned to see Queen Alexandra, and the first thing she said to me was: "And how is your father? We were all so sorry that your home-coming should have been so sad, and we have thought of you so much."

Others of my friends—true friends they were, too—had forgotten that poignant little episode at Albury; but Queen Alexandra had heard of it, and she had not forgotten. She knew the subject that was nearest to my heart, and she was the first person to ask me. I felt inclined to kiss her skirts.

London was very different in 1903 from the London of two years before, because the shadow of Queen Victoria's death, which had been closely followed by the grave illness of King Edward, had been removed, and coming back from Australia with its simplicity and its beloved provincialism, it seemed to me that I had landed in the midst of an immense week-end party, in which everybody was intent on getting the most out of life.

Among the most interesting friends whom I now met was Lord Marcus Beresford, whose brother Charlie had long been a friend of mine. I suppose that beyond a sense of humour we had nothing very much in common. His was a life led for sport, a life which had never known the struggles and tribulations which most men have endured. But Marcus, in spite of his good fortune, in spite of the fact that he always seemed to be on the sunny side of things, had a most unspoiled, almost childish, nature.

I was staying with Mrs. Hwfa Williams, whose husband has been of course for so many years the moving spirit of Sandown, and as I had never been to Sandown in my life, and was therefore regarded as the mug of the party, Marcus was told off to look after me. Now, quite frankly, racing rather bores me. I never can remember what is happening, which colours are whose, or what is the meaning of those very complicated mathematical calculations which the hoarse-voiced gentlemen on the stands shout out to the surrounding crowd. Perhaps that is the reason why I have only once been to the Derby, and I shall probably never go again, for my memory of it is not too agreeable. Count Albert Mensdorff, the Austrian Ambassador, was my cavalier on this occasion, and I can think of few more unpleasant experiences than struggling through the crowd in the sweltering heat, being hustled here, there and everywhere, and walking after infinite difficulty a quarter of a mile in half an hour in order to get to Mr. D'Arcy's stand. And when we did get there, poor Count Mensdorff was in a terrible state, for his beautiful gold watch had been stolen in our passage.

However, I was perfectly willing, when we arrived at Sandown, to go off under Marcus' wing, and I was quite determined to have a flutter as well. And so when we reached the paddock, I eagerly scanned the race card which he gave me.

Suddenly, to my surprise and delight, out of the long list of fantastic names of the horses, I saw one that was very familiar indeed—Caruso! That was the animal for me. So I turned to Marcus and said:

"I simply must put a fiver on Caruso. I should feel I wasn't being friendly if I don't."

Marcus looked at me with an expression almost of pity on his face.

"Caruso," he said. "Don't be an ass. Caruso is an absolute outsider. You'll lose your money."

I said: "I will."

"You're a fool," said Marcus.

However, I insisted, and so eventually he had to give way, and he hurried on ahead through the crowd to a little group of bookies.

"Now look here," he said. "This is Madame Melba, and she has never been here before. She wishes to back Caruso." Here there was a look of blissful joy on the bookies' faces. "Now," added Marcus, "you've got to give her a hundred to one. I guarantee he won't win."

"Don't you be so sure," I said from the background.

One of the bookies came forward, removed his hat, and bowed low, saying that he would be delighted to take my bet. And so I made it.

Marcus turned to me. "Well, are you satisfied now?"

"Quite," I replied.

"Very well, then. You'd better come and see Caruso in the flesh."

He steered me through the crowd towards the paddock. There in the saddling paddock was a strange-looking, lanky animal, with large black blinkers over its eyes, that appeared to be in an exceedingly bad temper. It was kicking out in all directions, and generally causing the greatest commotion.

"What an awful beast," I said. "Don't tell me that that is Caruso."

"It certainly is Caruso," said Marcus. "You said you were satisfied."

"And so I am," I replied, bravely.

I went back to the stand holding my head high, to witness the utter defeat of Caruso. In fact, I am not sure that you could call it a defeat, for I believe that after a few high kicks he bolted in a different direction to the rest of his fellows.

But the finishing touch came when I looked once more at my race card, and noticed, with a feeling of almost personal responsibility, that Caruso was "out of"—Melba!

However, a few months afterwards, when I had forgotten the whole question, I received a wire from Marcus saying: "Caruso won yesterday. Don't you wish you had backed the brute?"

Equally delightful was Marcus' brother, Charlie, and as for Lady Charles, she was one of those refreshing people who do not care "tuppence" for the opinion of other people. She was a great patron of the opera, and sometimes she would go in a tea gown and a tiara, a combination which would cause most women to faint with horror. But she didn't care. She simply said to herself: "If I choose to wear a tiara with my tea gowns, nobody can stop me." And nobody did.

A wonderful story was running round London at this time concerning Lady Charles Beresford, and as far as I know it is true. She had long wished to have her portrait painted by Sargent, and when the picture was actually finished, she was infuriated. For Sargent had given her, as plain as Punch, two sets of eyebrows. As a matter of fact, she had two sets of eyebrows—those with which she had been endowed by nature, and those which she put on herself. But nobody likes to be reminded of their little idiosyncrasies, and so the picture was hidden away.

I shall never forget the last time that I saw Charlie Beresford. It was at a farewell lunch which he and Lady Charles gave to me before I went abroad. He had never seemed better or in higher spirits; but when it was over and when I had to go, he took me into his study and as we were saying good-bye he bent over me and said:

"Kiss me, little woman. One never knows."

I looked at him, wondering what he had meant, and said: "Why do you say that?"

He looked over my shoulder, and a strange light seemed to come into his eyes. "One never knows," he repeated, and that was all.

I had hardly been away a week when to the grief of countless of his friends, Charlie Beresford died suddenly after a shoot at the Duke of Portland's.

I wonder if it is only my imagination, or if the personalities of the men in those days really were richer than so many whom one meets to-day? Nowadays it often occurs to me that people are made after a pattern—dressing alike, talking alike, walking alike, and even thinking alike. But then the Edwardians were individualists. They had a character and a personality of their own, and they let you know it.

Certainly no man I have ever met was in the least like Alfred de Rothschild. Alfred has figured in countless memoirs, but I don't think anybody has yet paid adequate tribute to the predominant trait in his character, which was his generosity.

A friend of mine once said to me: "I wonder how many women in London would be having wax fruit on their tables if it weren't for Alfred." She was thinking of the manifold raids which he used to make on his hot-houses at Halton in order to supply some hostess or other with an adequate stock of fruit for her parties. I am afraid that Alfred must have received a good many broad hints from some of his friends.

But there were some of us, who, though we did not hint that we wanted presents, simply could not avoid receiving them from him if he liked us. He would ring me up and say:

"I hear you're giving a party to-night."

"Yes!" I would answer, knowing what was coming.

"I'm going to send you along something for it."

"Please don't bother," I would begin, but he had rung off before he had time to listen to my protests. And the something always turned up, whether in the shape of fruit or wine or orchids.

One of Alfred's favourite gifts was an immense chocolate cake, in the making of which his chef was supposed to be supreme.

Staying at Halton, Alfred's great big, typically "Rothschild" house in the country was at once extremely luxurious and extremely strenuous. We would go down for week-ends, taking a special train on Saturday, and although everything seemed to be done for our comfort I should, myself, have arranged much of the programme in a different manner, had I had the chance. One of the main disadvantages to me, at any rate, was the fact that we never dined until 9.30, sometimes even at 9.40. It is true that we never had tea till six, but it seems to be part of human nature to be hungry round about half-past eight. That, at least, was how many of us felt, and I wonder how many of Alfred's guests, like myself, who had dressed too early, would while away the extra hour by discreetly repairing to his or her bedroom to munch a dry biscuit or two. In fact, it became quite a common thing for those who were going to stay with Alfred de Rothschild to take down a little extra nourishment to fill in the gaps.

One of the most fascinating things at Halton was Alfred's little Circus, in which he collected various animals from all quarters of the world. It was his whim that we should inspect this Circus on Sunday. It was usually also arranged that after tea we should go to the dog kennels (which were situated on a neighbouring hill), driving in charming little pony carriages. These pony carriages were always kept in a state of exquisite gloss, and Alfred was very offended if any of us chose to use our legs instead of driving in them. I am afraid that I often sinned in this respect, for it seemed to me a little ridiculous to drive in a pony carriage when one might quite well have walked. But as soon as Alfred was inspecting his little Circus he could think of nothing else; for he thought that all the animals knew and loved him because they followed him about like dogs. I don't think anybody had the heart to point out to him that possibly some of their love was of the cupboard variety and was due to the fact that his pockets were always full of sugar and apples and carrots.

While I am writing of Alfred I cannot help recalling an incident which occurred when we were watching the *Walkyrie* together at Covent Garden. According to his usual custom, he was sitting at the back of the box, and I was so absorbed in the music that I had almost forgotten his existence. Suddenly, however, I was rudely reminded of it by a strange noise, which whatever else it might have been, was certainly not Wagner. It seemed to come from behind me, and, looking round, I saw that it came from Alfred. His mouth was wide open, and from it were coming a series of powerful snores.

I had hardly turned round before he woke up. He blinked, leant forward, and then said, suddenly: "What key are they playing in?"

I told him that I was not sure, but that he had certainly been snoring in a different one.

Still, in spite of these minor eccentricities, Alfred was a wonderful host, and I wish that he were alive to-day, to give us some more of those parties. He had a gift of surrounding himself with charming people, and everybody behaved under his roof as though they had known each other all their lives. One of the most frequent visitors to Halton was Lord Lonsdale, and I shall never forget an occasion when he said to me, quite casually:

"Do you play croquet?"

"Yes," I said, "let's have a game."

We went out, and I had the first shot. I never had another. Lord Lonsdale went on till he had finished the game. I told him that was a shabby trick to play on a poor defenceless woman.

Yes, Alfred adored his celebrities. And he was never happier than when he was bringing together two people who had not hitherto made one another's acquaintance. I had long wanted to meet Cecil Rhodes, and perhaps Alfred knew of this. He rang me up one day and told me that Cecil Rhodes was dining with him that night, and that if I would come too, he would take me in to dinner. Knowing that Rhodes' visits to London were as erratic and as brief as lightning, I put off another engagement and accepted the invitation.

When I arrived at Seamore Place, Rhodes was led up to me by Alfred, rather in the manner of a wild lion who had at last been brought to bay by a very diminutive

Samson. He said a few conventional words to me and then much to my disappointment, relapsed into silence. This silence lasted while we were going in to dinner, and when after at least two courses I found that he still remained mute, I became so bored that I gave him up as a bad job and turned to my neighbour.

Suddenly, without any warning, a deep voice thundered in my ear. It was Cecil Rhodes, waking up from his reverie.

"Madame Melba, which is it that appeals to you most, the art or the applause?"

"How dare you ask me such a question?" I said. The question in any case would have struck me as odd, but coming, as it did, after this long silence, it was positively extraordinary.

He partly turned away, and I could hear him mumbling to himself. "I was wrong, yes, I was wrong." I did not attempt to ask him in what way he was wrong. Although I was intensely interested to see what he would say next, I was determined not to give him any encouragement.

Then he turned to me quickly, and with his hand up to his mouth, said in a loud whisper: "I apologize. After all, it's the *power* that we like—the power!"

And there was a light of domination in his eyes.

CHAPTER XX

PÊCHE MELBA—OSCAR HAMMERSTEIN

I WONDER if the younger generation of to-day, who sail through London's great hotels, taking for granted their perfect *cuisines,* their absolute cleanliness, and their charming decoration, realize that they owe all this luxury to a thin, silent Swiss, with dark, close-cropped hair, who appeared in London in the twilight of the *fin de siècle,* and who was called—Ritz?

Ritz ought to have a monument to him in one of the public squares of London, and underneath, as a motto, there might be written: "He made us comfortable." For Ritz revolutionized London hotels. To think of them as they used to be is like recalling a bad dream. The cooking was execrable, the carpets were dirty, the linen was mediæval, the service was an insult. I remember, for example, giving a very important supper at an hotel whose name may be left to the obscurity it deserves. I say "important" because a certain great person was there who had very decided opinions on what he liked. After half an hour of indifferent food, the lights went out, and we ate half-cold *entrées* by candle light—a depressing occupation. After this fiasco, I left this hotel and took rooms, for the first time, in the Savoy, a smaller edition of the present hotel, and one which was in every way up to the modern standard. And I felt after my previous experiences as though I had landed in Paradise.

Nor was I alone in this connection, for soon all London began to foregather there as a matter of course.

Having proved his worth, Ritz spread his wings, became a little less thin, wore a diamond tie-pin, and opened the doors of the Carlton Hotel to a delighted London. His next venture was a Ritz in Paris, of which I was one of the very first clients. Soon he had a whole chain of hotels, all of unvarying excellence.

But success turned his head. He grew bloated. He lost his keen sense of responsibility, and though things were still done beautifully, it was not he who saw to them as of old. Somebody said to me: "I think Ritz is losing his head. He's grown terribly fat and he says the most extraordinary things." And soon afterwards we heard an amazing story which confirmed our worst suspicions. I believe it has never been printed, so I will give it here.

One day Ritz was informed that in a week's time the Prince of Wales was going to honour him by dining at one of his hotels. At once he drove to a big firm in Regent Street, entered the shop, called for the manager, and said:

"The Prince of Wales is dining with me next week. I want a very fine set of gold plate for the occasion."

Arrangements were made, an estimate approved, and the manager thought the business was completed. But Ritz continued to walk round the shop, looking with a wild eye at things that came his way.

"And of course," he suddenly added, "everything else in the room must be gold too."

The little group of salesmen looked at him in astonishment.

"Everything else?" they said.

"Certainly. I must have gold carpets, gold furniture,

gold curtains—all solid gold. See to it." And he turned on his heel and vanished from the shop.

I never heard if he obtained his gold carpets, but I heard shortly afterwards that he was very ill, having jumped into a boiling bath, and almost scalded himself to death.

The last time I saw Ritz was at the Ritz in Paris. I was talking to Elles, that most excellent of all head waiters, who has since died, and I saw Ritz enter the room. "Bring him over," I asked, and Elles brought him over, saying, "Madame Melba has just arrived from Australia." He talked vaguely and uncertainly for a few minutes, and then took his leave. But I afterwards heard that he did not know who I was. Immediately he had left my table he had said:

"Madame Melba? I haven't been talking to her. I didn't even know she was staying in the hotel."

The Savoy, then as now, was an ideal place for giving supper parties after the opera. I remember a party I gave there after the first night of *Aïda,* when I sat down in costume. I don't particularly like the idea of make-up still on, but I feel that with *Aïda* one might make an exception, for if I had begun to remove the black, my guests would have been kept waiting a very long time indeed. It was a penance, that make-up for *Aïda,* and though I adored the music, it was largely because of the make-up that I ceased to sing the rôle. If I had been less conscientious I suppose I could have worn gloves, as I have sometimes seen done. But I could not bring myself to do that.

Yes, I suppose—to return to Ritz—that we may regard him, from the point of view of the epicure, as the herald of a new era in the history of civilization as we know it. However, his rise coincided with the rise of a great many other new tendencies, not nearly so agreeable.

One of the troubles that confront a celebrity in the twentieth century is that, though he or she may have the highest ideals of his art, the loftiest conception of his calling, his name may at any moment be vulgarized by the craving of modern " Big Business " to turn all things to the uses of advertisement.

It was not so in the old days. Michael Angelo did not have to shudder at seeing his name on, for example, a tin of boot polish. There were no such things as " Shakespeare Cigarettes " or " Byron Bootlaces," and even the great singers of the past—Patti, for example, or Jenny Lind—lived in an age when, as yet, their names were known for their singing only and not for their patronage of cold cream or anti-nerve tonic.

And here, if I may, I should like to meet in advance a criticism which has probably occurred to you. " How," you may say, " can Melba talk like this when she herself has allowed her name to be associated with so mundane a thing as a sweet? How can she condemn modern advertisement when *Pêche Melba* figures on every menu in almost every restaurant all over the world? "

The criticism is a plausible one, and so let me tell you the story of the peaches.

I was lunching alone in a little room upstairs at the Savoy Hotel on one of those glorious mornings in early spring when London is the nearest approach to paradise that most of us ever attain. I was particularly hungry, and I was given a most excellent luncheon. Towards the end of it there arrived a little silver dish, which was uncovered before me with a message that Mr. Escoffier had prepared it specially for me. And much as Eve tasted the first apple, I tasted the first *Pêche Melba* in the world.

"It's delicious," I said. "Ask Mr. Escoffier what it is called."

Word came back that it had no name, but that Mr. Escoffier would be honoured if he might call it *Pêche Melba.* I said that he might with the greatest pleasure, and thought no more of it. But very soon afterwards, *Pêche Melba* was the rage of London.

Escoffier is an artist in his own materials if ever there was one. I once tried to calculate exactly how much he would have made had he charged a royalty of one penny on every dozen *Pêche Melba* that were consumed, but I gave it up when I realized that it would total many millions of pounds. And not only was he the originator of *Pêche Melba* but of *Poire Melba, Fraises Melba,* and all the other dishes that followed in its train.

I have told this story in full because I am always receiving messages from *chefs* in hotels all over the world, that *they* were the originators of *Pêche Melba.* Whether they think that my memory is particularly short, or whether they imagine I am merely a fool, I don't know, but I have had quite fierce arguments about it. Only the other day, in Paris, Escoffier came to me in great concern saying that some American journalist had published a story in which he (Escoffier) was reputed to have denied calling his creation after me, or denied creating it at all—I forget which. It does not matter, but I think we should give credit where credit is due. And it certainly is due to Escoffier.

However, though I have no objection to *Pêche Melba,* I have the strongest objection to my name being calmly taken for any object which the proprietor considers suitable—from scent to hairpins. America is particularly prone to this sort of piracy. I was wandering down a street in New York one day when I suddenly stopped short before an immense drug store, across the windows of which were splashed glaring advertisements of Melba perfume. "Ah!" I said to myself, "I think I deserve a bottle of this." And so I went inside.

I said: "May I smell the perfume Melba?"

"Certainly," said the assistant, and sprayed some on my wrist.

One sniff was enough. I hated the stuff.

Then I humbly asked who had given them permission to call this "creation" Melba.

"Oh, that's all right," drawled the assistant. "We've found out that her name is Mrs. Armstrong, and we've just as much right to call this stuff Melba as she has."

"I'm Madame Melba," I said quietly. "I think you might have asked my permission."

The assistant shrugged his shoulders. "It ain't necessary, Madame," was his only reply.

I expressed my opinion of his methods fairly freely, and left the shop a baffled woman. But I very soon made sure that the incident did not repeat itself, by patenting my name throughout the United States.

But there, I suppose nearly every celebrity has suffered similarly, and considering everything I do not think I have come off so badly. As a matter of fact, the only famous musical name that I can recall as being unassociated with any popular scent, cigarette, soap or what not, is Paderewski. Probably the Kings of Commerce felt that a Paderewski pipe or a Paderewski polish would defeat its own ends.

Speaking of Paderewski makes me think of Quarrywood Cottage, the little house which I took for the season of 1904 at Marlow, and where he would sometimes come down to visit me. It was an ideal place for entertaining—the shadowed lawn that stretched to the river, the cool rooms where one could sup after the opera, the little launch, by name *Mimi,* that was always waiting to take us up stream into the green reaches of the Thames.

On one occasion when a world-famous pianist came down to Quarrywood, I had arranged that as soon as he arrived we should go on the river. But to my consternation he was, as always, perfectly dressed, but in a manner more suitable to the city than the country. He had on an immaculate frock-coat and a glistening top-hat.

Before telling what happened, I really must apologize to A, as I will call him. If he were a less great man, I wouldn't tell it, but A can stand up to any storm, whatever it may be.

Besides, I afterwards learnt that he had had no time to change, and had come in this costume specially in order to avoid being late. Not many artists are so considerate.

However, I did not know this at the time, and I said to Madame Nikisch, who, with her husband, was of the party:

"We can't help the frock-coat. But do try to persuade him to put on another hat. You see, one doesn't wear them on the river in England."

"I perfectly comprehend," said Madame Nikisch. And she went up to A forthwith. The following dialogue ensued:

Madame Nikisch: "It is so hot on the river. Will you not change your hat?"

A: "Thank you, I am quite cool."

Madame Nikisch: "I suffer for you. That great black hat!"

A: "There is no need. I am completely comfortable."

All her insinuations, all her suggestions, were of no avail, and so after this we gave it up in despair, and took him on the river, hat and all, where he sat, bolt upright. It seemed to me that his hat dominated the whole view, and as I feared, the small boys made it a target of all their choicest epithets.

"'Ullo, long 'air!" they shouted.

"Where d'you get that 'at?"

Naturally, we made a pretence of not noticing this unchivalrous behaviour of England's youth, and talked feverishly at each outburst. But suddenly A turned to me, took off his hat, and with a gentle smile said:

"If you do not care, *I* don't."

I need hardly say that it didn't matter to me what A wore. He is one of the world's greatest geniuses to whom I pay devout homage. And I should be perfectly content to go out with him even if he chose to wear a fireman's helmet. I was only considering his own feelings.

Having told this story against a pianist, it is only fair to tell one against myself. One day my sisters were at one of Paderewski's concerts together, and as he came on to the platform, a woman behind them said in a loud whisper: "Isn't he wonderful? I hear he's going to marry Melba!"

"My word!" said her companion, "what a lot of money they'll make between them."

But, alas! Paderewski never asked me to marry him. I warn him that he would have been accepted on the spot!

My visits to Marlow were in the nature of brief respites in a life that was becoming every year more arduous. I had now been working continuously for nearly twenty years (I am taking the reader with me towards the end of 1906), and I thought that unless I soon had a little peace and quiet I should be worn out. It was only too probable that if I had stopped working for a few months, I should very soon have been chafing with restless energy to be at it again. But the fact remains that when I went to Paris in 1906 for the Autumn season, I had made up my mind that I would not visit America for at least a year, and that I would cut down my work in Europe to a minimum.

And yet, in December, I was to find myself engaged in the biggest operatic battle that America has ever known, and not only engaged in it, but loving it. What was the explanation of the change? The explanation was the dogged determination of that most American of Americans, Mr. Oscar Hammerstein—the only man who ever made me change my mind.

One day, when I was in my flat in Paris, thinking what fun I was going to have in my coming season, Mr. Hammerstein called. I had an idea of what he wanted, and I wouldn't see him.

Hammerstein went straight off to Mr. Maurice Grau, who, sad to say, was very ill at the time, and persuaded him to give him a letter to me. In view of the letter, I felt obliged to give him an appointment. But I kept on saying to myself: "I'm not going to America. I'm not going to America."

When Hammerstein arrived, my first impression was of a determined man of Jewish persuasion, shortish, thin and dark, with piercing black eyes. He carried a top-hat with a very wide brim in his hand, and he addressed me in a strong American accent.

Hammerstein: "I'm out to do the big thing in opera. I am building the biggest and finest opera house in the world. And I can't do without you."

The famous concert, the gracious Diva, and the Captain of the Campania. Mid Ocean. May 25th 1898.

Chauncey M. Depew.

CHAUNCEY M. DEPEW

Myself: " In what way do you want me to help you?"

Hammerstein: " I want you to come and sing."

Myself: " I'm very sorry, but I have no intention of going to New York next year."

Hammerstein: " I can't do without you."

Myself: " That's a great pity, because I'm not going."

Hammerstein: " I shall give you fifteen hundred dollars a night."

Myself: " Please don't discuss terms, Mr. Hammerstein, because I assure you that is useless."

Hammerstein: " Oh, you'll come all right. [A pause.] What do you say to two thousand?"

Myself: " If you offer me twenty thousand I shall still say the same thing."

Hammerstein: " It'll be the biggest thing you have done yet. Oscar Hammerstein says so."

Myself: " And Nellie Melba says 'No.' I have no intention of going. Good-morning, Mr. Hammerstein."

Had anybody else been so importunate, I should probably have been very angry. But there was a naïve determination about Mr. Hammerstein which appealed to my own character. He knew what he wanted, and did not hesitate to say so. We therefore parted good friends, and I regarded the matter as closed.

Not so Mr. Hammerstein. At intervals of six days during the next month he either called, wrote notes or telephoned, always prefacing his remarks by " Now that you have decided to come to America . . ." I merely sat tight and set my lips. On one occasion, I remember, he obtained an entry into my rooms while I was in my bath. Not in the least deterred he came and battered at the door.

Hammerstein: " Are you coming to America?"

Myself (between splashes): " No!"

Hammerstein: "I'll give you two thousand five hundred a night."

Myself: "Not for ten times the money."

Hammerstein: "And you can sing as many nights as you like."

Myself: "Go away."

Shortly after that, Mr. Hammerstein decided on his Napoleonic *coup*. I had just breakfasted and was sitting down, reading *Le Figaro,* when he burst into my rooms in a great hurry.

Hammerstein: "It's all settled. You're to have three thousand dollars a night."

Myself: "But I've told you a hundred times——"

Hammerstein (interrupting) : "Never mind about that. Three thousand dollars a night, and you open in *Traviata.*"

Here, to my astonishment, he drew from his pocket a bundle of thousand-franc notes and began scattering them over the floor like cards, until the carpet was littered with them. I was so surprised that I could say or do nothing, and before I could call him back, he had swept out of the room like a whirlwind, crying that he had to catch his train, and had no time to wait.

I packed up the notes, smiling quietly, and found that in all he had strewn my carpet with one hundred thousand francs. To-day it may not sound such a very vast sum, but then it meant four thousand pounds. And even nowadays one does not go strewing thousands of pounds on people's carpets.

I took the notes at the earliest possible opportunity to the Rothschild Bank, telling them that they were not mine, and that they must be kept safely until Mr. Hammerstein called for them.

However, he did not call for them. Instead, he called once again for me, in the early morning.

Hammerstein: " Well, and so you've made up your mind at last. Didn't Oscar Hammerstein say you would? "

Myself: " He did, and Oscar Hammerstein was wrong. As I've told you before, I am *not* going to America."

Hammerstein: " Oh, yes, you are. You've got all my money."

Myself: " The money is in the bank. It has nothing to do with me."

Hammerstein: " Was there ever such a woman? Still you'll come. Mark my words."

For once in a way, Mr. Hammerstein was right. I went to America, for him, nor did I ever regret doing so. For not only was I to experience one of the most brilliant epochs in my career, but I was to know the exhilaration of battles, rivalry, difficulties galore. And I love a good fight.

CHAPTER XXI

SINGING FOR HAMMERSTEIN—SINGING FOR GRAMOPHONES—PROPOSALS

BATTLE was in the air when in December, 1906, I arrived in America. I had realized, before I left England, that there were stormy times ahead. Hammerstein had sent me a sheaf of cables, and the whole trend of them was to show me that we were in for a fight. After all, this was natural enough. For years the Metropolitan Opera House had stood unchallenged. Like a lodestar it had attracted all the great artists of the past. It had had no rival; in fact, it might almost be described as a national institution. And now a new Opera House had sprung into being.

It was already, after only a few weeks of existence, on the verge of collapse. Candid friends in America had cabled me, time and again, that it would be madness for me to come out, and to associate myself with such an obvious failure. The receipts had fallen and fallen, until, on December 12th, they stood at the ridiculously low figure of barely over £200. It seemed that the Metropolitan stood supreme, unchallenged, that the great financiers of New York, whose interests were so largely bound up with that of the old house, had won.

Should I be able to win through? Should I be strong enough to draw away some of the massed forces of the Metropolitan, or would the great opera public of

America keep faithful to their old home? That remained to be seen.

As soon as I stepped out of the ship, sniffing with delight the clean sparkling air which seems peculiar to New York, a swarm of reporters descended on me. Every paper in the States seemed to be represented, and the babel of tongues was indescribable.

Did I realize that most people said I was about to ruin my career in America?

Had I any surprises up my sleeve?

How much was I being paid to sing for Hammerstein?

How many times a week should I sing?

Was I singing for Hammerstein because he paid me more than the Metropolitan?

Did I know that the Metropolitan was furious at my impudence?

To all these questions I merely replied that I knew nothing, that I was simply going to sing, that if people wanted to hear me, they would come, and if they did not, they would stay away. It made no sort of difference to me whether I sang in the Metropolitan, the Manhattan or a barn. As for anybody being furious, that was ridiculous.

I found the same air of excitement waiting for me at my hotel. One of my first visitors was Mrs. Jack Gardner, who ran into my room, holding out her hands. "My dear," she said, "we're all *thrilled*, and the Metropolitan are beside themselves with rage. However, they're massing all their available forces against you"—and here she mentioned the names of some other stars who were singing for "the old firm."

Another visitor was Mrs. Le Roy Edgar, who seemed even more excited over the battle than myself. She told me that New York society was talking of nothing else but the coming war, and that my first night promised to be one of the most remarkable in the whole history of the American stage.

Meanwhile, down at the theatre, all was pandemonium. It had been found necessary to provide a great many extra chairs to accommodate the crowd, yet, the day before my opening performance, half the chairs in the stalls had not yet been fixed up. They were arriving in vans all the time the rehearsal was in progress and I had to sing *Traviata* to the accompaniment of a perpetual storm of hammers. I left the theatre with a sinking heart. Should we ever pull through?

The day of the first night arrived. My telephone rang so incessantly that I eventually took off the receiver and told my maid to cover the bell of my front door with wadding. Finally, as I could get no peace, I went for a long drive down the Hudson Road, and came back feeling fresh, and ready for the worst—or the best.

Poor Hammerstein! I shall never forget his look of agitation and fatigue as he met me at the stage door. He had, a few weeks previously, fallen out of a box into the stalls during a rehearsal and had sustained a severe concussion from which it took him a long time to recover. In fact, he was never quite the same again. To-night, he was trembling with emotion.

"Every seat's sold," he said. "By Jove, I'm going to win out."

I felt so moved that I could only shake him by the hand. He looked at me anxiously. "For God's sake, keep well, won't you?"

I laughed. "I'll do my darnedest," I said; "angels can't do more."

"Come on the stage and listen to them," said Hammerstein, impulsively.

I followed him and heard a dull roar of conversation, that sort of roar which tells of a packed house, and sends the blood coursing quickly through an artist's veins. When I went to my dressing-room, and began to make up, I noticed that my hands, too, were trembling. But it was not from fright. It was from sheer exhilaration. Or—I wonder again, was it?

The orchestra struck up the overture, the curtain rose, and from my position in the wings I could see many familiar faces that were pillars of the Metropolitan. They had deserted their old home to hear me. Very well, I should sing as I had never sung before. I stepped on to the stage, and, contrary to all operatic custom, a storm of applause burst out like a clap of thunder. Silence again, and I heard my voice ring out. In thirty seconds—I must say it, though it may sound boastful—I knew that I had won. The rest of the performance was one long triumph, and when it was over, I walked through the corridors full of massed bouquets.

I felt the emotion which Cecil Rhodes described to me as the supreme sensation of life—power!

Perhaps you may think that I was unduly harsh with the Metropolitan. I do not think so. If there was to be a battle, it must be a battle to the finish, and throughout this struggle I felt that I was fighting not only for myself but for the freedom of the artist. If I had been one of the regular staff of the Metropolitan, I should have had to sing when and where they wanted. My rôles would have been dictated for me. I should have been at their beck and call. No artist gives her best under those conditions. I said to myself: "I am Melba. I shall sing when and where I like, and I shall sing in my own way."

It may sound arrogant, but arrogance of that sort is not a bad way to get things done.

After the first performance, it was evident that we had succeeded beyond our wildest dreams. On the Melba nights the gaps among the Metropolitan audiences were so great that it seemed as though they would be forced to do something desperate. In fact, some of the directors of the Metropolitan called on me at my flat—and very charming, gallant, American gentlemen they were, and one of them, acting as spokesman, said:

"Why don't you come and direct the Metropolitan for us, Madame?"

It was said in a laughing way, but perhaps there was more than mere jest in it. At any rate, I roared with laughter, and refused the proffered honour. Had I accepted it, I am quite certain that I should not have been alive to-day.

However, victory did not come at all easily to us. If I attempted to describe all the difficulties, this book would never have been finished. One of them, however, is typical.

We determined to do *La Bohême.* Puccini's finest opera has always been one of my favourites, containing, as it does, so many exquisite opportunities for *bel canto.* However, we could not get the music because it was possessed by the Metropolitan, and in some roundabout way they also possessed, I believe, certain rights of production.

Hammerstein came round to see me.

"What's this about doing *Bohême?*" he said.

I told him that I was longing to do it. "It's one of my favourite rôles," I said. "But how can we get round the Metropolitan? How can we get the music?"

"Leave that to me," said Hammerstein. "I may

have to go to Italy for it. I may have to fly to the moon for it. But I'll get it."

And he did get it, by what mysterious influences I never discovered. We were in transports of joy, until there suddenly arrived another difficulty. Campanini, the conductor, would not conduct it, although he was perfectly willing to rehearse it. He had scruples, had Campanini. He was also afraid of Ricordi, the music publisher, who was running round New York, in company with others, threatening lawsuits if we gave *Bohême*. In addition to which, quantities of anonymous letters were constantly arriving for myself, threatening the direst perils if I appeared as Mimi.

However, eventually we triumphed over Campanini's scruples, we held rehearsals *in camera,* writing in some of the minor orchestral phrases which were missing, and we gave one of the best performances of *Bohême* in which it has ever been my privilege to sing.

It was while I was singing for Hammerstein that a very strange and uncanny experience occurred that has often made me wonder if music has in it some power greater than that of merely stirring the emotions, if indeed it can actually transport one to another sphere.

The occasion of which I speak was my first hearing of Wagner's *Parsifal.* The performance was given at eleven o'clock in the morning. I was very tired, having been singing in *Traviata* the night before, and had it not been for the fact that I had been given a box, and felt that it would be ungracious not to use it, I should certainly not have gone at all.

However, I dragged myself to the opera, sat down wearily in the box, and gazed over in the direction of the orchestra. I was in a very nervous condition, and the fact that the *chef d'orchestre* had a bald head annoyed me in a ridiculous manner. I felt that I wanted to hit that bald head, to throw things at it, to cover it up. And then, suddenly there came the music.

I cannot explain quite what happened to me during the unforgettable act that followed. One cannot crystallize these things in prose. It was not only the bald head that vanished. The theatre ceased to exist, I ceased to exist —I was a disembodied spirit, floating in realms of pure music. But I do remember that at the end of the act, when the curtain fell, and the house remained wrapped in silence—I put my hand up to my head and felt that I had a hat on. A hat? What was a hat? It seemed something unreal, grotesque. And then Ada Sassoli, that great little harpist, sitting by me, said something which made me realize I was on earth. She took my hand, and at the touch of the warm, human contact, I leant back in my chair and sobbed.

The next thing I remember is that I was being led out by my friends, and walked up and down the snow-covered pavements, for a quarter of an hour. All the time I felt gradually that I was returning to earth. But from where? To what strange sphere had that music transported me? I suppose that I shall never know. But I do know that the coming back was infinitely painful, and that when I afterwards found myself forced to go out to lunch, the tinkling of the little orchestra in the restaurant was so torturing that unless I had asked them to stop I believe I should have gone mad.

Let me leave this emotional atmosphere for a moment and take you with me to a slightly more peaceful occupation (though by no means so peaceful as you might imagine), the making of gramophone records. It was now that I really began to take gramophones seriously. I say "seriously" because my first experiments in this direction were disastrous. They had come to me two years before in London, and after a great deal of persuasion, and a promise that, if I didn't like the records, they should be destroyed, I consented to sing. And so they arrived one day in my house in Great Cumberland Place, with many mysterious-looking instruments, and after turning the house upside down, I sang.

"Never again," I said to myself, as I listened to the scratching, screeching result. "Don't tell me I sing like that, or I shall go away and live on a desert island, out of sheer pity for the unfortunate people who have to listen to me." The records were therefore destroyed.

But the gramophone people (with whom the Victor Talking Machine Company were now associated) persisted. Never have I known such courtesy combined with such persuasion. They simply would not leave me alone. They said that no great artist, with the exception of Tamagno, had ever sung for the gramophone, and that if I would only give them another chance, with their greatly improved apparatus, they were sure that I would be delighted.

I did, and I was. I have always been one for "having a shot at things," and I am glad that I had a shot at this. I was no longer ashamed of my records. I was delighted with them. And I think you ought to know something of the manner in which they were made.

The headquarters of the Company were at Camden, on the other side of the river from Philadelphia, and there on the first occasion, in a little room barred from all outside sounds, I went through one of the most trying ordeals of my career. You who sit back by your firesides listening in tranquillity to our songs and our arias, and imagining that they were sung without nervousness, without any of the tremors that a great audience inspires, have little idea that to sing to the gramophone is, in reality, one of the most nerve-racking ordeals.

Let us suppose that I am making a record with an *obbligato* of flute, and a piano accompaniment. I stand against the wall, in front of a hole which I know to be the thin end of a trumpet leading to the recording apparatus. This apparatus is in the adjoining room, so that all I can see of the work is glimpsed through the tiny hole. In my own room, a tube ending in a trumpet hangs over the piano.

We get ready to sing, the flutist coming as close to me as possible without actually treading on my toes. I glare fixedly at the tiny hole. "Buzz" goes an instrument in the adjoining room. That means "Stand by." "Buzz, buzz!" That is for "Get ready." "Buzz, buzz, buzz!" That is the signal for the beginning.

A slight whirring noise comes from the other room, the pianist starts to play, the flute blows in my ear, and I begin to sing. There is no audience to cheer me on, only the sight of a little square window. But there is, in my mind's eye, an audience far greater than that of any operatic hall, and I know that if I make the slightest mistake, the faintest error in breathing, there it will remain, mercilessly reproduced, to all eternity.

What makes the whole thing even worse is the unusual "technique" which it is necessary to observe in making every record. For example, one must lean right back when taking a top note, or the record will jar. And at the end one must stand rigidly still and silent until the signal comes to "stand at ease." I shall never forget that once after making what I believe would have been the most beautiful record, I stumbled backwards over a chair, and said "Damn" in an all too audible voice. That "damn," when the record was played over, came out with a terrible clarity, making me feel much as a sinner must on the Day of Judgment.

No, singing for the gramophone could not be described as a rest cure.

One of the most curious features which the gramophone brought into my life was a succession of marriage proposals from people who had heard my records, but who had never even seen me. There was something almost uncanny in the idea of some man in the remote prairies sitting down in front of a little instrument, listening to the echo of my voice, feeling that he had found his ideal woman and writing to tell her so.

One of the most persistent (and also most alarming) admirers I have ever met, thrust himself upon my attention in Milan when I had just made my début at La Scala.

He was a young man, bearing a great Italian name, and I can see him as I write, standing outside my dressing-room, with fiery eyes fixed upon me with an expression that made me feel I should not like to be left alone with him for long.

I may or may not be right, but I should diagnose his case, in view of his amazing behaviour afterwards, as one of footlights love. Everybody was talking about me at the time in Milan. People cried "*Eccola la Melba*" as I passed by in the street, they bombarded me with flowers after each performance, and this young man evidently thought how marvellous it would be to have his name coupled with that of the idol of the day, and thinking so, fell in love.

I went to Venice to get rid of him. But he followed me there. He waited in the arches of the Piazza, in the narrow street outside my hotel, he even took to finding out where my gondola was lying, getting into it and hiding in the bottom, to my intense alarm. And one day he took out a mother-of-pearl pistol and put it to his head, vowing he would blow his brains out if I did not repay his attentions. Luckily, I seized the pistol in time, and secreted it in my bag.

In view of what had happened, my surprise and anger may be judged when one day I received in my hotel a visit from a dark, scowling man who announced himself brusquely as the uncle of ——, and upbraided me for leading his nephew astray.

"Leading him astray!" I cried. "I like that! I would give a great deal to get rid of him."

He refused to believe me. "I have great power in Venice," he said, "and unless you leave him alone, I shall take steps to make you do so."

CHAPTER XXII

TOURING THE BACK-BLOCKS

I AM now going to take you in spirit, for a breath of fresh air, far away from clever men and great musicians, from vast cities and easy comforts. And you will have to content yourself through most of this chapter with simple, unadulterated humanity.

I had longed for many years to be able to get away from the beaten track, and to tour the back-blocks of Australia—perhaps the most remote outposts of the white race in any part of the world. And now in September, 1909, I was able to fulfil my ambition, and to start out on a tour which, beginning at the old gold-mining town of Ballarat, was to extend into the country far beyond the regions usually visited even by the smallest and most intrepid travelling circus.

Mark Twain would have enjoyed himself on that tour, for if you want to see human nature at its simplest, you *must* go way back over the blue mountains into the burnt-up wastes where life is solitary and arduous, where roads are narrow and rocky, and trains few and far between, and where the only means of communication is on horseback for the young (oh! the straight, supple backs of my Australian bushmen) and by buggy for the old.

I know you will believe me when I tell you that I started that tour with an emotion which I had not felt during many of my greatest successes in Europe or

America. What would they think of me? Would they really come to hear? Would they like the songs I was going to sing them, or would they prefer something simpler, something easier to understand?

I need not have asked these questions, for I never had a more appreciative audience. From outlying stations they came, from remote homes in the wildness of the bush, in carts, in trucks, and often enough on foot, over distances of hundreds of miles. At every stopping place the village halls were packed, and at each place where I arrived they gave me a reception of which even royalty could not have complained. Memories come so thick and fast that I cannot give a consecutive account of the tour. I must just set down happenings as they occur to me, painting the pictures as they flash through my mind.

Here is a typical day. The tiny train puffs slowly into the station of ——, and as I look out of the window, I hear shrill cheers from an array of all the local school-children, lined up to meet me. I get out, and the sun-burnt Mayor, followed by equally sunburnt Councillors, advances and tells me that the city of —— (I see that city out of the corner of my eye, with its straggling shops and iron roofs) is honoured to receive me. A darling little lady, clothed by the local dressmaker in the pretty faded stuffs of twenty years before, drops me a curtsy and presses into my hand a bouquet of glorious flowers, mixed in an indescribable clash of colour, but precious to me none the less.

The school children sing "God save the King," the sunburnt Mayor stands erect, and then we jumble over the rough roads to the one and only hotel. Oh, those hotels of the Australian Bush! What have I not learnt from them! So clean, so shabby, with such an amazing ignorance of comfort, such an astounding ugliness of furniture, and from time to time, such treasures hidden away in their depths. Sheraton book-cases brought out by some ancestor from the home in the old country, pieces of Chippendale doing yeoman service in the kitchen, old first editions, dusty and forgotten, on bedroom shelves.

I always used to arrive a day before the concert, not only in order to have a good night's rest, but because I used to love to see the country round, and to mix with the life of the people as they lived it. The concert was such an event in their monotonous lives, and they put their utmost being into making the best of the twenty-four hours during which I was with them. If there was a newspaper, its tiny columns would be devoted entirely to highly-coloured accounts of my doings. But sometimes there was not a newspaper, and we had to rely on the town-crier. I shall never forget when, at one town, as dusk was falling, the town-crier came to John Lemmone, my manager, and said, in Irish brogue:

"Will you be afther wantin' the bell, to-night?"

"Certainly," said John.

"Roight you are," replied the crier. "You come with me, and listen to how Oi do it."

He walked down the street, ringing his bell, and soon a crowd had collected. "Oyez! Oyez!" he cried. "She's arrived. She's here."

A little cheer greeted these remarks.

"She's nothin' to *me,* you know," he continued. "I don't know anythin' about her. But when I tell you that she's sung before all the crowned heads of Sydney, she ought to be good enough for this one-horse town."

After the audience had assimilated this information, he continued:

"We also have with us, Mr. John Lemon, the world's champion fruiterer." (He meant flautist.)

I must ask you to believe me that this really is true. I have a vivid imagination, but not quite so vivid as all that!

Night falls, and I retire to my hotel, to sleep soundly on the local bed reserved for celebrities, whether it be hard as a plank or so soft and feathery that I am almost smothered. And then when I wake up at dawn, I lie back and listen, for already the carts and trucks and bullock-waggons have started to roll in from the outlying districts—all expectant for the great event, my humble concert. And sometimes, in those early hours, a lump used to come into my throat as I thought of the gift which God had given me, the strange power which could draw all these simple, wondering people, from miles and miles, to listen to me, Nellie Mitchell that was, the tomboy who used to fall into the mud rather than go to church.

Naturally enough, the local halls were never large enough to hold all the audiences. We packed the people as tight as sardines, we put them in rows along the window ledges, we allowed them to invade the platform, but still they came unsatisfied. On one occasion, when every possible seat had been taken, the doors were closed and I came on to sing. As I stepped on to the platform, after the applause had subsided into silence, I noticed, under my feet, a strange bumping noise, as though a miniature earthquake was in progress.

This went on without stopping, and I managed to ask John in a whisper what was happening. He whispered back that he had just discovered that the hall was built on piles, owing to the ravages of a certain wood-eating white ant, and that underneath were lying dozens of people who had been unable to obtain admission. The space was so restricted that they were unable to sit up, far less stand, and so there they were, lying down and bumping their heads.

John went out one night just before we had begun, when every seat had been taken and when even the gangways were packed to suffocation, and found that all round the wooden hall, in the road, on the grass behind, and seated along the fences was a vast, silent audience of country people, all of whom had wished to obtain seats and had been turned away. However, nothing would have induced them to go, for they knew that, the hall being of wood, they could hear at least something of my singing. The first bars of the accompaniment had been struck and they were all as silent as the grave. Not a cough, not even the striking of a match.

He was so touched that when the song was over he came in to me and suggested that we should open the doors. "Of course," I said, for I had heard the applause thundering in from outside the walls, and had been moved by the devotion of the silent unseen audience. So we opened the doors.

Immediately there was pandemonium. A rush was made for the entrance, chairs were overturned, women fainted and screamed, wild "cooees" echoed to the roof, and it was nearly half an hour before, with the assistance of the police, order was restored. We were a little more careful about opening the doors after that.

Here is a story which, if only one had the pen of a Balzac, would deserve to become a classic. We were giving a performance in ——, a typical little town which, for reasons which will shortly be apparent, is best left unnamed. As usual, all the seats had been sold out.

But in this particular town, certain of the leading citizens, not only men but women, were of a ca' canny sort, and were by no means prepared to pay for admission.

"We don't see why we should pay to hear *her,*" they said to themselves. And so, one of the more ingenious of the ca' canny brotherhood hit upon a plan. Instead of paying for admission, they would ascend to the roof by means of a ladder, which the old gardener, by some oversight, had left against the wall. The roof had a broad skylight in the middle, which, as the weather was almost unbearably hot, had been left open.

All went well for them at the first. They dressed themselves in their Sunday best, walked soberly with the rest of the audience to the hall and then at a convenient moment slipped round to the back and ascended by means of the ladder. Nobody suspected them.

However, Fate intervened. It happened that the caretaker, who was an old and querulous man, on this particular evening was bitten with the ca' canny feeling himself. With so many strangers about, and with such vast crowds invading his premises, had he not better put his ladder in the tool-shed at once? He concluded that he had. And so he went round to the back of the hall, shouldered the ladder, locked it up and then, I imagine, either came to listen to the concert or went to bed.

The concert ended and the audience dispersed. The ladies and gentlemen on the roof waited till all was silent and deserted, congratulating themselves that their ten-and-sixpences were still intact in their pockets. They then prepared to descend. Alas! the ladder was gone. They could not get down. There was a sheer drop of twenty-five feet which no respectable citizen, even if he were not in his Sunday best, was prepared to face. They cursed and swore, and then settled down for the night, which had begun to turn chilly. It was not till nearly five in the morning that they managed to attract the attention of a policeman, who found the ladder and fetched them down.

I can well believe that that policeman lived comfortably on blackmail for the rest of his life. However, the occasion did not repeat itself, for it was a complete exception to the general rule. Usually, people were not only willing to pay but would come long distances and suffer great hardships in order to attend the concerts. Once at the little town of Bathurst, I was greeted at the end of the concert by a little party of folk who had come all the way from Goodooga. That meant that they had undergone first of all a journey of 100 miles by coach, and afterwards of 300 miles by train. Moreover, they had to wait till five in the morning before they could get another train to start them on their journey home. I felt it was a privilege to give them supper before they started.

What rich veins of humour we struck! Take the case of an old man of seventy, whom we found waiting outside the hall one cold night in April. He had a face that Dickens would have loved, and he called out as we passed:

"I've walked eighteen miles to hear ye. And it was worth it. You're all prizes, and no blanks. And mind you," he added, holding on to my arm, "I know a bit about singing. I was in a circus meself once."

Another thing which reads more like the pages of a comic novel occurred at a town where the hotel was very dilapidated. The landlady had prepared for our arrival by purchasing a brand-new suite of furniture for my sitting-room. I was touched by this attention, but even more touched when, at the end of our stay, I found that this furniture had been put down on the bill. As usual, John coped with the difficulty. "We shall be delighted to pay for the furniture," he said, "only of course if we do that, we shall take it away with us."

That had not occurred to the landlady. "But I want it myself," she said. Our meanness must have astonished her. However, after a great deal of argument, she decided that, as she was to keep the furniture, she would also have to pay for it.

It was in this same town (which seemed to be suffering from a general state of decay) that an extraordinary accident occurred. In the afternoon I paid a visit to the concert hall which had been specially built in our honour, to see that all was well, and as I entered the door, a tremendous crash occurred. Fearing that the roof was falling, I rushed outside. However, the ensuing silence reassured us, and again we ventured in, to find that the piano had fallen right through the stage. We were lucky to find a village carpenter who told us that he had "an ear for music" and who succeeded in patching up the piano in time for the performance.

In spite of this minor dilapidation, the concert was one of the most successful of our whole tour. When we arrived back at the hotel, it was half-past ten. We were preceded in the lounge by a party of concert-goers, who had left their father at home. He looked up at them and said: "What? Back already? She's done you all right." I may add in self-defence that our concerts always finished comparatively early because we never allowed any intervals. We used to try to create an atmosphere, and once we had got it, to keep it. Intervals were fatally disturbing.

I cannot convey to you how much those concerts meant to the local inhabitants. Little men who had all their lives longed to hear good music at last found their ambition gratified, and I hear that they talk about them to this day. As for the local critics—needless to say it was a golden day for them, and they used as much ink in writing about me as if I had been an earthquake.

One day, there was a timid knock on the door at the end of one of our concerts, and John, hearing, said: "Come in." The head of a very diminutive man appeared in the opening.

"Yes?" said John. "What can we do for you?"

The little man came forward, and in a burst of confidence remarked: "I'm the musical critic of the 'Mudgee Guardian.'"

It sounded very imposing.

"And I want to know the name of the encore pieces."

John gave them to him, and they were duly noted down, after a great deal of spelling out. And then John said: "You know, we didn't play what was on the programme for the first number."

The little man scratched his head, and then smiled. "I'd have fallen in there, wouldn't I?" he chuckled. "What did you play?"

"Tschaikowsky's *Paraphrase on Eugene Onegen.*"

"Crikey!" and with one wild look around him, the little man disappeared.

Needless to say, in the primitive accommodation which was at our disposal, I constantly found myself in danger of strong draughts, which blew in from defective doors, from holes in the wall, from any and every unexpected place. I was sitting one evening before a concert in a little ante-room when I felt a piercing blast of cold air blow down my neck.

"John," I said, "there's a draught."

"That's very funny," he replied, "because I shut the window myself only a minute ago."

"Well, it's open now. Do go and see."

He went to the window, and sure enough it *was* open. Wondering if he were suddenly losing his memory, John shut it.

A minute later I felt the cold air once more. "John," I cried, "that dreadful draught is coming in again. Are you sure you shut the window properly?"

"Positive," said John. "But I'll go and have another look, if you like."

He went to the window. It was open wide. And now John smelt a rat. He poked his head out of the window, and there, crouched in the pouring rain, were two little urchins who had come on the chance of hearing something of the concert.

"Oh, do let them in," I said; and John let them in.

As soon as they had entered, one of them looked at me, nudged his friend, and said: "She don't want us to sing in the chorus, do she?"

I told them to sit over in the corner and to be very quiet, and when the concert was over, I went up to them and said: "Now, boys, you owe me a guinea each."

Entirely unabashed, the smallest of the urchins stepped forward and said, with a charming smile: "Madame, we owe you much more than that." I often wonder what has happened to that little boy. He ought to have got on in life.

It was a joy to me to learn, when I returned from the Bush to the civilization of Melbourne, that Lord Kitchener was staying at Government House. I had often met him before (I think the first time was at tea at the Astors' house in London) and each time I saw him I was more impressed.

To meet Lord Kitchener was to meet a new force in life. Though he was the gentlest of men, with the voice rather of a poet than of a soldier, he radiated strength. He did not bluster or pose, or put on airs—he simply *was* strength. And another impression he always conveyed to me was one of loneliness. In spite of his brilliant career he remained a solitary figure.

When he arrived in Melbourne the whole city went mad with excitement. Flags appeared in all the streets, the newspapers published eulogistic articles, and people fought for the honour of having him at their table. I remained at Coombe and did not join in the fray. I knew that he would have his every hour occupied, and thought he would not wish to be bothered with me.

However, several days after his arrival, I received a note from him. It read very simply: "Don't you think you've been very unkind not to send one word of welcome on my arrival in your country? Please come and dine with us at Government House to-morrow. We want you."

Of course, to that note there was only one reply, and when I arrived next day at Government House, I was indeed glad that I had come, for I had never seen him in such good spirits before. The first thing he said to me was: "I'm going to a Lord Mayor's show to-night, and you've got to be my A.D.C." I clicked my heels together and said that I would be delighted, though I could not help thinking that the idea of Kitchener at a Lord Mayor's show was rather like Daniel in the lions' den.

After dinner, when Lord Kitchener, the Governor-General, and the Governor of Victoria came in from the dining-room, they all approached me and with one accord pretended to fall on their knees. I looked at them in astonishment before I realized what this meant. Then I laughed and said:

"I know what you want, but I won't." The men

looked at each other as though to ask what was to be done next. Then Kitchener looked me straight in the eyes.

"Madame Melba, I've been an exile for eight years. Won't you—won't you sing me just one verse of 'Home Sweet Home'?"

"I can't resist that," I answered. I went to the piano, and I sang, the same song which I had sung many times before to countless thousands in all parts of the world, but perhaps this time the meaning was a little deeper, the sweetness of the melody more poignant, for I was singing for "an exile" and I too had known what exile meant.

When the song was finished, I looked across at Kitchener. He did not speak, but there were two big tears on his cheeks. He came over to me and kissed my hand. And when, in after years, I have heard people say that Kitchener had no heart, I think of that moment.

Very different was the Kitchener whom the public knew. He could be as stern, as unbending as any man in the world; so much so, in fact, that when after dinner we set off (I in the function of A.D.C.) to the Lord Mayor's show, I said to him before we started:

"Now, I want you to make them all love you to-night."

"Well," he said, "you're my A.D.C. What do you want me to do?"

"Smile," I answered, "and show your teeth. Never stop smiling. Like this, you know"—and I grinned at him from ear to ear.

He burst out laughing, and kept up the same spirit of joviality all the evening, even during the not very exciting procedure when we stood on the dais together while I whispered all the names of the local celebrities who were approaching.

When it was all over, and we stepped into our motor, he said:

"Well, did I please you?"

"Wonderful!" I replied.

"I've done everything," he added, "except gnaw a bone."

An unforgettable evening for me. I never saw him again.

Although he does not really fit into this part of the story, I cannot help thinking, as I write of Lord Kitchener, of that other great soldier, Lord Roberts. Many of the reputed characteristics of famous men are only the inventions of the press or the public, but certainly there was no fiction about Lord Roberts' famous fear of cats. He had what I can only describe as a sixth sense where cats were concerned, that is to say, he not only disliked them, but could sense their presence in a room with uncanny precision.

One night I was dining at Carlton House Terrace with Lady Mount Stephen. Lord Roberts was expected, and it had therefore been necessary to see that there were no cats lurking in the background. I said to Gean Mount Stephen: "Are you sure they're all put away?"

"Positive," she replied. "We found three, and they're all locked up in a room at the top of the house."

Lord Roberts arrived, and all went well until we entered the dining-room. And then, almost before he had sat down, he looked at his hostess, with an expression almost of fear in his little beady eyes.

"I'm sorry, but there's a cat in the room," he said, sharply. Gean was astonished.

"I assure you there isn't," she replied. "We've been

all over the house searching for cats, and they're safely reposing in an attic at the top of the house."

"I am convinced there *is* a cat in the room, all the same," repeated Lord Roberts. "I don't know where, but it's *somewhere*. Would you very much mind having it taken away."

To humour him, Gean told a footman to search the room. He did so, and as he drew aside one of the curtains, there was revealed a large black cat, which somehow had strayed in, and was blinking up with green eyes.

After that, we never again argued with Lord Roberts on the subject of cats.

CHAPTER XXIII

LORD MOUNT STEPHEN—LORD NORTHCLIFFE—LORD SANDWICH

WHENEVER I am told that England is on the verge of a revolution (and people seem very fond of giving me that information nowadays) I find myself looking back in imagination to those days in May, 1910, which marked the end of the reign of Edward VII. A shadow hung over England, deepening quickly as the crisis became more acute. It was no mere mockery of grief, no official "organized" mourning, it was a very real sadness which entered into the hearts even of those who had never seen the King.

On the night on which the King died, I had been preparing to give a concert next day, and as the bulletins became more and more grave, I was torn with anxiety as to whether I should postpone it. Had I consulted only my own wishes, I should have put it off at once, but to postpone a concert is not so simple as all that—it means the disorganization of the plans of countless other people. However, I did postpone it, for the King died.

I shall always remember that last night of the reign of King Edward. I was in my hotel and I could not sleep. I lay back listening to the noises in the street, listening always to the subdued hush that seemed, in some way, to indicate the passing of a great man. Three times in the night my little maid came in to see me—herself equally unable to rest. And then in the morning the news came through.

I gave my concert a month later. The whole audience was dressed in black, and the impression was unforgettable. And in the few concerts and private parties that were given in the subsequent months, I don't think I have ever seen the women looking more beautiful. Faces that had seemed dull and commonplace, attained a sort of radiance, in this sombre setting, that was unforgettable. But it was not merely a question of the colour of their clothes, for the colour actually seemed, for a space, to have gone out of their lives also. And it was the same all over England.

It needs an Englishman, I think, to understand this grief, because Edward VII was a typical Englishman, with an Englishman's faults, as well as his virtues, and that will be the final judgment of history upon him.

What an amazing gallery of fine men and noble women the Edwardians appear, looking back at them in perspective. I do not mean only the men who were born to greatness, but the men who achieved it. They had a glamour about them which is sadly lacking in some of the *nouveaux riches* of to-day.

Lord Mount Stephen for example. Of all the men I have ever met, Lord Mount Stephen was the only one who really reminded me of my father. He had the same shrewd humour, the same absolute directness; and, like my father, he had begun life as a penniless boy and had gradually worked up to a position of prominence. And when I think that this great man was largely instrumental in building the Canadian Pacific Railway and bringing untold prosperity to lands which would otherwise have remained desolate, I feel proud indeed of being a Scotchwoman.

Lord Mount Stephen was not a man to boast about his own achievements, but he did tell me during one of his rare moments of expansion something of the romance of his early career. And it is a story of such bravery and such ingenuity that I think it is worth putting on permanent record.

"Running bare-foot over the stubble," he said, "is the first memory I have, and in a way it is one of the sweetest memories of all. I used to earn a shilling from the Laird (the old Duke of Richmond) in those days for going twelve miles to carry a letter. And very lucky I thought myself to get it. Those shillings I earned were the best-earned money I ever made, because, as you may know yourself, if you want to get over stubble with bare feet, the only way of doing it is to run. It's when you drop into a walk that you start to feel it.

"Later on," he went on simply, "I decided I would set out for London, having come to the conclusion that there was not enough scope for the capital I had saved out of my shilling letter journeys if I remained where I was. So I started off south, still walking at first, and then going in the "Parliamentary" train, which was about the slowest thing in creation. However, I did eventually get there, and I hadn't been there long before I got a job in a wholesale cloth merchant's at £20 a year. And as I was lodged and boarded as well, I saved that £20 a year and began to think myself a capitalist." He paused and smiled. "Pawsons was the name of that shop," he said. "It's in St. Paul's Churchyard, just the same to-day.

"But"—and here a sort of mist gathered in his eyes—"I was not really happy in London. I could not get enough potatoes. I just used to stand outside the windows of the greengrocers and look at the potatoes, all brown and earthy in their boxes, and then I used to sigh and tighten my belt, and think what a fine place Scotland was, where you could have as many potatoes as you could carry away with you for a halfpenny.

"And then I got out to Canada in a sailing vessel which took three months to cross over, and worked like a young devil in another cloth business with a cousin of mine. Clever? No. There was no cleverness in it. A man would just have to be born asleep if he could not have got on in Canada in those days."

I asked him if he liked it. His lips set in a tight line. "I didn't think about that," he said.

I was perpetually entertained by the running chaff and dialogue which was always going on between Lord Mount Stephen and his wife at Brockett. We would all three wander out into the garden for a walk by the side of the delightful lake which stretched away on one side of the grounds, when suddenly he would look out across the water, grip his wife by the arm, and say:

"Gean, there's a new punt on the lake. What a dreadfully extravagant baggage you are. I've never seen it before. I suppose you bought it. Where did you get it, and what do you want it for?"

Or at dinner, as soon as the soup was served, he would put on a mock frown and say:

"Gean, I have not seen these plates before. You have been buying more rubbish. What is the meaning of it?"

One night Gean Mount Stephen was showing me her jewels. She had a most charming way of showing them, dragging them rather diffidently from their boxes and holding up diamonds and pearls and emeralds to the light, rather as a child would hold up a new toy. Among them I noticed two superb rows of diamonds.

"Do be really pompous to-night," I said, "and wear them both."

She shrank back with a little gesture of dissent and shook her head, saying:

" Oh, no, his Lordship never allows me to wear more than one of them at a time."

" Oh, don't bother about that just for once," I said. " Put them on, and see if he will notice them." And after a little persuasion she did.

All went well during dinner, and she sat at the end of the table, glittering with diamonds, and secretly revelling in her naughtiness. But afterwards, when he came into the drawing-room, Lord Mount Stephen pointed his finger at her, and said:

" Gean, haven't I told you not to wear all those diamonds round your neck? "

I pleaded guilty to making her wear them, and I said rather indignantly: " Why did you give her two rows of diamonds, if she is not allowed to wear them? "

He frowned at me and said: " You are making a great mistake. I will tell you how I came to buy those diamonds. I'd already given her one row. And then I went into Christie's one afternoon and I saw that necklace, and I said to the dealer: ' How much do you think they will fetch? ' He told me. Well, like a stupid old fool, I told him, ' If you can get it for £5,000 less, I will have it.' I forgot all about the darned thing, but when it was brought to me I had to pay for it, so I shoved it in my dispatch box.

" But trust a woman to find out if there are any jewels about the house! I was working in my study with the dispatch box open one day, when in comes Gean, starts muddling round, finds the box, and says: ' Oh, what's in this? ' ' I don't know,' I said, being busy at the time.

" So she opened it, and then I had to answer some questions. ' Who are these for? ' says she. ' Why didn't you tell me about them before? What do you keep diamonds like these in your dispatch box for?' So I told her the whole story, and I said she could have them; but I had to make one condition, just to save my own face, and that was that she should never wear the two at once. She promised she never would, and now she goes and breaks her promise. Oh, she's a wicked woman!"

One met every type of man and woman at Brockett. That was the charm of it—the charm of the unexpected. One day a Canadian friend arrived from the other side of the water. I forget his name, but I know that he had been a companion of Lord Mount Stephen's in his early struggles, and that as such he was received with open arms.

His arrival created something of a sensation, because he came in an exceptionally tall top-hat, and a very long frock coat, and linen so highly starched that he looked as if he were about to suffocate. This costume, especially when one compared it with one's own comfortable country clothes, made conversation a little difficult, and it grew worse as the day went on until evening, when the wearer of it took me into dinner. He relapsed into a state of absolute silence. At last in desperation I thought of the most obvious question I could ask him, and then turning to him I said:

"What do you think of our English country-house life?"

He looked me straight in the eye as though he were delivering a sentence of death, and he said in a gruff voice:

"Madam, I think it is most educational."

Whether he thawed at all when he was alone with Lord Mount Stephen I do not know, but I do remember that when the time came for him to go, Lord Mount

Stephen shook him by the hand and said: "What's the matter with you, mon? You have been *blithering* ever since you came into the house."

One day I asked Lord Mount Stephen how he had come to choose his title. He roared with laughter and said:

"I got it from a mountain. But I gave it to the mountain first."

I asked him what he meant. "Well, you see," he said, "we Scotsmen who helped to build the Canadian Pacific used to lend our names to some of the big ranges on the route. My name was Stephen, so my own particular mountain was called Mount Stephen. A fine name I thought it, too," he added, "but on the very first time I went out in the street with my new name, I saw an old coal cart with the owner's name 'Mount Stephen' written all over it. What d'you think of that?"

It was Lord Mount Stephen who cured me of a misunderstanding which, I am quite sure, must be common to many millions of people. We always used to sit in the porch at Brockett, and one day, in answer to a long-standing request, I sang "Comin' thro' the Rye" for his especial benefit. I can see him to this day, nodding his dear old head in time to the music, with the sunlight streaming on his face, while I stood in front of him and sang.

When I had finished, and he had thanked me, with that wonderful old-world courtesy of his, he suddenly said: "I suppose you're like all the rest of them? You think 'Comin' thro' the Rye' means 'Comin' through a field of rye?'"

"Well, doesn't it?"

He shook his head solemnly. "It does not. It means comin' thro' a bur-r-rn. The Rye is the name of a

Scotch burn." He looked up at me with a twinkle in his eye. "And you with a Scotch father!"

I tremble to think of the number of oleographs of plump young ladies wading through fields of rye which will have to be destroyed when this revelation is published.

Writing of Lord Mount Stephen makes me think of another self-made man, no less great, but, oh, how different—Lord Northcliffe. He was only young Mr. Alfred Harmsworth when I first met him, but he was already a celebrity and was well on in the triumphant campaign which was to capture the English press. I remember that as I drove to his house in Berkeley Square, I read for the first time a copy of "The Evening News," and was amused by the audacity which he had introduced into journalism. It was as though a young giant had suddenly entered Fleet Street, sweeping away all that displeased him—the dull leaders, the stodgy headlines and uninspired criticism—and had set forth what he had to say with a shout of joy.

I was greeted in the hall of Harmsworth's house by a good-looking young man, clean shaven, with an engaging smile, a broad forehead and eyes that darted hither and thither like a bird's. He shook me warmly by the hand, and I said: "I don't think I know your father yet." "My f her?" he replied, "but I thought you'd come to see me. I'm Alfred Harmsworth."

We became firm friends, in spite of my blunder. In fact, I think he liked to be thought younger than he really was. One of the first things he said to me was "I shan't even allow a man over forty to work in my office. Old men are no use in journalism. It's cruel, but it's true. Old men haven't the courage, and what's more, they write themselves out. They go on repeating themselves. And so, when a man gets old, I shall give him a pension and set him free." I think that, inevitably, he changed his opinion when he himself reached that age.

Alfred Harmsworth was always a true friend. He had a habit of ringing one up, very early in the morning, before most people's breakfast, and asking if he could do anything for one. He was quite hurt if you said "No," and never more happy than if he could help. On one occasion he did me a service for which I am eternally grateful. My son George was in Texas, when suddenly the news came through that there had been a terrible earthquake. Whole streets had been destroyed and hundreds of people killed. In desperation I rang up Harmsworth and prayed him that if it was humanly possible, he should find out what had happened to my son. "That's all right," came back his quiet voice over the telephone. "Don't you worry; I'll let you know in twenty-four hours."

He set his cables working, ordered foreign correspondents to make exhaustive inquiries, and before the twenty-four hours had elapsed he rang me up to tell me that my son was unhurt. "I told you I should find out," he said, "and I always keep my word."

He did, and for a long time he kept his youth, even to an amusing little love of practical jokes. Once, when I was in Paris, at the time he was given his title, Lord Northcliffe was announced. "Lord Northcliffe?" I said. "I don't know who he is. Tell him I am not in."

"But I must see you," came a voice from behind the screen.

Very much annoyed at being worried by a stranger, I got up, prepared to tell him what I thought of him, walked behind the screen, and saw the laughing face of Alfred Harmsworth.

"It's only me," he said. "I'm Lord Northcliffe. And I wanted to hear how my new name sounded."

Legend has concentrated so exclusively on the business side of Northcliffe's character, that he has come to be generally regarded as a man without any artistic nature at all, as a sort of inhuman journalistic machine, gifted with an abnormal capacity for work. How false that legend is!

The very first time I visited him when he had moved into his new house in Carlton House Terrace, he gave me proof of that love of beauty for which most of the world did not credit him. As I stepped into his dining-room, the first thing I noticed was a collection of marvellous pictures on the walls. I cannot give a detailed account of them, but I know they made an instantaneous impression on me.

"These pictures," I said, "they're wonderful. Where did you get them?"

"I bought them with the house. They were part of the furniture."

A look of disappointment came over my face, and Northcliffe must have seen it, for he laughed and said:

"Oh, I'm not quite such a barbarian as you think. I bought the house because of the *pictures,* not the pictures because of the house!"

I felt that it was very like him to buy a whole house because of something it contained.

On another occasion, he gave me proof of his artistic instinct and proof of his friendship at the same time. I had been singing Juliet at Covent Garden, and I know that I had been singing as usual. On the following day, however, a very scathing notice appeared in the *Daily Mail,* telling the world in general that I had given a remarkably poor performance. I read the notice, shrugged my shoulders, and thought nothing more about it.

Suddenly the telephone bell rang. It was Northcliffe.

"I want to have tea with you to-day," he said, characteristically.

I told him to come along at half-past four. He bustled in, punctual as usual, shook my hand, and without more ado said:

"Did you read the *Daily Mail* criticism this morning?"

I told him that I had done, and that I was not in the least angry about it.

"Do you know the name of the critic?" he continued.

"No."

"You haven't ever offended him?"

"Not that I know of."

"Well, anyway, he's sacked. Lady Northcliffe and I were in the house last night and you sang beautifully. His criticism was malicious and unfair. I'm not going to have that sort of thing in my papers. And so I sacked him. I'm sorry."

Nobody who knew the triumph of young Harmsworth could fail to feel deeply the tragedy of Lord Northcliffe. That last world-tour of his was the final gesture of a great man, but of a man already under sentence of death. When he arrived in Australia he came straight up to stay with me at Coombe, and I could hardly prevent myself crying out in pity, and alarm. The slim alert figure had grown heavy and swollen, the keen face was puffy and sagged, the bright darting eyes had lost their lustre. He gave me the impression of a man whose whole body was poisoned, as indeed it was.

The sparkle, too, had gone out of his talk, though there were flashes of the old brilliance, like a giant reviving. He would sit down, after dinner, for a long time silent—almost asleep—listening to what others were saying. And then suddenly he would plunge into the conversation, contradict us all, and with a few quick staccato sentences indicate a train of thought which was fresh and stimulating. Then, he would sigh, and again relapse into silence. The only thing which made me feel that perhaps after all he was not as ill as he looked was the tremendous energy with which he played with my little grand-daughter, Pamela. But his love for children was, after all, a characteristic which I have noticed in many great men, and he played with a feverish anxiety, as though he had little time to lose. Six months later he was dead.

There is nothing like contrast in autobiography, and I have been feeling as I wrote the last few lines, the need of a little humorous relief. Nor do I think that contrast, provided one keeps fairly within the limits of chronological sequence, is so very inartistic. And certainly there could be no greater contrast than between Lord Northcliffe and the man of whom I am now going to write—Lord Sandwich—that strange exotic figure whom one knew so well in those days before the war, and who might well have stepped straight out of the pages of Thackeray.

I learnt on my first visit to Hinchingbrooke that though the late Lord Sandwich was one of the most delightful companions in the world, he was also at times one of the worst tempered. I arrived at Hinchingbrooke soon after lunch and as it was a very hot day, and tennis seemed too strenuous, we decided to play croquet. I had never looked upon this game as one of very tremendous importance, and though Sandwich was my partner I could not interest myself in it to the extent of stopping conversation, and therefore chattered gaily. I began to drop behind the others and suddenly Sandwich, who was on the other side of the lawn, shouted out: "If you would stop talking for two seconds, you might perhaps sometimes go through a hoop."

Needless to say, we lost. And then, to my astonishment, I saw Lord Sandwich run across the lawn, seize the balls, and hurl them furiously into the lake. I learnt that this was his invariable custom when he lost a game. However, half an hour later he was his old self, and was showing me Hinchingbrooke as though nothing had happened.

Another of his eccentricities was that he attached an unusual importance to punctuality. He used to say to his butler: "When I say eight o'clock I mean eight o'clock, and not one minute past eight." Being equally punctual myself, I had no fear of offending him in this respect. But on one occasion I had been out motoring in the country when, about six miles from home, the car broke down. After considerable delay, I managed to get a motor-bicycle with a side-car, and by the time I reached Hinchingbrooke it was already eight o'clock.

When I came down to dinner, Sandwich was so annoyed that, although I was sitting next to him, he would not say a word to me. At length, he turned to me and with more than his usual stutter said:

Sandwich: "D-d-d'you know whom I considered the g-g-greatest singer in the world?"

Myself: "No. Who?"

Sandwich: "I think the g-g-greatest singer in the world was m-my m-m-mother."

Myself: "Then I wish I might have heard her. She could have given me lessons."

At that he laughed, and all was well.

Lord Sandwich had very determined ideas as to the

correct dress which was necessary for his guests who were staying at Hinchingbrooke. In particular, it greatly annoyed him if the women wore hats during lunch. Most of us were warned about this little peculiarity as soon as we arrived, but sometimes we were apt to forget it. And one day when we had been out for a walk, and returned just as luncheon was ready, we all went into the dining room with our hats on.

Lord Sandwich sat at the end of the table with an expression of deep gloom on his face. Suddenly after taking a sweeping glance at us all munching our food quite innocently, he turned to the butler and said:

"Bring me my hat!"

The butler, who must have been used to strange orders, gravely went to the door to fetch it. Just as he was going out, Lord Sandwich shouted: "*You* put on a hat, too."

"Yes, sir," said the butler.

"And," added his master, "the footmen can also get their hats and wear them."

During the whole of this remarkable procedure, I had been wondering whether I was supposed to laugh or to take no notice. But as the prevailing atmosphere of the table continued to be one of deep gravity, I said nothing.

In a few moments the butler returned, wearing a smart grey Homberg hat, which looked ridiculously out of place with his black clothes. He was followed by a couple of sheepish footmen, one of them in a slouch hat, the other in a cap. But nobody looked more fantastic than Lord Sandwich, who was handed a tweed cap on a silver tray. This he put on, tugged it over his eyes, and glared fiercely in front of him, as though to say, "Now criticize me—if you dare!"

CHAPTER XXIV

THE WAR

WE are only just beginning to realize, once again, that all Germans and Austrians are not necessarily fiends, and that there is not really so yawning a gulf fixed between them and the rest of humanity as some of us appeared, not long ago, to imagine. And yet, when I recall those days before the war—and how swiftly they seemed to pass—it is still with something of a shock that I realize that some of my best friends were later on the sworn enemies of England. I think that those memories of German and Austrian friends bring home to one more clearly than anything else the horror which we have not yet succeeded in forgetting.

I suppose that few men occupied a more difficult position in the war than Kreisler, nor acquitted himself so honourably in it. He fought for his country, and after he had been wounded he came back to America and gave every penny that he earned to the Red Cross. I consider it an honour to have sung with him at one of these charity concerts. Kreisler! He has the heart of a child, and the sensitiveness of a child as well. But what a god on the violin!

Nor was there a more charming companion, for example, than Count Albert Mensdorff, the Austrian Ambassador, whom I used frequently to see in those last days of peace. He was not only a charming companion but a very useful friend, as I had discovered during a rather unpleasant experience which had occurred to me in America.

The service he did me was of an unusual nature. I had a maid, an Austrian girl, who, although a very faithful and a very excellent servant, was sometimes a little peculiar in her manner. She used to make strange remarks apropos of nothing, and stand suddenly still, staring into vacancy. I was willing to put up with these peculiarities, but when I took her to America she began to behave in so extraordinary a way that I became somewhat alarmed.

One morning, just as I was preparing to go out, she walked into my room and said:

"I am Mary Magdalene. I have just kissed Jesus' feet."

"Really?" I said, edging away from her. "How very interesting."

She nodded gravely, and repeated her remark, while I was all the time walking slowly backwards. Fortunately my secretary was in the next room. I called her, and together we reasoned with the girl, and within a few hours we had her in the care of a keeper.

I decided that my only course was to send the girl home to Austria, where she could be looked after properly. I therefore wrote to Mensdorff to know if he would help me. He not only made all arrangements, but a little later when I wished to know how she was, he went to great pains to discover her exact situation, her state of health, and other details.

On my very last day in England before the war, Mensdorff gave a farewell luncheon to me, and whatever else we talked about at that luncheon it was certainly not even remotely connected with the possibility of war. When I took my leave he said: "When are you coming back?"

"In a few months."

"We'll have another one then. Will you come?"

"Rather!" I said. But I never saw him again.

From London I went to Paris, prepared to enjoy

myself before my trip home to Australia. How wonderful those last weeks in Paris were! Looking back on it to-day, it seems almost as though we were all like the revellers at some great ball, dancing faster and faster, more and more madly in the last hours before the coming of dawn. Of course, the simile cannot bear examination, since we had no hint of the coming catastrophe. We imagined that life would go on like this, for ever.

And yet, there now came my way one of the most remarkable prophecies that I have ever heard, from the mouth of one who was not usually much given to prophesying—Lord Bertie, our Ambassador.

It happened like this. I had given a party for Gladys de Grey (whom I must now call Gladys Ripon) at my flat, of which Lord Bertie had apparently heard. At least, when he came to tea with me two days later, we had not been talking for more than ten minutes before his voice suddenly changed and a shadow came over his face.

Lord Bertie: "I see all you middle-aged women were dancing here the other day."

Myself: "We can't help being middle-aged. Have you any objection?"

Lord Bertie: "No. But are you well up in your Roman history?"

Myself: "I shouldn't like to pass an exam in it."

Lord Bertie: "Do you know that before the fall of the Roman Empire the women of Rome were behaving just like the women of to-day? Do you know that they were indulging in every extravagance, wearing green wigs, red wigs, painting their faces, caring for nothing but pleasure? dancing all day and all night? And do you know what came of it?"

There was a pause. Then very slowly and emphatically he said: "*Dancing feet bring war.*"

I shivered a little, for there seemed something more in his words than the mere statement of fact. But such is the constitution of human nature that they soon passed out of mind. It was not till war had actually been declared, and was raging in all its violence that I recalled Lord Bertie's words, and when I wrote to him I sadly reminded him of them, and asked if, when he said them, he actually knew facts that were denied to me.

"No," he wrote back. "I knew nothing. The sky was absolutely without a cloud. But though I knew no facts, I felt——" And he did not finish the sentence.

The month of August in Australia is wattle month. Perhaps that may not mean very much to an Englishman or an American, but to an Australian it brings with it a rush of fragrance, a vision of tossing, golden branches, a breath of home itself. And in August, 1914, as I remember, the wattle was particularly beautiful. All the wattles round Coombe seemed filled with beacons of light, ranging from the palest shades of yellow to the deepest hues of gold, and outside my dining-room on the lawn a great wattle tree which had been there since the house was built, was the finest of them all.

I have often wondered, looking back on the tragic sequence of events that followed August 4th, 1914, whether the various nations of the world were affected psychologically by the season in which the catastrophe occurred. In England, of course, it was hot and thundery, and indeed in all the countries which were to participate in the struggle. But over Australia hung the first hint of Spring. And to me there will always be a memory of Spring associated with that dark epoch, a memory which seems somehow to soften in some slight degree the horror of it all.

We none of us, in those early days, took the war seriously. In fact, it was not till after the struggle was over that we really understood the horror (and the heroism) of it all. Not until 1922, for instance, did I hear at first hand a story which gave us a true insight into the amazing courage of the Belgian people.

It was Max, the famous Burgomaster of Brussels, who told it to me. At first he was reluctant to talk about himself, for I believe he had been cross-examined by curious busybodies and insatiable reporters until he must have felt almost murderous. But when he saw that I did not wish to draw him out against his will, he began to talk, and as he did so, it seemed as though a vivid light was being thrown back on those amazing days of 1914.

"When the Germans came to the Hôtel de Ville," he said, "one of their first demands was for a dozen beds to be installed without a moment's delay. They expected me to rush off at once to order them, but I quietly went on with my duties, and then departed to order, not twelve beds, but thirteen. As soon as this was discovered, I was summoned before the commanding officer.

"'You have ordered thirteen beds?' he demanded.

"'Certainly,' I replied.

"'I ordered only twelve. For whom is the thirteenth bed?'

"'That's for me,' I said. And I slept in it too," he chuckled, "though how I managed it, I never quite realize, for after all we were powerless before them.

"The next day," continued Max, "there was a conference in one of the committee rooms of the Hôtel de Ville, to deal with certain urgent matters of neutrality. I shall never forget the little room, filled with officials, German officers in their swaggering uniforms, and among others, the American Ambassador. As soon as the conference began, the German commanding officer drew a revolver from his pocket, and threw it down in front of him. The incident would probably have passed unnoticed had not the American Ambassador, who was sitting opposite, at once dived his hand into his own pocket, and brought out another revolver, slightly larger than that of the German's.

"There was a moment's silence, and then the German officer growled:

"'What are you doing?'

"'Well, and what are *you* doing?' drawled the American.

"'You are not at war,' said the German.

"The American looked him straight in the eyes. 'No,' he said, 'we're not at war with you. But when a man puts a gun on the table, I do the same.'

"The German glared. The American smiled. The gun remained."

However, in 1914, we thought it would "all be over" in a few weeks, and I remember my feeling of incredulous astonishment when Lord Kitchener announced that the struggle would last at least three years—a feeling almost as though he had said something alarmist—something needlessly and foolishly pessimistic. How it gradually dawned on us, I don't think, even to this day, we quite realize. We women saw our men off with smiling faces, and did our crying in our bedrooms. But even so, we refused to admit things. We refused to face the black, endless horror of it all for fear of going mad. The only sign that we knew more than we would admit was in the universal desire, even of the most useless of us, to *do* something—something practical, anything that would stop us thinking.

I was seized with that desire myself. My concerts—

and they were legion—in aid of the Red Cross, and other war charities—did not seem to fill the gap which I so longed to fill. If anything, they reminded me by the very closeness of their association with our cause, of exactly the things that were, day and night, preying upon my mind. And so I tried to knit. Pathetic memory! The wool I wasted, the number of stitches I dropped, the scarves that unravelled themselves at the slightest touch, the socks that would never have fitted any human being! If everybody had been as inefficient as I was, our poor armies would have been going about with bare feet.

Knitting became almost an obsession with me. Not my own knitting, I mean, but other people's. One's whole life seemed to be dominated by the monotonous rhythm of those eternal needles. It seemed to click with my music, to turn every *tempo* into a ragtime. On one of my first concerts after the declaration of the war, I noticed, as soon as I had stepped on to the platform, that almost every woman in the audience seemed to be knitting. I stood there, feeling suddenly isolated, incapable of singing, shut off from the usual circle of sympathy which every artist tries to create. The first bars were played of my accompaniment. They meant nothing to me. Still that terrible clicking, that distracting flash of needles continued. And suddenly I stepped forward, spread out my hands, and cried:

"Stop! Please stop! You are driving me mad."

Like magic, the needles dropped. Every eye riveted itself upon me. I laughed nervously.

"I know the soldiers will forgive me," I said, "if I ask you, just for a few moments, to stop. It is almost driving me mad." They stopped, of course.

My nephew, who was a brother of Gerald Patterson (of tennis fame), was fifteen when the War broke out.

He immediately went down to the nearest recruiting station, and told them with a gruff voice and as elderly a bearing as he could assume, that he was twenty-one. I am afraid that his conspicuously youthful schoolboy complexion aroused the suspicions of the recruiting sergeants, for when they began to question him a little and discovered that he was my nephew, they rang me up to ask me how old he really was.

"He is only fifteen," I cried. "Don't tell me that you are going to put him into the army!"

There was a laugh from the other end of the telephone. "We thought as much, Madame," they said. "But we would like to tell you that he is a sportsman."

He was. For as soon as he discovered that it was useless for him to try to enlist, he begged from his father a small plot of the kitchen garden, and throughout the War you might have seen that small boy, in rain and sunshine, digging away breathlessly to plant the vegetables which he sent to the soldiers, as though on his efforts depended the entire food supply of the Allies.

How endless and appalling was the strain—so monotonous that it is difficult to pick out isolated incidents from this uniformity of disaster. I remember, however, that Sir Ronald Munro-Ferguson, whom you will probably recall more easily by his present title of Lord Novar, was Governor-General in those days, and now and then he would come up and stay with me at Coombe, to rest from the arduous labours which the War entailed. If it had not been for these rare rests I do not believe he would have escaped some sort of a breakdown, for he was the hardest worker I ever knew. But I think he regarded Coombe as a little oasis. One morning, when he and Lady Helen had been staying with me, an urgent message arrived from Melbourne, saying that there was an important meeting that he must attend at Government House at eleven o'clock. I sent immediately to inform him of the fact, and when he could not be found I began to hunt for him myself. Over the whole house I went calling, out into the garden, into the paddocks, and eventually as a forlorn hope, I thought I would try the outhouses. And there I found the Governor-General in his shirt-sleeves, chopping wood with the odd man. The odd man did not look very embarrassed, nor did the Governor-General.

"Don't tell me you are going to take me away," he said. "I have been having such a good time with my new friend here."

I think that of all the many delightful children's stories I have heard, none made me laugh so much as one in which I myself played a small part at that time. At Government House were staying the little eight-year-old Veronica, whose father was Lord Dufferin, and Basil, her brother, who is now Lord Ava. They were both charming, unaffected children, whose only weakness, if you can call it a weakness, was an excess of curiosity.

One day a very distinguished and powerful Maharajah who happened to be visiting Melbourne at the time was asked to tea, and before he arrived Lady Helen called both children to her and explained that Maharajahs were not quite the same colour as they were—in fact, I remember that she described him as being of something the same hue as a chocolate cake which they had eaten in the nursery the day before—but that they must take no notice.

The Maharajah arrived, and the children behaved themselves admirably. However, just as he was going to make some remark to Veronica, there was a moment's silence, and then in a piercingly distinct voice Veronica said:

"I think I have had the pleasure of meeting you on

the P. & O. steamer." (I may say, for those who do not see the point of this story, that all the servants employed on the P. & O. lines in the lesser-paid occupations are Lascars.)

It was at this time that I received the proudest compliment which I have ever been paid. I had been giving a great many concerts for the Allies, and at one of them at Melbourne I sold a flag which had originally cost a guinea for the very creditable sum of two thousand two hundred pounds. I may mention, incidentally, that after it had been sold, nobody claimed it. As I came out of the concert afterwards, flushed with pleasure at the result of my efforts, my dear old Scottish clergyman, by name the Rev. Dr. Marshall, approached me, and in his broad burr he said:

"Madame, you have been called many flattering names in the course of your career. Do you know what I call you?"

I laughed and said I had no idea.

"I call you the 'Empress of Pickpockets,'" he said.

I am afraid I was the Empress of Pickpockets. I used to go up to people in the streets—people, that is to say, whom I knew to be rich, and to be able to afford to lose something—and I would say to them:

"I am Nellie Melba. I want you to promise to give me everything in your pocket book, before you look inside to see how much you have got." I do not think I had one refusal throughout the whole course of the War, but I did have a certain amount of difficulty in persuading a man, who discovered, when he opened his pocketbook, that inside were two £100 notes whose existence he had forgotten at the time of giving his promise.

I am only too aware of the shortcomings of my memories of this period. I say to myself, here was I travelling in the United States, in Australia, in Canada, in the most thrilling time of history, and yet all I have to say seems trifling and of little account. The explanation is that, quite frankly, I find it difficult to talk about the War at all. When so many great sacrifices were being made, when so many gallant deeds were being achieved, to write of my small efforts, my hopes and tribulations, seems almost impertinent. However, one thing at least I can look back upon with some small gratification, and that is, that I am reminded even as I dip my pen into the ink, that my handwriting was completely ruined by the war. One reason for this was that wherever I went, whether it was in Australia, Canada or the United States, I was always being asked to sign autographs which would be sold for the benefit of the soldiers. I signed and signed, until I could sign no more. For one concert alone I wrote over a thousand letters in my own hand, and the comparatively sober and dignified "Nellie Melba" with which I started the War, had degenerated at the end of it into a flourishing and untidy parody of its former self.

Let me just add, not in any boastful spirit, but as a means of thanking those who helped me, that I made through the War over £100,000 which I was enabled to hand to the Red Cross, as a slight tribute from one who cared.

The candles were lit round my dinner table, the first glass of wine had been drunk, on this day of November 11th, 1918, when suddenly the telephone bell rang, and my butler came into the room and told me that the commandant of one of the destroyers in the harbour wished to speak to me. At once I went outside, and there in that darkened hall, over a wire that seemed to buzz and whirr as though it had caught something of the thrill of the message that he was delivering, I was told that peace had come at last. I let the receiver drop, and stood there for a moment motionless. And then, in a sort of wild joy I screamed, and ran back to tell the others.

They sprang to their feet and clustered round me. What did I know? Could I tell them any more? Had I any definite information? I shook my head. All I knew was that we had peace, and that Death had ceased to take his toll.

Suddenly I remembered that all the little villages round about, all the tiny townships whose methods of communication were still as crude as they had been fifty years ago, would still be in ignorance. So I ordered my car, and as soon as it was ready we all got into it and whirled down to the village of Lilydale. Never shall I forget sweeping up the deserted street to the old fire-bell standing rusty and usually forgotten under the tall gum-tree. I jumped out of the car, seized the rope and pulled and pulled and pulled, till the whole night rang with the echoes of it. For a few minutes there was no response; and then, one by one, they started to come out.

"Melba's here," they said to one another as they clustered round.

"Don't bother about Melba," I cried out; and I can't remember whether I was laughing or sobbing. "It's peace!"

Like a flame in the woods when the Bush is scorching, and the wind high, the word "peace" rushed round the village. It seemed hardly out of my mouth before other bells had begun to ring, and soon in that little village of the Australian Bush a strange shrill clamour of bells, like some unearthly chorus, was pealing to the skies.

It was the same all the way down the road, and when

tired out, we drove back, still from tiny houses on distant hills lights were shining brightly, and as we swept through the villages bells were still pealing.

The next morning I rose at four o'clock and went outside for a walk. The events of the night before seemed some grotesque dream. I wandered round the lawn, and I found myself standing under the great wattle. How fresh and exquisite it was in this early breath of summer. It seemed to me like a promise of life renewed.

When I got down to Melbourne early in the morning, the streets were full of people shouting and crying and waving flags. A service was being held in the Town Hall. All difference of creed or of sect had been forgotten, and the place was full to overflowing—so full, indeed, that when I attempted to enter I found at first that it was impossible. However, a friendly policeman pushed me through the mob, and I found myself on the stage. They cried out my name, but I shook my head. There was nothing I could say.

Then suddenly I thought of the gift which God had given me—the gift of song. Surely, if ever there was a time in my life when it was needed, now was that time. I had been told time and again in the past that I had brought hope and beauty into the lives of men and women through that gift. Let me only try to do it now! Impulsively I turned to a clergyman, who was by my side, and put my hand on his arm, but before I could ask the question he had asked it of me.

"You must sing, Madame Melba," he said. "You must sing as you never sang before." And I found myself singing the National Anthem, at first a solitary voice, as it seemed, floating out into the great spaces, and then but one of an immense chorus that welled up like an organ. When it was over everybody was crying.

CHAPTER XXV

CHARLIE CHAPLIN

One cannot live for four years in a state of acute nervous tension without paying the price in some form or another. and even to recall, in the comparative peace and quiet of the present, these times of torment makes my heart beat quickly, and my hand tremble. And so, at the risk of being thought irreverent, I am going to plunge without any premeditation into a totally different atmosphere, to cheer up, not only those who may read these words, but myself, who am writing them. In fact, I am going to give you a tonic. The name of that tonic is—Charlie Chaplin.

I had long had a great desire to meet Charlie Chaplin, and as soon as we arrived at Los Angeles, on my long-delayed journey home, I set out for his studio in company with Lady Susan Fitzclarence (now Lady Susan Birch), my great friend.

No celebrity whom I have ever met so completely falsified my preconceived notions of them as Charlie Chaplin. He was then at the pinnacle of his fame as a comedian—a pinnacle which he still occupies in solitary state. But how little the world knew of the real man who was hidden behind the mask of humour!

I had expected, first of all, to meet an ugly, grotesque figure. Instead there advanced towards me a smiling, handsome, young man, small, but perfectly made, with flashing eyes and beautiful teeth. He was dressed quietly

CHARLES CHAPLIN, CALIFORNIA, 1919

and well, and he spoke in a low musical voice that seemed to belong more to an English public schoolboy than to a knockabout comedian.

But it was not the superficial Charlie Chaplin that most surprised me, but the character of the man as revealed by his conversation. Instead of a brilliant clown, I found myself face to face with a philosopher, with a serious, almost melancholy attitude to life.

"Ah, Madame Melba," was one of the first things he said to me, "*you* should be happy. You have been able to express *every* emotion. You have laughed in *The Barber of Seville,* and you have wept in *Othello.* But suppose that you had never been allowed to weep? Suppose, like myself, that you had always been forced to laugh?" He paused, and then said abruptly: "I would give my soul to play *Hamlet.*"

A few minutes later he was again as bright as a child. He had just bought a new motor-car, and danced round his new toy as if he had never seen a car before. He patted the radiator, poked his nose underneath, and blew the horn, pretending to be very alarmed at each blast which it gave. Finally, he invited us to come for a drive, and as we clambered in he said vaguely: "Will you accept this present which I have had prepared for you?"

I looked down and discovered to my delight a beautiful rug of fox-tails on my knees.

We dined with Charlie Chaplin that night at the Raymond Hotel, Pasadena, and here he expanded, and told me more about his early struggles. "My first engagement in America," he said, "was with William Gillette, and I received three dollars a week for my pains. Those three dollars a week were the best-earned money I ever made. I was supposed to be a burglar and every night I clambered in at the window in the second act. I'm not heavy, but the window was particularly fragile, and I was afraid that it would break. The nervous strain was terrible."

More reminiscences, and then, for the first time, I had a taste of the Chaplin of the film. The waiter presented the bill, Charlie produced a wallet, opened it, and found it empty. With a sigh he put both hands in his pockets and drew them out filled to the brim with silver dollar pieces. Many of these scattered over the floor, involving much scrambling under the table-cloth. Eventually, after a great deal of argument and addition, the bill was paid, the waiter departing with a plate that was heavily loaded with coins.

I had laughed so much at the inimitable stock of "business" which had accompanied this procedure that I felt quite tired and said:

"Let us go and get some fresh air."

Charlie Chaplin smiled and shook his head, pointing at the same time to some small boys who had miraculously appeared from nowhere, and who were scrambling about on the floor in search of loot.

"You don't want me to offend my penny public?" he said, simply.

On my next visit to Charlie Chaplin's studio, I not only had a good insight into one of the reasons for his success but I had the unexpected honour of taking part in a film with him myself. He was creating at this time a picture called "The Cure." The immense studio was a bustle of activity and the powerful arc lights were centred on Charlie Chaplin who was supposed to be drinking some medicine out of a mug. A simple operation, you might imagine, but Charlie Chaplin, like all true artists, was not satisfied with anything but the best. Over and over again he drank, and was still displeased. Then suddenly he altered his position slightly, gave a new twist of his hand, shouted to the photographers and the picture was taken. An hour's hard work for less than a minute's effect! He came towards me wiping his face and said:

"I think your first film was very good."

"What do you mean?" I said.

For answer he pointed to a blank screen. There suddenly flashed across it a picture of myself, taken in the studio on my last visit, in which I had pretended to slap Chaplin's face, and had followed it up by chasing him round the room. All these activities had been duly registered by the camera, and when the short comedy was over Chaplin smiled at me mischievously and said:

"There's a small part in my next piece that would just suit you."

How charming was this little colony of film stars! I have memories of it very different from the lurid pictures of drugged, abandoned orgies to which we have recently been treated by the more sensational sections of the Press. I have never met, for example, a more delightful couple, more utterly unsophisticated, than Mary Pickford and Douglas Fairbanks. I don't think they had been long married when they came my way, and they were so wrapped up in one another that sometimes Mary would stop in the middle of a sentence, look shyly at her husband, who was probably leaping over a wall or jumping a hedge, and say softly, "Isn't he wonderful?"

In spite of the colossal sums of money which these two young geniuses were earning, they were entirely devoid of affectation. I shall never forget a little episode which occurred when Lady Susan asked Mary Pickford for a photograph.

"Of course," she said, and ran to a bureau where there was a stock of photographs six feet high, all waiting to be dispatched to ardent admirers. She chose a particularly nice one.

"Would you like me to sign it for you?"

"Please," said Lady Susan.

Mary dipped the pen in the ink. There was a pause, and she frowned prettily. Then she looked up shyly at Lady Susan, and said, very seriously:

"Would you please tell me how to write your name? You see—I'm not used to meeting Royalty."

In the same spirit of complete simplicity, she told us how, when she had been asked to go to New York to meet President Wilson, her great ambition was that her mother should go too, and how she had spent hours in discussing what would be the most suitable dresses for them both to wear. I never heard if Mrs. Pickford went, but I hope so, for she was a charming woman.

Our last day in Los Angeles was again spent with Charlie Chaplin. Susan had discovered to her great joy, that in a tiny cottage there was living an old woman rejoicing in the name of Kitty Mulberry, who had long been in the service of the Hardwicke family and who had actually nursed her when she was a baby. This news was communicated to Charlie Chaplin, who was thrilled. "We must go down and have tea with Kitty Mulberry," he said, and leapt away to send the old lady a wire.

I have never seen him more delightfully happy than at this reunion. The old lady, who was like a lovely, faded picture among her roses and her pots and pans, was in the seventh heaven at the visit. To receive a visit not only from little Lady Susan, but also from two other "lesser celebrities," was almost more than she could bear, and she had provided a tea that would have satisfied the requirements of a small army. Charlie was determined that she should not be disappointed, and partook of bread and butter, eggs, rock cake and steaming cups of tea until I feared for his health. Finally, when he could eat no more, he sat back and munched lumps of sugar, watching us, I will believe, with tears in his eyes.

The visit, I am glad to say, had the happiest results, for shortly afterwards, Kitty was reinstated in England, to spend the rest of her days in the heart of the Hardwicke family, whose interests she has always served so loyally.

CHAPTER XXVI

POST-WAR LONDON—ROYALTIES—INDIA

AND now for England again.

I do not suppose I shall ever recapture the same thrill which I experienced when, the War over, I started on my journey for home. It was with a feeling almost of fear that I looked forward to the future, fear not for myself, but for England. What would England be like? Would my friends still remember me? Would there still be any smiles left in the streets? Would there still be any of that old gaiety which we had so loved in the days of the London that had gone? Or would the whole country be given up to mourning—the ghost of its former self?

All these questions were running through my head as I eventually went on board the liner in New York. It was in January of 1919, one of the coldest months that have ever been known. And as I entered my cabin, I noticed that all the windows had been broken in. I went outside and walked down the decks, noticing on every hand evidences of the rough usages to which the vessel had recently been put. The paint was old and chipped, the chairs were rocky, the decks were lacerated, there was none of that feeling which one used to have of being on board some wonderful floating hotel. I found the steward, and told him of my predicament, which he seemed to take quite as a matter of course, and with an encouraging smile he said that he would clear out of his own cabin for me. And so I slept in that.

When I arrived at Liverpool, it was almost as much as I could do to prevent myself from breaking down altogether. Almost as I stepped on to the deck, from the grey and desolate sky overhead a few tiny flakes of snow were drifting down, and it seemed to me by some queer twist of the brain that this was intended as a welcome. English snow! What memories it brought back; memories stretching right back to the days when as a young singer I had looked out with wondering eyes from the window of a hansom cab, as I trotted through the first snow-storm I had ever known, on my way to a concert. And now, I put out my hand and took on the tip of my finger one of the flakes which had landed on my fur, and ate it. I shall never forget to this day the cool tang of that northern snow and the sudden feeling of "getting back" that it gave me.

I knew, of course, that London would be changed. I recalled with a sudden shock my last birthday party which I had given in May of 1914, when the Marquis de Soveral, Count Mensdorff, Mrs. Hwfa Williams, Lady de Grey, and so many others had been present. There had been in all some twenty men, of whom sixteen were eligible for military service, and as I ran through their names in my head, I discovered that of these sixteen, ten had been killed. And how well I remember Lady Juliet Duff and her husband dancing together, with an expression of such happiness on their faces. He was one of the first to go.

Sometimes I think that those who remained, crippled and maimed for life, were figures of even greater tragedy than those who had gone for ever. And among those who had lingered on in a living death was that gallant gentleman, Major Robin Grey.

Before Robin's death, which was really due to the

years of torture which he had spent as a prisoner of war in Germany, he had sent me a letter from his nursing home telling me that he was going to have an operation, and that he hadn't told me before because he knew I was giving a concert, and he didn't wish me to be worried. "Don't worry," he said. "I am only going to have a spring cleaning."

A week later I picked up the paper and read that Robin had died.

I went to the tragic little ceremony at the Guards' Chapel, and as the gun carriage wound slowly on its sad way to the cemetery, I walked to Buckingham Palace, where I was helping Princess Mary with her singing. Mechanically I entered the room where the lesson was to take place, and Princess Mary handed me the song she wished to sing. I looked at it, and as I did so, I felt as though somebody had stabbed me to the heart. By one of those grim coincidences which life sometimes offers us, the song she had chosen was:

"What's this dull town to me?
Robin's not here."

But London! It was not until I had been for several days in London that I realized the yawning gulf which separated this new, untidy, haphazard metropolis, so grey and so strange, from the London which I had known.

"Don't you find London very dirty?" said the Queen to me, on the first occasion when I had the honour of seeing Her Majesty at Buckingham Palace after the War. And I was forced to admit that I did.

It is an ironic comment on the frailty of human nature that the change should be most graphically brought home to me by a simple question of food. Adelina Duchess

MELBA AS MIMI IN LA BOHÊME

of Bedford rang me up a day or two after my arrival, and asked me to lunch at a restaurant. No sooner had we sat down to lunch than she produced two little gold pots, and placed them with a gesture of triumph before her on the table.

"Whatever are these?" I said, because I am a curious individual, and want to know what is going on in the world.

"Ah!" said the Duchess. "That's something you won't often see in London."

"Really!" I exclaimed. "Do let me look."

Very gravely she took off the lids of the two little pots and disclosed a small piece of butter and some sugar. I looked at her in astonishment. Had everybody gone mad? What I saw before me was obviously sugar and butter, and yet it was being produced as though it were some rare delicacy.

Then I remembered, and the memory made me almost cry. In Australia, and in America, we had had as much butter, as much sugar, as much everything as we wanted, and the delight on the faces of those around me at being greeted with such a simple commodity was infinitely pathetic. That lunch was full of surprises. We had paper table-napkins, and when eventually coffee was served, the *maître d'hôtel* discovered to his consternation that the restaurant had no sugar spoons. I think that was what hit his honest heart as hardly as anything else; but he rose to the emergency and gave us salt spoons instead.

I remember going back to my club in Dover Street after that lunch and asking myself: Is there anything I can do to help London to regain something of its old charm? Is there any way in which I can try to make people forget? And it was really this feeling that was uppermost in my mind when later on I accepted the honour of opening Covent Garden after the War.

That first night at Covent Garden will always stand out as one of the supreme memories of my life. To drive to the old stage door, to walk upstairs and down the long corridor to a dressing-room at the end of the passage; to sit down before the same mirror; to make up again; to put on once more the simple dress of Mimi—all as though nothing had happened, as though I had only been away for a holiday—and yet, to feel around me, in every shadow cast by the lights, in every bustling noise outside the door, in the very air that I breathed—ghosts. "It is not you," I said to myself, as I peered into the glass. "It cannot be Melba. It is somebody else. So many have gone, so many new faces have come—it can't be that you have remained."

I am standing outside the door of the attic in which the students of *Bohême* have been making revel. From inside I can hear Rudolpho sing his phrase *non sono in vena,* followed by the sudden sweeping change of key in the orchestra. And then I am mechanically finding myself singing, *Scusi!* And I open the door, to step once more on that stage which has been for me the scene of so much that is wonderful in life.

Rudolpho runs forward and gives me his arm, and I sink into the chair, the candle dropping from my hand, a few phrases coming from long habit to my lips. But it is more than the simulated exhaustion of Mimi, the little seamstress, which has gripped me now. For I find myself looking into the great space of the auditorium, and feeling once again that I am singing to an audience of ghosts. Lady de Grey had gone, Alfred de Rothschild had gone, and so many others, all gone; and yet I felt them there, I seemed in my imagination to see their faces again, looking out from the shadows in their boxes, and it was for them rather than for this great audience that I sang.

It was that night at Covent Garden which made me realize the full extent to which London had changed. It is true that I could remember no occasions on which I received, in the professional sense of the word, a greater ovation. No occasion, indeed, on which I have ever been more satisfied, as far as one ever is satisfied, with my performance. But though there was as much, if not more enthusiasm, than before, there was so little of the old brilliance. Can you imagine in the old days, men walking into Covent Garden on a Melba Night, or on any other night, and sitting in the stalls in shabby tweed coats? Yes, that is what I saw on this night, and though I have no objection to brown tweed coats, or to shabbiness, I could not help feeling a sensation almost of resentment that men who could afford to pay for stalls could not also afford to wear the proper clothes.

It was not, however, so much a mere question of material things, but a question of spirit. London just then, to one who had known it at its best and come back to see it in its worst, provided a constant succession of shocks, and none were more startling than in the realm of art. I have often wished when I heard some young singers to whom God has given divine voices, uttering songs which they have obviously not studied, slipshod in phrasing, in breathing, in the very spirit even of the words, that they too might have had, as I did, a course of Marchesi. She at least would have taught them that no one is an artist who has not taken infinite pains, that there is no other sure road to success, and that detail, detail, detail, must be the rule by which their lives are guided.

You cannot take Art flippantly, and flippancy seems just at the moment to be the order of the day. I think that the most flippant and the most idiotic remark I ever heard in my life was made by an American woman not long ago about Covent Garden. Imagining that she was being clever, she turned to me and said: "I always think Covent Garden rather like a Punch and Judy show."

It may surprise you to learn that I refrained from giving her a smack on the face, and merely countered her with another flippancy, in which I referred to the boxes at the Metropolitan Opera House in New York, as bearing a distinct resemblance to brass bedsteads.

With extravagance piled upon extravagance, and life growing faster and faster, louder and louder, is it so very surprising that our satirists, dramatic and otherwise, have found such rich material on which to pour their sarcasm? I often wonder what English society would be like if we had not had, quietly and almost unnoticeably before it, the eternal example of our Royal family—always simple, always kindly and warm-hearted, always sincere.

I had a very touching example of this simplicity when, in the July of 1921, I was summoned to Marlborough House to see Queen Alexandra, just before my departure for Norway. Queen Alexandra had been very ill, and I imagined, when I was received by the lady-in-waiting, Miss Charlotte Knollys, that I had only been asked in order to deliver some message or take some little present to the Queen of Norway, who is Queen Alexandra's daughter.

However, Her Majesty insisted on seeing me. The doors were flung open, and I perceived, in the shaded light of the sitting-room, the frail beloved figure of the dowager Queen, supporting herself on two sticks.

"So you're going to see Maud," she said. "You must give her my best love."

As I curtsied, I tried to remember who Maud was, and it was only after Queen Alexandra had entrusted me with a great many messages to "Maud," that I realized she was speaking of the Queen of Norway herself.

"And now," said Queen Alexandra, "my daughter-in-law is in the next room, and wishes so much to see you. *She* will have messages for Maud too."

Royal relationships have never been my strong point, and at the mention of the word "daughter-in-law" I again racked my brains to think who it could be. The difficulty was soon solved for me, for as I walked into the room I saw the Queen of England, with Princess Mary and Prince Henry, who was introduced to me as "our sporting son," and I laughed at myself for being so foolish as to forget.

Whenever it is my privilege to meet the Queen, I marvel afresh at the wonderful dignity of her carriage. It is not an assumed dignity. It is always there. I have seen Her Majesty sitting down at an absolutely informal tea-party, and there is always the same beautiful carriage of the shoulders, the same proud bearing of the neck, and that same wonderful smile. She never allows herself, even for an instant, to lose her distinction, and yet she combines it, in an almost miraculous way, with perfect ease.

We had a delightful talk, and every member of the Royal Family seemed thrilled that I was going to meet "Maud."

Suddenly Her Majesty turned to me, and said:

"Of course, you'll be seeing George too!"

Now I thought to myself, I *am* finished. I felt certain that Her Majesty did not mean King George, and for the life of me I could not think who the other George was. I thought of all the Georges I had ever known, and they seemed to stretch to infinity. I was about to murmur something quite inconsequent, when Prince Henry pulled me out of my predicament by saying: "My middy brother, you know."

I shall never forget that little party, not because of its royalty, but because it seemed to me to be typical of an ideal English family life.

When I eventually arrived in Norway, I found that my hosts, the Baron and Baroness de Wedel, whom I shall always count among my dearest friends, were the possessors of a very beautiful country-house. It was situated some miles outside Christiania, among hills and pine forests which seemed to have been specially created not only for singers with lungs, but singers with eyes as well. I may also add, singers with appetites, for I shall never forget the plates of raspberries and gooseberries they used to send up to my room for breakfast. But when I arrived I was so tired after the journey that I had no inclination to look at scenery and I was therefore a little taken back when I learnt that the King and the Queen and Prince Olaf were dining that night.

How I got through that dinner I shall never realize, for in spite of the charm of the King and Queen and the effervescent spirits of Prince Olaf, my head was heavy with sleep, and my eyelids had an almost irresistible tendency to droop. However, all went well, and dinner was over at half-past ten. But after I had sung, we began to dance.

I danced in a dream, and made conversation, growing sleepier and sleepier every minute, until finally I could bear it no longer. Greatly daring, therefore, I went up to the Queen, and said: "Your Majesty, I do hope you'll forgive me if I'm doing wrong, but I am terribly tired after my long journey. Would you be so good as to excuse me?"

The Queen was all contrition.

"Oh *dear!*" she said, "of course. I had no idea you were tired. Please, please go," and then she added: "I go to so few dances here, and I love staying late."

I can quite believe what Her Majesty told me, for dining and dancing seems to last longer in Norway than in any other country I have ever visited, not excluding Russia. Many is the dance I attended in which we were considered to leave "early" although it was not till six o'clock in the morning that we drove home through the brilliant sunshine. A nice Judy I must have looked.

At this time there occurred a concert which, they tell me, was the biggest musical event that Norway has ever known. It arose from the suggestion of the Baron de Wedel that I should give a concert in aid of the Norwegian sailors, who, though they had not actually been at war, had suffered many casualties. Needless to say I accepted with great enthusiasm, and the Baron and I immediately began to work together.

If I may say so, we made rather a powerful combination, and as for the generosity of the Norwegians, it cannot be surpassed by any nation in the world. As soon as we had told the director of the theatre our plans he generously told us that we could have the theatre for nothing. It was the same with the orchestra. And the newspapers gave me more publicity—all for nothing—than I have ever had in my life. Finally, when the King and Queen had granted their patronage, it seemed inevitable that the concert should be an immense success.

It was. The estimate of 12,000 kronen, which, we had been informed, was all the money we could possibly get into the theatre, was very greatly exceeded. And when it was all over, I laughingly turned to the Baron and said, " If only you weren't such a distinguished diplomat, I would have liked you to be my impresario for ever."

Among my great friends who were present on this occasion was Mr. Gronvold, the life-long friend of Grieg, whose life he wrote. He came up to me and paid me one of the most original compliments I have ever received, saying, " Melba, when you sing, I have cold down the back, and hot in the heart." He has become very dear to me—in fact, I often call him, for fun—" My love." For he is such a lovable man.

While I was singing, a message was handed up to me from Prince George, who had arrived on his ship just in time to come along. It read very simply:

Dear Madame Melba,—Do please sing one verse of " Home, Sweet Home."—George.

Needless to say, I did as I was asked.

I realized after this concert that simplicity was not confined to the English Royal Family. I was summoned to the Royal Box, and after the King had decorated me, he told me an amusing little story which seemed to illustrate the feelings of any young man who was called unexpectedly (as he was himself) to be King.

" I used to be in the Navy myself, you know," he said, " in my humble days. Well, there was a friend there—a first-class sailor, whom I spotted at once as a future admiral. In fact, I used to say to him: ' I'll have to be calling you " Sir " one day, I suppose.'

" Then," he continued, " I became King. I forgot all about him in the excitement of the occasion, but the very first person I saw after my coronation was my friend. He had the laugh on me. He came right up to me and said: 'I have the honour of calling *you* "Sir,"' he said."

Still a bird of passage! I wonder, as I near the end of these memories, if I shall ever rest, or if there will always remain in me some spirit of adventure urging me out to distant lands. I sometimes almost wish that, for a few months at least, I could cease to be so violently interested in everything that comes along. I say to myself: "Now, here, I am in London (or in Paris, or in California, or wherever else I may happen to be) and here I am going to stay." And then, there comes a letter from some dear friend telling me that the sun is shining in Florence, or that the sea is bluer than ever at Honolulu, and off I go, at a moment's notice. Only the other day a cable arrived from China asking me to give a series of concerts in that disturbed country. I was on the point of accepting, when my doctors told me that it would be tantamount to suicide. So I regretfully declined. But I should love to sing in China, should love, even, to climb to the top of some remote mountain in Tibet and sing psalms with the Grand Lama.

The nearest approach I have ever made to singing songs in Tibet was I imagine when, not very long afterwards, I visited India (on my way home from Australia) and sang a long trill in the Taj Mahal. It was in some ways the most uncanny sensation I have ever experienced. The moonlight, the warm, scented darkness, the soft radiance of marble, and then—my voice echoing out in a trill which never seemed to stop. It went on, long after I had finished, until it seemed that all round my head were circling flocks of clamorous birds.

India affects different people in different ways. For some it is like a poet's dream—a realization of all that they have dreamt of in Beauty—for others it is a mere hell of malaria and mosquitoes. Some seem to be affected, the moment they set foot on its soil, by the mystic atmosphere of the East, others merely treat it as a commercial proposition, a country of infinite possibilities for making money.

Frankly, the predominant emotion that comes to me when I recall India is a feeling akin to fear. I think of the teeming masses of natives dominated by so pathetically few of our own race, I think of the dark customs, the inscrutable eyes, the uncanny luxuriance of it all—and I shiver a little.

Perhaps my first experience in India may be accountable for a little of this feeling. I had received a telegram from Lord Reading, the Viceroy, asking me to stay with Their Excellencies at Simla, and when I arrived at Bombay, I found that all my means of transit had been arranged so that I should travel with every comfort.

But no amount of comfort or of civilization in India can ever be for me more than a veneer over the unfathomable depths beneath. At Delhi the train stopped, and I thought that I would stretch my legs and go for a walk with the A.D.C. Dusk was falling quickly and we had not gone far before I heard a strange chanting, rising and falling like a dirge. I looked round quickly, and there, coming out of the shadows, was the naked corpse of a native, borne aloft on a bier. " Don't look," said the A.D.C. quickly. There was no need to tell me that. I had seen enough. And I shall wish, to this day, that I had stayed in the train.

Another experience which I had, at Bombay, was even worse. I was walking along a street in —— when suddenly from the skies a strange object fell with a thud only a few yards away from me. I realized with a thrill of horror that it was a human arm. I was standing near to a high tower on which they bury—or rather, fail to bury their dead. The bodies are left in the open air, for the vultures to devour, and from there this hideous thing had come.

After this gloomy introduction, let me take you with me to a scene of a very different sort—one of those rich settings which India alone can provide. I shall never forget my first dinner at Simla. We enter a room of immense size—as large, as it seemed to me, as a fair-sized church. Although the lights are bright, in this immensity they seem almost dim, and in the shadows, rows of native servants are lined up, all in red and gold, their black heads bent low, and their faces covered with their hands, for they may not look at their master. And then, like one man, the line sways up again, the faces are uncovered, and silently they move off on their duties.

Certainly if you like pomp you have it to the full in India.

India is a place of perpetual surprises and I had one of them soon after I left Simla, for the Viceroy had kindly arranged that I should go to Delhi and visit a Maharajah there—" to get some local colour," as he put it.

I shall never forget the moment that I met him, coming down the steps of his palace to greet me. But it was not the Maharajah who captured my attention. A large tiger cub glided at his heels, and fixed me with an expression far too playful to be pleasant.

Forgetting all else, I said, in a somewhat husky voice:

" Don't you keep it on a chain? "

He smiled at me, and answered: " Certainly not. He's as tame as you are."

I was a little reassured by the *perfect English* in which this was spoken. (I found out afterwards that he had been educated at Wellington.) It seemed to place the tiger on a more normal basis. But I would not accompany him on a tour of inspection till it was safely locked up.

However much you may Anglicize an Indian, he remains an Indian.

Even though much of the furniture in the Maharajah's palace was English, it seemed by its very surroundings to have acquired an Oriental character. We lunched together, a quite simple English lunch, but the Maharajah would not eat with us. He merely talked. And afterwards, when we went over to his other palace, there was a wonderful lake, dark, mysterious, inviting one to plunge into its depths, until one realized with a thrill of disquiet, that it was full of crocodiles.

I am afraid that the most vivid impression I carried away from that visit was not the Maharajah's fleet of 80 motor-cars, nor his many elephants, nor his quantities of peacocks. It was the sight of his bed, which appeared to me to be as large as an average bedroom. My host had only one wife, but a dozen could have slept in that bed without becoming aware of one another's existence.

CHAPTER XXVII

MY COUNTRY AND MY ART

NOBODY wants to read about illness, and I am not going to bore you with mine. During the greater part of my life I have been blessed (touch wood!) with the most wonderful health, being the possessor of an iron constitution, which I had inherited from my Daddy. I remember that not long ago an American doctor who was examining me said: "Of course, there is no reason why you should ever die at all, Melba. There is absolutely nothing the matter with you. I have looked, and I have searched my darnedest, but you are just one hundred per cent. sound."

But now came a time when for days I lay under the shadow of death. I need not go into details about operations or treatments, because, as I said above, nothing is so boring as the description of other people's ailments. But it is necessary to mention the fact that in 1922 I was very ill, simply because it throws a light on these last pages of my life.

Never having been ill before, I suppose that I must have been a very bad patient, because, after an operation which had lasted two and a half hours, the first thing I said on coming round was: "Shall I be able to sing at Covent Garden in three weeks?" I think my nurses and advisers were so surprised by the question that they did not know what reply to make, but they certainly gave me the impression that I should not only not be able to sing, but that I should probably not be able even to walk. However, I did sing in six weeks, and unless the critics were particularly kind, I sang pretty well. However, I realize now that it was a silly thing to do, and that he or she who takes liberties with Nature is bound eventually to be called to account.

But I did not realize it then. I sat down at my writing desk, and busied myself all day long with plans and organizations for a farewell opera season in Australia. How much ink was expended in that task I do not know, but it must have been a great deal, because I think that I used up at least two pieces of pumice stone in removing the stains of it from my fingers. I simply cannot write with a pen, and even the indelible pencil with which these words are being written occasionally leaves its mark.

"You must not do it," all my friends said to me. "You are not strong enough yet. You must wait and see, say, two years, before you attempt such a vast undertaking." I looked these counsellors straight in the face, and I said, "I am going to do it. I have promised, and I shall keep my promise." And keep my promise I did.

I set out from England in the September of 1923, and I realized as soon as I was on the Atlantic that I needed a rest. For weeks before my operation I had been travelling around Italy, ransacking the Continent, for the greatest artists I could find, and even trying in a moment of abandoned enthusiasm to see if I could not take half the orchestra of La Scala over to Australia, so that my countrymen could see what good music could be. All that, as well as a subsequent trial, did tell upon me, and was beginning to show its mark. However, I struggled on, only to be met, when I landed in Australia, with further difficulties.

Australia, I discovered, had also changed. For years,

of course, Labour had been in power; but Labour during the War and immediately after it was not so aggressive as I now discovered it to be. A few hotheads who desired to cause trouble and who were acting not so much for their country as for their party, discovered that I had made arrangements to bring out some Italian singers, a few Italian instrumentalists, and an Italian stage director and ballet mistress. They suddenly seized upon this, and tried to make it into a public scandal. "Look at Melba," they cried, "who calls herself a patriot, and yet goes out of the way to flood Australia with Dagoes just in order to put money into her own pocket. We'll strike. We won't let them land. We'll wreck the theatre if they ever appear. We'll boycott her. We'll ostracize her."

I sat tight. I did not reply to their criticism. I only deplored their ignorance and their stupidity. I was also, I admit, a little hurt to think that I, who had worked so hard for Australia, should receive so little gratitude from these few fools who had never been outside their own country, and whose one idea was to make a noise. It was useless to argue with them. It was useless to point out, for example, that one could not, even if one would, produce an entire season of opera in Italian and in French, entirely from the local talent to be obtained from the new conservatoires of Melbourne and Sydney. It was equally useless to point out to them that if anybody should be the loser by the project, that person would be myself, and those who were associated with me. You cannot transport a bevy of sopranos, tenors, basses and instrumentalists, from Italy to Australia, without paying for it. However, I said nothing. I let them have their say, and finally, through sheer exhaustion, they talked themselves out.

Now let me, being an honest woman, speak straight out about this question of Australia. It is to me the most beloved country in the world; and for that reason I cannot bear to see Australia day by day thwarting its own development, and throttling its very existence.

Think for a moment of this country. It is larger than the United States. It has boundless natural wealth, infinite resources, and yet it has a population less than that of the single city of London. Parts of the northern territory, which are as big as France and Germany put together, have a population of only 1,100 and even that population is slowly decreasing. The distribution of the population is even more deplorable than the scarcity of it. For of the six millions which compose Australian inhabitants, over one million are in Sydney, another million is in Melbourne, and three other cities hold between them a third million. That leaves some three million scattered over an area which, I repeat, is bigger than the United States. What is the reason of it?

I do not wish to maintain for one instant that the reason is entirely Australia's fault. Australia is a young country which has not had time to develop and which has been constantly handicapped by the fact that it is so far away from the Mother Country. But I do not think that any thinking man will deny that there have been many occasions when my fellow-countrymen have been given the opportunity of developing themselves, and when they have thrust it aside. As long as we have the Labour Party in Australia, so long will there be a natural prejudice against immigration, on the grounds that if the country is flooded with immigrants, those who are already there in possession will find the struggle for life increasingly hard. There seems to be firmly rooted in a certain type of Australian mentality the idea that development

MELBA AS DESDEMONA IN HER FAREWELL OPERA SEASON 1924

means unemployment—surely one of the strangest paradoxes that has ever dwelt even in a Labour member's mind. It is this shortsightedness which makes a city like Melbourne the dull city which it is to-day. A city where you begin the day by being told in your hotel that on account of trade union regulations you cannot be served with breakfast before eight o'clock, and in which you end it in some uninspiring restaurant which is struggling hard to hold up its head against quantities of restrictions. One of the last things I read in an Australian paper before returning home was that if a certain American jazz band was allowed to land, all the other jazz bands in the continent would go on strike. The jazz band did not land, and as a result the dancers of Australia are still dancing to the tunes which have long ago been mercifully forgotten in the countries of Europe.

However—enough of criticism. I wish to take you in imagination to one of my rehearsals at an opera, because I feel that there should be set down some permanent record of the methods in which I and those who belonged to the same school of training are accustomed to conduct such enterprises.

The first rule in opera is the first rule of life, a very simple and possibly unexciting rule, for which I shall receive no thanks. That is, see to everything yourself. You must not only sing; you must not only act; you must also be stage manager, press agent, artistic adviser. And more: if you desire the season to run without any murders, or assaults, you must be mother, father and sister, all rolled into one. And I cannot help thinking that it would be a good thing if you have a bed fixed up in one of the boxes, so that you will be always on the spot, from morning till night, and from night till morning.

See to everything yourself. You would not dream how

easy it is for things to go wrong. I shall never forget the shock I received in the first act of *Lucia* when the Italian chorus came on. I had been ill, and had been unable to attend rehearsals. They were supposed to be dressed as Scottish warriors, and I think I can most tactfully express my criticism by remarking that I am sure that no Scottish warrior even in the time of Sir Walter Scott would have permitted himself to appear with baggy tights beneath his kilt. I have dreamed nightmares about those tights. They were pink, and white, and even yellow. They sagged at the knees, and hung in folds around the calves of the less generously proportioned chorus-men. The kilt was, I am quite sure, to the Italian temperament, a mystery beyond solution. One man, for example, had, in a moment of independence, conceived the idea that his sporran would be more decorative if it dangled gracefully from his hip, and it was in this manner that he made his appearance on the first night.

As for one's voice—that is a subject of such infinite detail that it would require a separate volume all to itself. I want, later on, to try and give to young singers, far more fully than I have yet given, a permanent record of all that my years of song have taught me. I am the more encouraged to do so because all those who have had the opportunity of studying the method which I began as a student with Marchesi and have been perfecting ever since, have proved, without a solitary exception, that there is no method that can touch it for bringing out the full beauty of the human voice, and preserving it for the longest possible period.

You cannot take liberties with your voice. You must always regard it as your most precious possession, a possession, moreover, of infinite delicacy, which the slightest false treatment may injure. Whenever I am singing in the evening—and throughout my entire career I have always kept to the same routine—I rise early, breakfast lightly, then warm my voice by a few scales and exercises. The only meal of the day of any importance is lunch, and even that must be light, and with no sort of wine, with no salt, with only the most easily digested dishes. After lunch I go out for a short walk, and then I rest. At five o'clock I am up again, and I go through the pretence of eating an apple, sometimes an omelette, with a little water. And that is all I have until after the opera.

Even then, I avoid suppers. A heavy meal, just before going to bed, when the mind is still excited by the glamour of a long performance, is a fatal mistake. It merely disturbs the whole system and leads to bad dreams. Eat a raw apple and a slice of brown bread, and you will wake up in the morning feeling as fit as a fiddle.

As long as man is man and woman is woman, that will be the ideal routine for them to adopt. You cannot eat, and be merry, on the days when you are singing. The human body is not made that way. It may be a pity, but there it is.

I always like to arrive at the theatre two hours before the performance. I hate slipshod methods of making-up. If an artist is to present a really artistic appearance on the stage; if her face is to look natural and not a mass of paint; if her wigs are to be properly adjusted, if her hands are to be powdered, her dresses to be accurate and in order, she will find that an hour and a half is none too much for all these manifold tasks; moreover, she should allow herself time to go through her rôle, word for word and note for note. There is no other way in which she can make absolutely certain that she remembers it. And when it is over she will find that half an hour's rest is more or less essential, if she is to sing her best.

Throughout every performance of this season, and whether I was ill or well, I kept to my routine. It was a hard struggle, because I was gradually getting weaker and weaker as a result of overstrain and worry. But how my audiences repaid me! They stayed up outside the theatre in the drizzling rain and the bitter cold all night, not even to buy tickets, but to have the privilege of buying a coupon which would enable them, if they were lucky, to buy tickets. There was one flower girl who spent (as she told me) thirty-six pounds on tickets to hear me sing, for the single season. There was a wounded soldier, practically penniless at the time, I believe, walked three miles on his one leg to hear me, and who sent me sixteen exquisite little bouquets, each tied with a different-coloured ribbon, and each representing one of the first nights in the various operas which I have either created or given in the course of my career. Dear Jim Styles! I am thinking of *you,* and I thank you. You have the soul of a poet, and I am honoured by your friendship.

As for my last night—how can I describe it? I have memories of bracing myself for a supreme effort after a long and painful illness, memories of feeling, with every note I sang, the sense of glory passing—not my own but that of the great days with which I had been associated, memories of a curtain of roses, towering itself gently between me and the vast audience, as though to give sweetness to my passing. My last night of Opera in Australia! Shall I say that it was the greatest of my life? And the saddest?

CHAPTER XXVIII

CONCLUSION

GOOD-BYE is of all words the hardest to say, when it is really good-bye and not *au revoir*. And for a singer I think it is even more difficult than for the ordinary run of mortals. It is not merely a question of anything so inevitable as losing one's voice. It is not merely a feeling of pique or bitterness at the thought that others are crowding along to occupy the stage which one once held alone. It is rather a feeling, as one says the word, that one is parting with thousands of friends—friends perhaps whom one has never met, of whose existence one will always be ignorant, but who are friends none the less.

It is the feeling that in some subtle way there is a link between the singer and her audience, that makes the severing of it so terribly painful. Now that I look back on my life, I remember so many hundreds of little details which go to show the strength of that link. One did not perhaps realize it at the time. I remember bunches of roses sent anonymously to my dressing-room in Paris night after night; roses which I would put on my dressing-table, which would blossom for a day or two and then die and be forgotten. I remember little presents from unknown worshippers which filled me with pleasure at the time, but which remained merely presents from the unknown, which never materialized into friendship. I remember, too, a wonderful copy, bound in heavy leather, of Gounod's *Faust* with an " M " and a Crown in gold stamped on the top of it, and underneath the words:

MELBA SUM ET REGNO.

I never knew from whom that came either. It was typical of a hundred other things which came my way.

However, if there is one thing which makes the saying of good-bye less difficult than it might otherwise have been, it is the fact that I can at least say it with a clear conscience. Let me speak quite frankly about this. I am perfectly aware that ever since I have been Melba, rumours have flown all over the world that I, like so many other artists, have been cruel, jealous, violently antagonistic to anybody who might endeavour to supplant me in the popular affection. I have been referred to in public and in private as "the hidden hand." I have never fully understood the direction in which my hidden hand was supposed to operate, but I gather that I am reputed to have instituted a sort of cabal at Covent Garden by which all those who endeavoured to obtain a hearing there were first of all referred to me, and then, if they showed promise, were summarily dismissed without a word of explanation. Professional singers will realize without any comments of mine how utterly fantastic and impossible such stories must be; but the general public who know nothing about the organization of an opera company, who have never been to Covent Garden except to sit in its stalls, are more easily deluded. It is the general public I love, not the professional musicians, and it is for them therefore that I am including in this latter chapter a copy of a letter from Mr. Harry Higgins, who has been for so many years the directing spirit of all that concerns Covent Garden. That letter I publish without comment for it will tell its own story:

7 Bloomsbury Square,
London, W.C.
May 21st, 1925.

My dear Dame Nelly,

When you were telling me of the book of reminiscences that you were about to publish, it struck me that you were a little hurt at suggestions that have come to your ears that you were in the habit of using your position at Covent Garden to influence the management either in favour or to the prejudice of some of the artists or those seeking to be engaged there.

I can honestly say that I have never known such to be the case, and after all no one had had from the very beginning of your career less cause to fear competition than you, apart from which you always appeared to me to wisely imitate the example of the gentleman who earned £10,000 a year by minding his own business.

In any case, if you were ever engaged in such machinations, you must have used very circuitous and not very successful methods, for they never came to my knowledge.

You know as well as I that inefficient artists are always ready to put forward every sort of excuse for their failure, and never attribute it to the obvious cause, their own incompetence, and I think that accounts for the rumours you referred to.

It is strange that although the outside public who interest themselves in such matters have an idea that I as a Director of the Opera am constantly involved in bitter controversies and angry disputes with the artists and members of the staff, I can only say that in all the years of my association with it, I have never had anything approaching a quarrel with any one of them, except in the case of one highly paid lady who wanted us to pay her Income Tax; and although a solicitor or perhaps because I am one, I have never yet been involved in a lawsuit in connection with our enterprise. Whether this was due to the forbearance of the members of the Company or to the tact of my colleagues and myself, I must leave it to you to say, but the fact remains that whatever troubles we have gone through, they have never arisen from any friction between employers and employees.

During the War a well-known and popular General inquired of a prima-donna—a mutual friend of ours—whether the intrigues among her colleagues were not of the most terrible description. "They were nothing," she replied, "compared to those among the Generals at the War Office," and I have no doubt she was right.

Do not therefore be annoyed or surprised at the imputations of the jealous and ill-informed. Your conscience on the point is, I am sure, quite clear, and if you had occasionally been guilty of the interference suggested, it would probably have saved me from some unfortunate errors of selection. I ought perhaps to complain that your abstention from it amounted to neglect of your duty to me!

I need hardly add that our invariably pleasant relations will always be among the most agreeable of my operatic recollections.

Yours most sincerely,
HARRY HIGGINS.

Somebody said to me the other day: "How different is the England to which you are saying good-bye to the England you first knew when you made your bow at Covent Garden in *Lucia*. So many illusions lost; so many glories gone; such a sad bewildered country, so bereft of the romantic things we used to know!"

I nodded, and said, "Yes, in some ways you are right. England and the rest of the world are different. But there are some things about England which I am sad to say are very much the same."

I smiled.

My friend was surprised. "You are *sad* to see that they are the same," he said. "What do you mean?"

"Look at the provinces," I said. "Do you realize that the provinces are asking for exactly the same things in music as they demanded forty years ago? Do you realize that when I go to big towns which possess, according to popular tradition, such excellent taste, I am compelled time and again to sing the same old songs, and that whenever I endeavour to put something new on the programmes, I am regarded as positively eccentric? Do you realize that even now, in this year of 1925, wherever I go I am being asked to sing Tosti's 'Good-Bye,' 'Comin' thro' the Rye,' and all the other old tunes that they have heard a thousand times? I try Debussy, I try Duparc, Ravel; I try anything and everything which strikes me as beautiful and fresh, and always I am greeted with the same response; enthusiastic, it is true, but tame compared with the positive uproar which I receive when I sing the old favourites."

Why is it that we are so behindhand in our musical imagination? Why is it, of all countries in the world, we go on with the same old things after the same old way, distrusting anything that is fresh, unwilling ever to make any experiments? When I come to America, when I sing in Paris, or in Italy, I am overwhelmed with requests to sing works by hitherto unknown composers. None of these requests ever come to me in

England. We are conservative to the point of madness.

This is not the time, in my last chapter, for bitterness, and although I could have mentioned a great many names of figures prominent in English musical life, who seem to me to be responsible for the dry rot which is setting in, I prefer to leave them out, in the anonymity which they deserve. But their faces float before me as I write: the faces of old men in academy after academy, grizzled haired, with set faces against innovation. I have dined next to such old men and have listened to them in utter astonishment as they went into ecstasies over some outworn thing by Mendelssohn, and growled and fidgeted when anybody attempted to play even some of the simpler melodies of Debussy. I have heard a man, who is reputed to be one of the greatest composers we have ever produced, admit his complete ignorance of the works even of such great geniuses as Chausson and Rimsky-Korsakoff. In the same breath I have heard these men declare that in their opinion we should allow no music to be played but British music; that we should rigorously close our doors to all foreign influences and live, apparently, on *Rule, Britannia* for the rest of our lives.

I have no patience with such an attitude. Art is not national. It is international. Music is not written in red, white and blue; it is written with the heart's blood of the composer, whether he be English or German, black or white. If I felt that there was the vaguest excuse for imagining that by closing our concert halls to any but English music we should thereby encourage English musicians, I should write differently, but the facts all point in the opposite direction. Germany does not shut her doors to British music; when there is any work of merit written in this island, she is the first to appreciate it at its true value. It is the same in Austria and France. That interesting composer, Mr. Josef Holbrooke, for example, had to go to Vienna for the first performance of one of his finest piano concertos. Why? Not because we are unwilling to listen to British music; but simply because the dreary grey-heads who have pushed themselves to a position of prominence in our musical world are unwilling to listen to anything which they imagine may have been written since the death of Queen Victoria.

No, I am frankly disappointed in the attitude of this country towards all things musical. It is partly, of course, our own fault—that lack of imagination which is at once our weakness and our strength, but it is also in no small degree the fault of a Government which, while it is willing to support any of the other arts to an almost unlimited extent, seems to imagine that a paltry £500 a year is sufficient for the encouragement of music—the greatest art of all.

There, I have said enough about that subject. I do not wish in these closing words to introduce any other controversial topic. I feel at the end of this autobiography like one who is saying good-bye to many friends, who recalls at the last moment so many things he might have said, so many words that he has left unspoken, so many stories that will have to remain for ever untold. I cannot crowd them all into a few last paragraphs. I can only, in imagination, wave my hand and smile, trusting that now you know me a little better than before.

I close my eyes, and it seems to me that life has been very wonderful, and is wonderful yet. I see the tall stark trees under which I played as a child with the blue hills beckoning to me beyond them, and the first heat of the Australian sunshine melting into the mists of the valley. I see the bustling London streets, down which I drove as a tremulous excited girl from Covent Garden, stretching before me dim and forbidding. I see the sparkle and glitter of Paris, when everything is new and fresh, when one drove down the Bois in an open carriage, a little proud, a little elated by success. I see America, comparatively raw and crude, growing, always growing, like a giant in its sleep—I see a sea of faces, so many of which I love, so many of which are gone. . . .

The face of my father bending over me as a child, the stern face of Madame Marchesi from the shadows of her little room in Paris, the face of my tiny son as I nursed him, with the hot rain dripping on the roof of my Queensland home; the face of a little woman whom I shall never know, who approached me one day in the snow outside the Opera House in Philadelphia and asked me for a red rose, and when I had given it to her, she said to me words which I shall never forget: "Bless you, my beautiful heart." And the face of Jean de Reszke . . .

Jean! I feel in some way that my last words shall be about you. Not because of all you have meant to me as an artist, but because your death was one of the few perfect things in life of which I have ever heard. Let me tell it—my last story.

I was in Paris when Jean died, and I confess with the utmost grief, I was one of the few—a very few people—who were there to follow him to his grave. It seemed to me tragic that a spirit which had at one time held the whole world in thrall should be going almost unmourned to its final resting-place. And then I heard of the manner of his death, and I was glad.

For twenty years Jean had not sung. The golden voice had been silent, and his days had been spent in giving the fruits of his experience to others. But towards the end he was forced to stay in bed, and as he sank lower and lower, his voice died away almost to a whisper. And then, suddenly, in his delirium a miracle was worked. His breathing became clearer and clearer; his youth seemed, as it were, to come back to him like a flowing tide; he sat up in bed crying "*Enfin j'ai retrouvé ma voix!*" And he sang.

For three days in that house of death Jean sang, and the whole house rang and echoed with his golden notes pouring out with all their former loveliness. He was dying every minute, and yet the song still poured on, rôle after rôle in which he had once been so superb. I suppose it was uncanny and incredible, yet to me it was only beautiful. It is how I should like, when my time comes, to die myself. For it makes me wonder if the gift which one had always regarded as transient, like the passing of the summer or the fading of the rose, may not, after all, have an eternal being.

INDEX